SPECIAL ISSUE

CASSANDRA'S CURSE: THE LAW AND FORESEEABLE FUTURE DISASTERS

STUDIES IN LAW, POLITICS, AND SOCIETY

Series Editor: Austin Sarat

Recent Volumes:

Volumes 1–2:	Edited by Rita J. Simon
Volume 3:	Edited by Steven Spitzer
Volumes 4–9:	Edited by Steven Spitzer and Andrew S. Scull
Volumes 10–16:	Edited by Susan S. Sibey and Austin Sarat
Volumes 17–33:	Edited by Austin Sarat and Patricia Ewick
Volumes 34–67:	Edited by Austin Sarat

STUDIES IN LAW, POLITICS, AND SOCIETY VOLUME 68

SPECIAL ISSUE CASSANDRA'S CURSE: THE LAW AND FORESEEABLE FUTURE DISASTERS

EDITED BY

AUSTIN SARAT

Department of Law, Jurisprudence & Social Thought and Political Science, Amherst College, USA

SPECIAL ISSUE EDITORS

LLOYD BURTON

Program Concentration in Emergency Management, School of Public Affairs, University of Colorado Denver, Denver, CO, USA

LISA GROW SUN

School of Law, Brigham Young University, Provo, UT, USA

Emerald

United Kingdom – North America – Japan
India – Malaysia – China

Emerald Group Publishing Limited
Howard House, Wagon Lane, Bingley BD16 1WA, UK

First edition 2015

British Library Cataloguing in Publication Data
A catalogue record for this book is available from the British Library

ISBN: 978-1-78560-299-3
ISSN: 1059-4337

CONTENTS

LIST OF CONTRIBUTORS

Lloyd Burton	School of Public Affairs, University of Colorado Denver, Denver, CO, USA
Oscar Capdeferro	Faculty of Law, University of Barcelona, Barcelona, Spain
Michael Eburn	ANU College of Law, The Australian National University, Canberra, Australia
Sabrina McCormick	Milkin Institute School of Public Health, Department of Environmental and Occupational Health, George Washington University, Washington, DC, USA
Masayuki Murayama	School of Law, Meji University, Tokyo, Japan
Alexandre Peñalver	Faculty of Law, University of Barcelona, Barcelona, Spain
Justin Pidot	Faculty, University of Denver Sturm College of Law, Denver, CO, USA
Juli Ponce	Faculty of Law, University of Barcelona, Barcelona, Spain
Susan M. Sterett	Center for Public Administration and Policy, Metropolitan Institute, Virginia Tech, Alexandria, VA, USA
Lisa Grow Sun	School of Law, Brigham Young University, Provo, UT, USA

EDITORIAL BOARD

INTRODUCTION: THE MYTHS WE LIVE (AND DIE) BY

Lloyd Burton and Lisa Grow Sun

ABSTRACT

Two meanings of the word myth *informed the origins of this volume and its constituent chapters: myth as an archetypical narrative that societies and cultures use to embody value-laden lessons about both the natural world and human nature (myths to live by); and myth as a nefarious fabrication that imperils those who believe it (myths to die by). Throughout this volume, we use the Greek myth of Cassandra – the heroine of Troy who unsuccessfully forewarned her community of avoidable future disaster – as an archetype for the often heroic efforts of those in our day who seek to forewarn us of altogether foreseeable future disasters associated with both natural forces and human contrivance. We also explore the deadly myths of delusion – those which weave an illusory cocoon of invincibility around those who increasingly inhabit increasingly disaster-prone landscapes. Each chapter in this volume tells stories about what happens when these two meanings of myth collide, and of how better heeding the message of present-day Cassandras might help us to dispel the myths of delusion.*

Keywords: Disaster myths; Cassandra Conundrum; law; values

Special Issue: Cassandra's Curse: The Law and Foreseeable Future Disasters
Studies in Law, Politics, and Society, Volume 68, 1–13

ISSN: 1059-4337/doi:10.1108/S1059-433720150000068001

THE GATHERING

In July of 2011, a gathering of Law and Society scholars from around the world took place at Oñati, in the Basque Autonomous Region of northern Spain. A college town since the 1500s, Oñati is also home to the International Institute for the Sociology of Law, which hosted this event, underwritten by a grant from the Law and Social Sciences Division of the U.S. National Science Foundation.

The invitational conference was titled "Workshop on Disasters and Sociolegal Studies." Those of us who attended focus our work on the relationship between disasters and legal systems: specifically, on (1) how law can actually make catastrophic disasters more likely to occur and (2) how law reform can be employed to minimize human suffering caused by future disasters. Several of us presented case studies of major disasters that had been preceded by credible experts predicting exactly what would later occur, but whose warnings were unheeded, ignored, or ridiculed by leaders in government, science, and industry.

Interaction at this meeting and commonalities in our research interests later led to the founding of the Collaborative Research Network on the Jurisprudence of Disasters within the Law and Society Association in 2012. And it was to selected members of this (now expanded) network that we issued invitations to contribute chapters to this volume.

THE MEANINGS OF *MYTH*

In common English usage, the term myth can have several meanings. One is its use in the title and themes for this volume: a story of archetypical personas (either deific or human) who behave in ways and with motives that we recognize in ourselves. We use the stories of these larger-than-life figures as a way of reminding ourselves of the relationship between motives, actions, and consequences. We learn vicariously – with less wear and tear on our bodies and psyches – the painful lessons that life circumstances teach them.

In *Myths to Live By* (1972), Joseph Campbell recounted some of these stories, in which protagonists face what seem like impossible odds to achieve noble ends. They respond to a call to action (whether the call originates externally or from their own conscience), go forth, and engage in heroic struggle. Sometimes they are honored and rewarded for their efforts.

In other stories, such as Cassandra's, they are punished and destroyed. Such myths can serve as either inspiration or as cautionary tales, and sometimes as both.

But another popular meaning of myth is that of a fabricated story intended to create a false or misleading impression among listeners, to achieve the storytellers' ends when they have decided that the truth will not suffice. It can also be a story that believers cling to and repeat to each other, to avoid acknowledging a painful or inconvenient truth that challenges some of their most strongly held preconceptions. Myths in this form enable denial. All these meanings of myth play an important role in this volume.

The Myth of Cassandra

Cassandra was a high-born princess in the kingdom of Troy, said to be second in beauty only to her sister Helen, the lust for whom led to the Trojan War and the downfall of the kingdom. The god Apollo sought Cassandra's favor by giving her the ability to foresee and foretell important future events. Cassandra declined his advances, and paid dearly for her independence, as often happened to forthright women in Greek myths. Since he could not take back his gift, Apollo then laid on her a curse, to the effect that no one would believe her warnings, and that her listeners would instead regard her cautions to be incredible.

It is not altogether clear in the original Cassandra myth whether Apollo caused others to see her as stark-raving mad, as an over-excitable woman the strength of whose emotions obscured her reason (clear evidence of the inferiority of her gender, in the ancient Greek view), or to see her as merely misguided, mistaken, or confused. In Virgil's Aeneid, Cassandra is one of several who tried to warn Trojan civic and military leaders of treachery within an offer of truce (the Trojan Horse), but she was the only woman who issued that warning. Perhaps these leaders preferred to think that they had actually prevailed against their Greek besiegers' war of attrition, and chose to perceive the Horse as a peace offering rather than a potential threat. As the soothsayer of Troy, Cassandra's warning was the most notable, and thus the one most in need of discrediting.

In the view of Campbell, Jung, and some other Western mythologists, archetypical figures such as Cassandra can represent patterns of thought and impulse within our own psyche. As such, Cassandra is the cautionary voice warning us not to be deluded by self-serving images of ourselves, our circumstances, or our environment that have little grounding in reality.

Of course, the voice of caution and of preventive intent is only one of several vying for our attention, whether within our own consciousness or in public discourse. In both contexts, heeding this voice first and foremost can lead to anxiety-ridden enervation: seeing threats everywhere, such that the only sensible course of action is to hide under a blanket in the fetal position.

Just as self-defeating, however, is refusing to even acknowledge – much less to prudently act upon – credible warnings of foreseeable future disasters. And it is in this regard that the other meanings of myth come into play.

Myths That Kill

In disaster management, the most dangerous myths are the ones that weave epistemic cocoons of delusion – that obscure awareness of the realities of disasters past and present in service of the interests of those perpetuating the myth. For example, the Trojans preferred to believe their own self-created myth of invincibility – that they had prevailed by their powers of fortitude, endurance, and courage over the Greeks bearing gifts. The price they paid for their delusion was the destruction of their society and the loss of their own lives.

Unfortunately, the field of contemporary disaster law and policy continues to be rife with such myths, and we describe several of them here in Cassandra's Curse. One is our modern version of the myth of invincibility.

In 1900, US government meteorologists were confidently predicting that a hurricane could never strike the Texas gulf coast, since in the brief period they had been collecting data, hurricanes had all veered north when they reached Florida. Thus, money shouldn't be wasted building seawalls, and residential development along the coast should proceed apace. Then came the Galveston Hurricane of 1900 (which most Texans still refer to as the "Galveston Flood"), with 15-foot storm surges that either killed at once or swept out to sea about 10,000 residents, and damaged or destroyed nearly all the structures on Galveston Island (Larson, 1999). Yet there are more homes in Galveston today than there were then, and the seawall they eventually did build is only two feet higher than the 1900 storm surge.

Now more than ever, this prodevelopment myth lures us like moths to the flame. Local governments and land developers actively encourage people to keep moving into some of our most disaster-prone landscapes, such as tinder-dry forests in the United States' Mountain West and the Australian bush, or storm-hammered low-lying coastal areas such as the U.S. Gulf Coast and Atlantic seaboard.

The loss of lives and property occasioned by such short-sighted land use decision making continues to rise as catastrophic natural disasters grow in both size and frequency. Ironically, it tends to be the purveyors of these fatal fantasies, whose environments have been made measurably more dangerous by climate change, who charge that climate change itself is a myth.

The chapter on Fukushima in this volume by Masayuki Murayama and Lloyd Burton speaks poignantly of another deadly myth. This is the "myth of safety" utility companies and government regulators carefully nurtured in order to convince the Japanese people to accept placement of one of the world's most potentially dangerous power-generation technologies in the midst of one of the world's most disaster-prone landscapes: the often tsunami-ravaged Sendai coast.

One of us (Lisa Grow Sun) recently published an article titled "Disaster Mythology and the Law" (Sun, 2011), in which she describes a persistent, pernicious, and deadly set of myths reinforcing the notion that urban catastrophes will inevitably lead to widespread civil unrest, mass hysteria, and waves of uncontained violent behavior besieging the populace. This notion persists, in spite of very substantial postdisaster research affirming that prosocial, neighbor-helping-neighbor behavior is the norm, and antisocial behavior is rare. Dating back to the U.S. Army's occupation of San Francisco after the 1906 earthquake, the overwhelming majority of deaths by gunfire after urban disasters have been soldiers or police shooting "looters," many of whom were actually residents trying to retrieve belongings and medicines, or survivors scavenging for bare necessities in abandoned and heavily damaged stores.

In the case of Hurricane Katrina in 2005, major national newspapers repeated so many unfounded rumors spawned by these myths that they eventually had to publicly retract their stories as both inaccurate and overblown. Even worse, these disaster myths can and have encouraged a legal and policy approach to disaster response that militarizes rather than socializes government response to catastrophe – exactly the opposite of the kinds of public policies that would actually help keep residents safer and more capable of community self-help in the aftermath of a major disaster.

THE CASSANDRA CONUNDRUM

The Tension Created By Credible Warnings

What all the chapters in this volume describe to one degree or another is what might be called the Cassandra Conundrum. This is the situation created when credible experts warn of a foreseeable future disaster, but leaders in government, science and technology, industry, and the news media choose to ignore, dismiss, minimize, or ridicule such warnings – and sometimes the warners as well. We have a credible warning on the one hand and institutional opposition or indifference on the other: thus, the conundrum. The public is left wondering who and what to believe.

The conundrum persists until either the warnings fade away if catastrophe does not ensue; or instead, the warnings are catapulted to the top of the policy agenda if more credible evidence (often in the form of the predicted disaster) bears them out. The conundrum persists during the period Burton refers to in his chapter as the "Cassandra Interval," while proponents of the threat message struggle to get it onto the policy agenda and the Powers That Be try to keep it off.

Examples of the Conundrum in Cassandra's Curse

Both hazard events and their effects on human populations are increasingly not only foreseeable, but foreseen. Although President Bush, in Katrina's aftermath, opined that he didn't think "anybody anticipated the breach of the levees" in New Orleans, levee failure had in fact been foreseen, not just by the National Hurricane Center and the National Weather Service in the days before Katrina made landfall, but by FEMA and other agencies for years, if not decades.

Indeed, while the 9/11 Commission identified the failure of "imagination" as the "most important failure" leading up to the terrorist attacks, the House Committee charged with investigating both preparation for and response to Katrina found that "Katrina was primarily a failure of initiative." While the House Report focused largely on the lack of initiative and leadership during the immediate response to Katrina, the same failure of initiative was on full display in many of the federal, state, and local decisions that set the stage for the Katrina disaster, including the heavy reliance on (poorly maintained) engineered solutions to risk, the failure to plan for evacuation of vulnerable populations, and land-use decisions.

Why are warnings about impending disasters so widely and frequently disregarded? Like Cassandra of Greek myth, those with the prescience to foresee disaster are often unable to persuade others of the truthfulness or importance of their message and, ultimately, unable to galvanize actions to mitigate the foreseen risks.

One prominent Cassandra of his day – Gilbert White, the father of modern floodplain management – wrote in his 1942 doctoral dissertation at the University of Chicago that "Floods are 'acts of god,' but flood losses are largely acts of man." His central insights, that human choices about where and how to live are the primary drivers of disaster risk and that human attempts to manage and control nature often exacerbate that risk, are now widely acknowledged in theory but still poorly implemented in practice. Burton's chapter tells the story of yet another Cassandra, Professor Harold Biswell, of the University of California, Berkeley's School of Forestry, whose work advocating prescribed burns took decades to gain traction against the common wisdom, and prevailing policy, of total fire suppression.

Of course, Cassandras are not always trained experts in disaster management or related fields. Indeed, for some types of disasters, particularly environmental and technological disasters, citizen scientists may play an increasingly important role in discovering, documenting, and demanding response to threats. The Louisiana Bucket Brigade, for example, has been at the forefront of the effort to collect data about the local effects of the BP oil spill on air, seafood, and soil and to demand redress for these harms.

Together, the chapters of this volume suggest that there are a multitude of reasons – apart from Apollo's curse – that Cassandra's warnings of impending disaster are so often disbelieved, ignored, or both. As both the chapter by Justin Pidot and the later chapter by Lisa Grow Sun and Sabrina McCormick suggest, the ways we talk about disaster, the metaphors we use, and the myths we believe can all undermine effective disaster policy. Moreover, as Burton's chapter suggests, strategies for mitigating disaster risk often threaten powerful vested interests. Indeed, the Powers That Be (PTB) may not be the only ones with incentives to preserve and justify the existing system. Social psychologists have postulated that individuals may be inclined to justify existing social systems, even when they are disadvantaged by those systems, to maintain a sense of stability and certainty (Napier et al., 2006). As Pidot argues, other cognitive errors, including reliance on heuristics, affect our ability to process disaster risk.

Overlapping government authority and jurisdictional boundaries may also complicate setting and implementing disaster policy. Policy consensus may likewise prove elusive in the face of disagreements over the proper role of government and differing views about how to prioritize public safety vis-a-vis other important values.

The relationship between government, community, and individual responsibility for disaster mitigation is also fraught with pitfalls.

As Michael Eburn's chapter demonstrates, as government assumes increased responsibility for disaster mitigation and response, an individual and community sense of responsibility may wane. The more the government does, the more the public expects it to do. In his view, the ambiguity over who has responsibility for what in the bushfire disaster management cycle is exacerbated by a relative lack of political consensus over management of Australia's bushlands generally. As is the case in the United States, most land use policies and decisions are made at relatively local levels of government, though it is the higher levels of government (state and national) that wind up bearing most of the responsibility for fighting the massive bushfires that threaten lives and property.

Likewise, as Pidot points out, government financing of disaster recovery can mute incentives for local and individual mitigation measures. Moreover, as Sun and McCormick suggest, government control over information and process, as well as the perpetuation of emergency measures long after the immediate disaster has passed, can sideline communities' participation in their own recovery.

Beginning the discussion of the many barriers to effective disaster policy, Pidot's chapter provides a thorough overview of the different types of obstacles that prevent effective mitigation of disaster risk. He divides these common impediments into three categories – symbolic, cognitive, and structural – and suggests that recognizing the common patterns will aid in developing appropriately tailored solutions.

The primary symbolic obstacle Pidot identifies – the one also discussed in Sun and McCormick's chapter – is the use of war metaphors in disaster response. This "rhetoric of conflict" frames many sensible disaster mitigation strategies, particularly retreat from hazardous areas, as unacceptable defeats and entrenches the "rebuild at all costs" mentality. Cognitive obstacles, in turn, problematize the very nature of "foreseeability," as reliance on heuristics and other cognitive errors cloud our perceptions of risk. Finally, structural obstacles, such as federal financing of disaster response and recovery, coupled with local control over land use decisions, make it difficult for both politicians and citizens to appreciate the true value of many mitigation measures.

Beyond the array of obstacles outlined by Pidot, there are also fundamental moral questions that shape and inform critical decisions about what mitigation measures should be taken and by whom. Three of the chapters in this volume explore this insight that, at the heart of the debate over appropriate precautions in the face of foreseeable disaster, are questions about values and how different individuals, communities, nations, and governments prioritize and harmonize these arguably conflicting values and moral commitments. Interestingly, all three of these chapters share a focus on government wildfire policy.

Burton's chapter takes on this question of value ordering most directly and explicitly. Building on the framework introduced by Philip Selznick's 1992 The Moral Commonwealth, he considers the critical, but sometimes competing, values that a moral community must honor. Applying that framework to disaster mitigation choices, he examines what the differing state approaches to wildfire mitigation rules in the fire-prone American West reveal about the value structures of those states. In particular, he concludes that those western states that impose mandatory common standards on all their localities prioritize the value of mutuality (including both our obligations to each other and government obligations to protect community health and welfare) over the values of autonomy, pluralism, and participation. In contrast, local option states, which empower, but do not require, localities to adopt enforceable rules, subordinate the mutuality value to concerns for local control, diversity of approach, and citizen participation.

Ultimately, Burton suggests that local option states may need to recalibrate the relative weight they give these values so that local option states meet basic obligations to their citizens. In his words, "These states are failing to honor the mutuality value at a level sufficient to protect the health, safety, and well-being of the citizens" they are permitting, and even encouraging, to live in particularly dangerous locales.

A second chapter, this one by Eburn, also grapples with the important role that values play in formulating disaster policy. Eburn's chapter traces the evolution of fire and other emergency services in Australia, from the late nineteenth century, when there was no expectation that the government at any level was responsible for protecting the community from fire, to today, when "emergency management is seen as a core or central government activity." Eburn notes, however, that since the 1990s the pendulum has swung back somewhat to the "self-help days of the past"; Australian emergency management has shifted from a government-centered model to a model that strives to make individuals and communities more resilient.

Eburn explains that Australia's new resilience strategy emphasizes informing and educating the public about risk and response and underscores that individuals must share responsibility with communities and the government for preparing for, responding to, and recovering from disasters. He explores various conceptions of this "shared responsibility" that might develop, concluding that both the allocation of responsibility between individuals, communities, and government, as well as the determination of "acceptable" levels of disaster risk are ultimately value questions that must be resolved through the political process. Politicians and the public must then be willing to accept the residual risk that remains.

Eburn's vision of appropriate disaster mitigation embraces a middle road between strict government mandates and complete government deference to individual risk preferences – an approach that he hopes leaves space for individuals and communities to make informed decisions about disaster risk, even if those decisions conflict with the way government decision makers would prioritize public safety and other values.

The following chapter on wildfire prevention and mitigation in Catalonia, Spain, by Juli Ponce, Alexandre Peñalver, Oscar Capdeferro, and Burton, provides a nice contrast with Eburn's description of the Australian conception of government responsibility for wildfires and other disasters. Ponce et al. describe the emergence of a positive government obligation, grounded in the case law of the European Court of Human Rights, to exercise due care to prevent and mitigate disasters. This emerging state obligation to protect human life and property rights from disaster contrasts with the Australian conception of shared responsibility and the devolution of more responsibility to individuals and local communities, though the differences in actual policy may ultimately be greater in theory than practice. In the wildfire mitigation research reported here, it is clear that the EU, in general, and Mediterranean Member States like Spain and its fire-prone provinces such as Catalonia, in particular, take a much more preventive and vigorous approach to land use regulation in high risk areas than that taken in the former British colonies, with their common law tradition.

Another common theme that runs through many of the chapters in this volume is that of government incapacity and incompetence. Sun and McCormick's chapter focuses on examples of government mismanagement of disaster response, which – like disasters themselves – exhibit some predictable patterns. They examine common disaster response failures, and consider how climate change may affect these forms of disaster mismanagement, which include poor assessment and prioritization of risks; marginalization of public participation and civic engagement in risk management and response; unnecessary continuation of emergency measures and emergency powers beyond the immediate emergency; and neglect of vulnerable populations.

Exploring both legal and structural remedies that might prevent some of these typical response failures, Sun and McCormick emphasize that, just as we must mitigate foreseeable disasters, we must mitigate foreseeable response failures. They suggest that a key step to countering these failures is recognizing that they "require their own preparation and mitigation strategies" integrated into all phases of emergency management.

More broadly, we must recognize that the many obstacles to effective disaster policy discussed throughout this volume require their own mitigation and management strategies. Thus, as Burton suggests, Cassandra must sound the warning, not only of impending hazards, but also of the many institutional failings that keep us from responding to those risks appropriately.

Susan M. Sterett's chapter also addresses issues of institutional capacity, exemplified by problems in appropriately addressing the needs of already disadvantaged persons displaced by the long-term consequences of catastrophic natural disasters. She notes how within our legal culture we expect those mistreated in such circumstances to either vindicate their rights in court (which almost none have the wherewithal to do), or passively accept their lot.

She offers the example of Katrina-displaced persons from poor New Orleans neighborhoods interred like war refugees in crumbling dormitory facilities surrounded by wire fencing and armed guards in a redeveloping area of Denver, Colorado. Alarmed by lurid (and later largely discredited) news reports of rampant lawlessness and mayhem in the streets of New Orleans, Denver authorities had feared that perhaps their city might suffer similar problems. As well-meaning as some of these relief efforts may have been, she points out, they also violated several international norms and declared rights of both foreign refugees and internally displaced persons. These displaced New Orleanians were, in short, victims not only of Katrina, but of some of the pernicious "disaster myths" of mayhem and necessary militarization about which Sun has written.

CAUSE FOR HOPE?

Just as the reasons for resisting Cassandra's warnings vary widely, so too do the potential solutions that move us forward, and the chapters in this volume consider a wide array of possible remedies. Taken together, the essays suggest that, in order to craft effective remedies, we need to take a broad view of how the many obstacles to effective disaster mitigation are interrelated and intertwined. For example, it makes sense to treat mitigation decisions as value choices and, hence, as political decisions that require us to live with the residual risk that remains once the community has sacrificed all it is willing to sacrifice in the name of public safety and loss prevention.

Yet, current political decisions by local communities about "acceptable" levels of risk may reflect government disaster policies that subsidize living in risky places every bit as much as they reflect true community ordering of values and preferences about how to trade-off public safety and property protection with other concerns. These decisions cannot be taken at face value as true indicators of community-value hierarchies if they are hopelessly skewed by pre- and post-disaster subsidies.

Nevertheless, differing cultural contexts and value hierarchies may well lead communities to choose quite different mitigation strategies. Centralized, prescriptive authority is not the only solution. Devolution of authority coupled with capacity building, may prove to be one effective approach.

On reflection, reading over the chapters comprising this volume leaves the impression that all of us who contributed to it are to some extent Cassandra's progeny. The challenge for us, as it was for her, is to do what we can to avoid having our warnings (mostly of institutional incapacity) go unheeded. That is one of the reasons we are grateful for the opportunity to assemble this scholarship. Some of us have already testified at government hearings and fielded numerous news media inquiries on the subject of foreseeable risk and what we are and are not doing about it. And we hope that public and institutional attention to these issues will continue to grow, along with the number of scholars interested in entering this area of inquiry and joining our network.

Our modest efforts have drawn inspiration from some of the great Cassandras of our time described in this volume, such as Gilbert White, Harold Biswell, and *Silent Spring* author Rachel Carson. These reformers managed to help bend the course of American environmental history. They stood up to Establishment criticism, and waged the "epic struggle" (as Joseph Campbell described it), using the soundness of their research as sword and shield, and ultimately shifted professional and public opinion from skepticism to support.

So, ultimately, we have as much cause for hope as for despair, even though most of the disasters we researched for our chapters are linked in one way or another to perhaps the greatest unfolding environmental challenge of our times: climate change induced by carbon-based fuels combustion. Warnings about climate change are not merely credible; they reflect broad scientific consensus that climate change is both occurring and increasing the likelihood of severe weather disasters, though ongoing science-based skepticism will continue to stimulate self-correction as warranted.

Thus, we may be in the midst of the greatest Cassandra Conundrum of all time. We have the (more than) credible threat on the one hand, and national and international institutional incapacity (so far) to respond effectively on the other. The heroic struggle is well under way, though various interest groups have their own views of who the heroes and villains may be.

As the Murayama and Burton chapter sets it out, two mythical figures vie for our attention. For much of our modern history, the voice of Prometheus has assured us that the power of fossil and nuclear fire is limitless, and has made us invincible to Nature's caprices. But now the voice of Cassandra (in the form of the entire global climate science community) tells us this myth of invincibility is a deadly delusion. We have collectively created the greatest human-caused environmental crisis in the history of our species, and only we can wisely resolve it. As individuals, communities, and nations, we must choose which voice we will heed.

REFERENCES

Campbell, J. (1972). *Myths to live by*. New York, NY: Viking.

Larson, E. (1999). *Isaac's storm*. New York, NY: Vintage.

Napier, J. L., Mandisodza, A. N., Andersen, S. M., & Jost, J. T. (2006). System justification in responding to the poor and displaced in the aftermath of Hurricane Katrina. *Analyses of Social Issues and Public Policy*, *6*, 64.

Sun, L. G. (2011). Disaster mythology and the law. *Cornell Law Review*, *96*(5), 1131–1208.

THE "CASSANDRA ZONE" AND LAW'S MORAL PURPOSE

Lloyd Burton

ABSTRACT

The Cassandra Zone is that time period – and the events that occur within it – from the voicing of the first credible warnings of foreseeable future disaster until society either awakens to the threat and proactively mitigates against it, or chooses to ignore such warnings and subsequently suffers the consequences when the foretold disaster comes to pass. Whether or not that society manages to learn from its own history of disaster and use the power of state to mitigate against foretold future ones is one of the definitive criteria for determining whether, in social theorist Phillip Selznick's terms, such a society can be deemed to constitute a moral community.

Keywords: United States wildfire mitigation; law; morality

INTRODUCTION

Along the northern California coast, early on an April morning in 1906, the earth literally fell apart. The San Andreas Fault ruptured, causing an instantaneous and massive shift in the tectonic plates along its seam. In the

Special Issue: Cassandra's Curse: The Law and Foreseeable Future Disasters
Studies in Law, Politics, and Society, Volume 68, 15–32

ISSN: 1059-4337/doi:10.1108/S1059-433720150000068002

meadowlands of Marin County north of San Francisco and the orchards of Santa Clara County to its south, trees fell and fence lines snapped.

But in the rickety wooden apartment buildings and tenements on unstable landfill south of Market Street in San Francisco, hundreds of low-income day laborers and service workers died as their dwellings collapsed upon them. Hundreds more perished in Chinatown, the waterfront, and every other part of the city where flimsy housing sat on equally insubstantial earth. Fire claimed most of the real estate during and after that calamitous event, but it was the earthquake that swiftly took most of the lives, as weak structures on unstable soils entombed their inhabitants (Butler, 2007).

In the weeks and months following the disaster, the business interests of the city mounted a concerted and ultimately successful effort to frame this catastrophe as just another major urban fire, and downplayed the deadly impact of the quake itself. They argued that such fires were regularly afflicting other fast growing and hastily constructed cities around the country, as the industrial revolution ballooned at a faster pace than municipal infrastructure's ability to accommodate it. All they needed was a better fire department and more reliable water pressure, they argued. Nothing to see here, folks. Time to move on (Hansen & Condon, 1989).

City leaders quickly proceeded to rebuild equally insubstantial structures on the same unstable soil, arguing to insurers and real estate investors that fires can happen anywhere, San Francisco was no different, and upgraded services and infrastructure would take care of the problem. By the time the city adopted a modest structural integrity code three years after the earthquake, the city's most unsafe structures had already been rebuilt on its most unsafe land (Smith, 2006).

As San Francisco's financial movers and shakers were working hard to erase public (and investor) memories of San Francisco as a place that literally moves and shakes, across the Bay in Berkeley, geologists at the University of California started working just as hard researching where, when, and why such catastrophic events were likely to strike the state in the future. They co-founded a geophysical research society within months of the San Francisco earthquake, and they began to issue sobering reports about the extent of seismic hazard in California (Geschwind, 2001).

Both the San Francisco area and greater Los Angeles – the two largest population centers in the state – lie above active fault zones, the geologists reported, and future earthquakes of varying degrees of magnitude were inevitable. Further, they discovered that other fault lines lay in areas where future land development was planned, such as the East Bay hills across from San Francisco and southern California's San Fernando Valley – areas that were equally at risk and equally in need of building standards to mitigate against future losses (Geschwind).

The world's best and most credible seismic hazard research notwithstanding, it took more deadly quakes to compel the Powers That Be to heed Cassandra's cry. The Long Beach tremblor of 1933 damaged or destroyed most of Los Angeles' brick schoolhouses – fortunately, not during the school day. So that same year state legislators adopted statewide standards for construction in areas of heightened seismic risk, starting with public school buildings. It had been more than a quarter of a century from the time of the San Francisco quake until the state government finally acknowledged the extent of the risk and that only effective statewide action could adequately protect Californians from the seismic hazards with which they lived (Davis, 1998).

Elsewhere in this volume, Justin Pidot's chapter illustrates how the politics and economics of disaster denial impede our ability to better plan for these inevitable events; while Sun and McCormick provide examples of failed past policies and the unlikelihood of near-term improvement, showing how disaster resilience is impossible as long as business and government leaders cling to persistent, unfounded, and largely self-serving disaster myths. Neither of these chapters offers much hope for near-term improvement in these dynamics, absent multiple near-term catastrophes of increasingly calamitous proportions.

But change does happen. This chapter in *Cassandra's Curse* opens with an accounting of how the sheer magnitude and deadly, destructive character of California's seismic events in combination with the science of their behavior finally overcame denial bias and led to effective seismic safety regulation. This sets the stage for the focus of this chapter, which is what happens from the first credible warnings of impending disaster to acknowledgment of that threat in public discourse through to eventual law and policy reform. In this writing, I refer to this period and the events that occur within it as the *Cassandra Zone*.

In the case of seismic hazard in California, it lasted for a generation, from 1906 to 1933. Every major business interest in the state benefiting from real estate development did everything possible to deny, denigrate, and dismiss the magnitude of the threat. This began with the publishing of false information about the death toll from the San Francisco quake: the "official" 1906 figure was 478, but more recent archival research shows it to have been well over 3,000 (Hansen and Condon). And the denial movement continued right up into the 1930s, when land values were depressed anyway and more quakes in urban areas demonstrated that urban California was a more dangerous place to live without seismic safety regulation than with it.

This same dynamic – of resistance to credible disaster threats by entrenched interests who benefit from the status quo – has played out over time in many different settings and with several forms of disaster (Steinberg, 2000). What follows below is a description of the parameters of this playing field – the Cassandra Zone – and the dynamics that take place within it in general terms. And following that is an application of the trope to the century-long struggle over the management of fire on the public lands of the American West.

The final installment of this study is a closer look at one of the disaster discourses that take place within the zone, which is law's moral purpose in protecting us from preventable disasters: awakening us from the dream of denial, and discouraging us from the market-driven tendencies to put ourselves in harm's way.

INCONVENIENT SCIENCE, THE CASSANDRA ZONE, AND THE POWERS THAT BE

The Cassandra Zone concept is based on a common grade school science project in which students plant and water a seed in a soil-filled container, and then keep a daily log of its growth processes over time. They track plant development from germination to sprouting to stalk growth and foliating to flowering and fruiting. Record keeping for this experiment includes plotting a growth curve, the horizontal axis being time and the vertical axis the various stages in plant development. The shape of the curve describes the plant's relative success in achieving its growth potential.

In defining the parameters of the Cassandra Zone, the horizontal axis is also time (whether measured in weeks, months, or years). The vertical axis (the growth stages) begins with the first warning of catastrophe, and then tracks the ascendance of the issue into public consciousness, public discourse, and policy response. The vertical growth rate can be affected by intervening events, such as scientific research tending to either legitimize or discredit the initial warning, or a disaster lending credence to Cassandra's message. Plotting these growth stages over time yields a curve, and the space beneath it constitutes the Cassandra Zone. This is the realm within which the merits of the warning are vetted, more research is done, intervening events are accounted for, and advocates both for and against heeding the warning with a policy response make their case.

Not all warnings of impending disaster are initially rejected. Some are immediately recognized as legitimate and swift action is taken. What makes a warning fall into the Cassandra category is that it is deliberately ignored or actively discredited by the Powers That Be. And more often than not, the same fate befalls the messenger as it does the message.

Early skirmishes in the conflict over early warnings of disaster sometimes include an assault on the credibility and the image of the forecaster. Apollo courted Cassandra with the gift of prophecy; when she rejected him, he cursed her by causing others to perceive her as deranged and her warnings as incredible; that is, as the kook on the corner.

If opposition to the foreteller's message is fierce, the Cassandra Zone can become a gladiatorial arena, in which the Powers That Be (PTB) are the lions, and Cassandra is the Christian. In Greek mythology, she warned the PTB (Trojan civic and military leaders) of treachery within an offer of truce. The treacherous victors whose maleficence she had predicted later seized, brutalized, and destroyed her, just as they did the city-state that refused to heed her warning.

In myth, the Trojans preferred to think they had actually prevailed by attrition over their Greek beseigers, rather than acknowledging the possibility that they were being fatally duped. In modern times, the PTB are the Establishment: government institutions whose competence is challenged by foretold disaster, leaders in the scientific community whose work might be questioned or partially disproven by new disaster-based hypotheses, and business interests (like the early 20th century San Francisco land developers) whose fortunes might be diminished.

The more gravely threatened the PTB understand themselves to be, the harder they will try to consign the foreteller to Cassandra's fate. For example, in *Secrets*, philosopher Sissela Bok (1983) recounts the sometimes career-ending consequences for whistleblowers in government and the corporate worlds who try to alert authorities and the public to impending calamity.

At least in the realm of potential natural disasters, credible early forecasters are seldom alone in their concerns. They are simply the first ones willing to give them voice. Having done so, they step into the Zone whose growth they have initiated, knowing they may indeed be risking Cassandra's fate, and that they might well be caricatured as the kook on the corner. But just as often, the courage of their reason-based convictions inspires others to join them in the arena, to have a hard look at the hypotheses and the data, and perhaps to add some of their own. And thus begins the image transformation of the messenger from kook to courageous crusader; and of the message from that of fretting on the fringe to a central policy concern. Little wonder then that many members of the scientific and technical communities want to stay as far away from the Zone as possible; it can make them professionally radioactive.

Sometimes orchestrated denial wins. Jared Diamond's book *Collapse* (2005) describes several historical cases of unheeded evidence of foretold natural disaster that triggered both environmental and societal collapse. In these cases, the curve defining the upper boundary of the Zone looks like the trajectory of a rocket whose guidance system fails on launch and crashes nose-first back to Earth.

Things didn't end well for these societies. They either chose not to heed clear warnings of impending disaster, or they did not have the institutional capacity to respond effectively. They collapsed as a result. By contrast, in the case of seismic safety regulation in California, the trajectory rose until it intersected with and culminated in disaster prevention law reform, maturing and fulfilling its growth potential.

As the following case study illustrates, we stand at such a crossroad in the realm of wildfire management in the American West, at the Wildlands-Urban Interface (the WUI, where residential development meets wild open space). By one estimate, about 85% of the private lands available for residential development in the western WUI are as-yet unexploited (Headwaters Economics, 2009); and state laws vary widely in terms of their use of their police powers to mitigate against wildfire disasters on private lands (Burton, 2013).

We failed to avert environmental catastrophe through soil conservation and agricultural price stabilization in the Dust Bowl of the 1930s, which triggered the greatest environmental collapse in American history to date (Egan, 2006). It took over a generation of government-guided and supported soil restoration practices and commodities market regulation for the landscape to partially recover. And some argue that given the rate at which the Ogallala Aquifer is being overdrafted now, we may be setting the stage for a recurrence. But at least with regard to wildfire in the urbanizing American West, we still have time. We can only hope that our most destructive exurban megafires are behind us rather than before us, though current trends suggest otherwise (Headwaters Economics).

FIRE AND THE FATE OF THE AMERICAN WEST

Laying the Great Fire

Massive fires in the forested mountains of the western United States are nothing new. Tree ring data show that they periodically swept through these ranges during times of multidecade droughts long before Europeans first began to settle there. But the same data also show that today's megafires, like coastal storms and tornadoes, are bigger and fiercer than ever before. And other research clearly points to climate change as the causative factor (Fraser, 2013).

The first of the Great Fires clearing the path for 20th century wildfire policy on the public lands started in the forests of eastern Washington, Idaho, and Montana in the summer of 1910. Dubbed the "Big Burn" (Egan, 2009), it blew up on an especially hot, dry, and windy August afternoon, when several lightning and locomotive-sparked spot fires exploded into conflagrations, and then joined forces until entire valleys and canyons were engulfed in flame.

Prevailing winds blew these miles-wide, 200-foot tall curtains of fire eastward toward remote mountain towns, burning some of them to the ground and killing some of their inhabitants. Nearly 100 government firefighters lost their lives in a vain effort to contain and to quench the largest wildlands firestorm in the history of the Mountain West; it would take the fall rains to do that (Egan).

This may have been the greatest environmental catastrophe to strike the western states so far, burning over three million acres of public and private forestland, but it could not have come at a better time for the fledgling United States Forest Service. Congress founded the Service in 1905 amid immense controversy over whether the forests on the public lands should be privatized or preserved in the public estate. Even as the agency took its first steps toward sustainable forest management, senators from the mountain states focused single-mindedly on destroying the conservation infrastructure the Theodore Roosevelt administration was working to foster (Egan).

Roosevelt named Gifford Pinchot, a fellow scion of a wealthy eastern family and a German-trained forester, as the first director of the Forest Service. Pinchot spent most of his first five years in office struggling to keep the new agency alive, as hostile western senators starved it of needed funding and tried to block its every effort at forest resource protection and fire suppression. And a few foresters lost their lives in the line of duty in these same states, killed by poachers or bootleg loggers (Egan).

When critics alleged that the Forest Service should have done a better job of fighting the Big Burn, Pinchot counterattacked with a vengeance. He charged that Forest Service enemies like Idaho Senator Heyburn had caused those deaths by not adequately funding the agency, and had "blood on their hands" (Egan, 2009, chapter 17). Congress voted a 100% increase in USFS fire-related infrastructure funding less than a year after the Big Burn.

As an astute forest scientist and keen naturalist, Pinchot knew that the forest ecology of the Mountain West was fire-dependent. (Years later, when redwoods stopped propagating in Yosemite National Park, fire suppression was discovered as the cause; the big trees needed fire for their cones to open.) And yet, the price he was willing to pay to get his Forest Service up and running was to promise the impossible: to ban fire from the nation's forests.

In retrospect, it seems almost as if he was making a deal with the Devil – the Fire Devil.

> GP: Fire Devil, for the time being, I really need for you to appear conquerable, so I can appear to conquer you.
>
> FD: Okay, Giff, I can do that for about two human generations. But all you're doing is laying down kindling for future fires all over the West that will make it look like Hell on Earth. After we're through pretending, I'll be making up for lost time.
>
> GP: I know, Luce. I'll be dead by then, but I hope my Forest Service won't.

And so both elements of the bargain came to pass. With its increased funding for fire suppression, the Forest Service went on the offensive, and dramatically decreased the incidence of large fires by attacking them immediately when they were still small. And with evidence of successful suppression came funding for more of the same. The post-World War II housing boom demanded record volumes of lumber. Campers could hike in the woods and sleep out at night unafraid of fire and unperturbed by smoke-filled skies. Smokey the Bear watched over us, keeping the Fire Devil at bay (Pyne, 2004).

What Pinchot probably did not countenance was the degree to which his successors and timber industry lobbyists would transform our national forests into tree farms feeding the forest products industry's production line. Half a century would pass from the time the Big Burn catapulted the Forest Service into the role of the nation's public lands fire department until a few silvacultural Cassandras started warning us of the dangers ahead, in forests carpeted by layers of deadfall and thick underbrush that in bygone times would have been swept away in annual groundfires. Now these millions of tons of duff were but kindling for the massive fires to come – fires that would rise up into the crowns of the forests and sweep across hundreds of thousands of acres of timberland annually, burning with the kind of unnatural intensity that would bake and sterilize the soil for at least the next half-century.

Calling Out Calamity

In retrospect, Pinchot's bargain seems ill-fated indeed, at least in terms of its environmental impact. Some argue in his defense that politically, it was absolutely necessary. As endangered as the Forest Service was at the outset, promising the impossible was probably the only way he could assure the agency's survival, so that the agency could help keep the national forests from being dismembered by privatizing western politicians and timber barons.

But even as Pinchot publicly advocated forest management goals he knew were ultimately illusory, critics both inside and outside the Forest Service privately voiced doubts about both the science and the logic of his position. Though fire suppression may have been the order of the day, national forest managers in remote areas and neighboring ranchers and timber companies whose private holdings adjoined public lands tended to look the other way when seasonal brushfires broke out in years of normal rainfall. They knew that these low-level fires were burning away the understory and deadfall that, if not removed by fire and released as nutrients back into the soil, might supply the kindling that during drought years would destroy the forests entirely (Biswell, 1989; Pyne, 2004).

With the Great Depression and New Deal public works programs, fire suppression in the back country gained new vigor. The array of surplus aircraft, communications gear, and field support infrastructure available after World War II and the Korean conflict equipped the Forest Service for an even more effective assault on the seasonal fires breaking out in the national forests. Fire suppression strategies and campaigns ruled the woods, with the effect that the forests became ever more vulnerable to the catastrophic fires that were to follow (Pyne, 2004, chapter 2).

As the threat grew, so too did the concerns of forest scientists who knew what was in store for these fuel-choked woodlands. By the late 1950s and early 1960s, field research was calling into serious question the Forest Service's total fire suppression policy. And the work of one respected forest scientist in particular was drawing more and more attention from both defenders and critics of the Forest Service mandate.

Professor Harold Biswell, of the University of California, Berkeley's School of Forestry, was conducting long-term field research on controlled burns being conducted in the low-elevation conifer forests of the Sierra Nevada by ranchers and resort owners who had learned the practice from their forbearers – and quite probably from the indigenous peoples who had originally inhabited the area. First studying their techniques and then refining them for application to different kinds of forests at different times of year, he perfected a process for replicating natural processes in several of California's mixed conifer forests.

The ultimate validation of his work came when a big fire moving through the national forests descended on Hoberg's Lodge in the Sierra Nevada's Madera County – private land in a ponderosa pine forest where Professor Biswell had been studying and supervising controlled burns for several years. When the fire reached lodge property, it went to ground, no longer having ground level fuels and ladder fuels to feed it. Though critics in the forest service and elsewhere argued that the fire abated because of changing wind conditions, the proof of controlled burning's effectiveness and total fire suppression's disastrous consequences was irrefutable (Agee, 1998).

What Biswell's work did during the 1950s and 1960s was to call out calamity. As bigger and fiercer fires were taking out bigger and bigger chunks of national forest, his controlled burn plots on private lands (at first, no public land management agency would host his experiments) remained unscathed. Attacks on his work from the timber industry, from suppression advocates both inside and outside the forest service, and from forestry school colleagues whose research was on the maximization of timber production were intense.

Late in his career, someone asked Prof. Biswell why he persisted with his work in the face of such uniform and hostile resistance from the PTB (including the dean of the UC Berkeley Forestry School, who warned him to stop talking publicly about his work and to develop another line of research). Among the answers he gave was that such opposition to credible, replicable, and defensible scientific research "made it interesting" (Biswell, 1989).

It takes a special kind of person to persevere in the face of such opposition. Obviously, he was not professionally risk-averse. The threats his dean made against him found their way to the head of the government agency that by then was funding his research; within days, the dean apologized in writing. Reflecting some of the spirit that drove his work, in his 1989 text on prescribed burning, Biswell published both the dean's threat and his apology (Biswell). Some are assigned the role of Cassandra, but take liberties with the original script, and transform their public image along the way. Harold Biswell was among them.

He also said he did the work because no one else was (his was the only such research being conducted in California), and because he believed in research on the possibility of "working in harmony with nature instead of against it." By the time he penned these words near the end of the 20th century, this was the ethic governing most public land management agencies, and seems self-evident. But a half-century earlier, such sentiments were considered soft-headed and heretical.

Through it all, Biswell bore the Cassandra mantle well. During his years in the Zone, his detractors referred to him derisively, and his colleagues and students affectionately, as "Harry the Torch." At a presentation in 1980 at Calaveras Big Trees State Park, an administrator with the California Division of Forestry remarked, "In the 50's, we were all making fun of Harry and fighting him. Now, 30 years later, we are all working for him" (Agee, 1998).

True to form, he continued to speak truth to power until near the end of his life, reprising his Cassandra role with regard to exurban fire danger, but this time to no avail. In his prescribed burn text, he warned of the growing threat of catastrophic and deadly fires in the wildlands–urban interface (WUI) in California and the need to thin vegetation there, including right outside his back door in the Berkeley-Oakland Hills. Otherwise, he warned, "many people could be killed in traffic jams on the narrow and crooked streets" trying to flee a catastrophic fire (Biswell, 1998, p. 76).

But the thinning he advocated on private property never took place, nor were measures taken to facilitate evacuation from the area. Three years after he voiced his warning, the deadliest (to residents) WUI wildfire in California history swept down from the ridge-tops of those very hills, killing 25 fleeing residents and destroying over $1.6 billion in residential property – California's first billion dollar WUI wildfire.

Professor Biswell died the following year, after witnessing the very catastrophe he had predicted but could not prevent in the hills near his home. A year after that, the California legislature adopted its first state-wide WUI wildfire mitigation law, incorporating much of his advice.

LAW'S MORAL PURPOSE

Values and Environmental Planning

What dissenters from the received orthodoxy do is to raise uncomfortable and unwelcome questions about the status quo, and by implication the judgments of the PTB who enforce and defend it. Though their concerns might first be voiced in dry, scientific terms, what contemporary Cassandras are ultimately calling into question is whether the authority government is exercising on the public's behalf is actually fulfilling law's moral purpose. Is its judgment worthy of the respect we accord the rule of law? Is it acting for the common good, or only the self-interest of the Powers That Be?

One of the reasons Harold Biswell's work caused such a furor was because of what it ultimately called into question. He kept his concerns focused on the role of fire on forested public lands, demonstrating how the Forest Service policy of suppressing all fire was doing more harm than good in the long run. He argued (and his arguments eventually carried the day) that fire needed to be respected as a necessary and essential force of nature in fire-dependent ecosystems, and that land managers needed to learn how to sometimes partner with it instead of always and only attacking it.

But the much broader issue – the one that eventually ground to a halt the dominant Forest Service paradigm of managing the forests only as fire-free timber factories for the forest products industry – was this: what role fire should play in managing the nation's forests depends on the ultimate purposes for which they are being managed (Pyne, 2004).

With the growing influence of the modern environmental movement in the 1960s, Congress passed the Wilderness Act in 1964 to make provision for establishing on all public lands vast areas in which no further resource-extractive activities could take place, thus reining in the Forest Service's dominant default option of managing for timber production and fire suppression. Then Congress proceeded to start creating wilderness areas within national forests that otherwise might have fallen to the logger's axe. And environmental groups started besieging the Forest Service with lawsuits intended to keep it from destroying pristine backcountry landscapes that might be declared wilderness areas in the future.

In the 1970s Congress thought it could solve the problem by adopting laws requiring the Forest Service to undertake ever-more elaborate planning processes encompassing the views of an ever-widening circle of interest groups. But all these requirements really did was to create an arena within which these contenders could fight each other to a draw, with the Forest Service as a hapless referee taking punches from all sides. Today's forest management plans tend to read more like treaties among war-weary combatants than the thoughtful, deliberative, science-based documents Congress may have hoped for when they wrote statutes such as the National Forest Management Act and Resource Planning Act.

An additional challenge facing public land managers at any level of government, from the US Forest Service to the East Bay Regional Park District managing the forested open space in the Berkeley and Oakland Hills, is how to articulate your fire-related land management plans with those of adjoining residential communities. Some of the foresters in the EBRPD were Biswell's students, and were taking his lessons to heart.

In the mid-1970s, a hard freeze killed over 90% of the eucalyptus trees in Tilden Park in the Berkeley Hills. The world's most flammable tree imported from the world's most flammable landscape (the Australian bush), the dead standing eukes could have created a firestorm the following summer and fall that could have devastated the region. So the park district went in and cut all the dead ones down. Since that time it has been doing what it can in the string of parks it manages atop the East Bay hills to keep deadfall to a minimum, and otherwise manage the parkland forests in as fire-protective mode as it is capable of doing.

But just across the road and downhill from the parks lies the most expensive private property in the East Bay – a mix of starkly modern and stately old shingled mansions with broad wooden decks and stunning views of the San Francisco Bay – homes overhung by huge and highly flammable eucalyptus and Monterey Pine trees These were the disasters-in-waiting Biswell warned of in his pleas over the years for the cities of Berkeley and Oakland to require mitigation measures in these fatally vulnerable neighborhoods.

His prescient warnings fell on deaf ears, and the lessons he was trying to teach his neighbors and their local governments went unlearned. In rejecting proposals for making the East Bay Hills more fire-safe in the 1980s, some of its residents responded the same way high-country residents in the rural Mountain West do: we moved here for the beauty of our surroundings. We'd rather take our chances with fire than modify our landscape to make it less likely.

An additional factor at work with residents of the East Bay was their relationship to other environmental risks. The Hayward Fault runs beneath the East Bay Hills, under some of the region's most valuable real estate, as well as under the football stadium at the uphill end of the UC-Berkeley campus. All of the faults in California's seismic mosaic periodically relieve the tectonic stresses upon them by periodically shifting – the intervals between them being well-documented. The longer the period between these adjustments, the bigger the shift. The Hayward Fault is now about 30 years overdue for a major "adjustment" (i.e., an earthquake at Richter magnitude 7 or above).

Residents of the East Bay Hills live with heightened risk already, and they know it. When the "big one" hits, it will quite probably rupture gas lines, ignite the eucalyptus and pines, and burn down everything that hasn't already fallen down. So for many Hill dwellers, the idea of cutting down some of their trees and replacing their redwood decks with more fire-resistant ones simply didn't seem worth the cost and the sacrifice.

Then came the 1991 Tunnel fire (so named for the highway tunnel running beneath the burn area), just as Biswell predicted it would. Over 3,500 residences were burned down and 25 residents lost their lives – most of them trying to flee in their cars or on foot – just as he foresaw and foretold. It's reasonable enough to assume that finally, then, Berkeley and Oakland would take steps to make the Hill neighborhoods safer and more fire-resilient. Reasonable, perhaps, but – facing concerted opposition from politically influential Hill dwellers – local governments mostly took baby steps, at least insofar as existing structures and vegetation were concerned (Hoffer, 2006). While new construction in the burned over areas needed to be fire-resistant, and new landscaping needed to take defensible space into account, residents in the unburned areas successfully fought off initial efforts to mandate removal or even the thinning of the eukes and Monterey pines, or removal of flammable understory shrub species. As a result, those areas remain nearly as vulnerable to fire now as they were in 1991 (Hoffer).

Applying Law's Moral Purpose to WUI Wildfire Mitigation

The deadly magnitude of the 1991 Tunnel Fire, combined with local governments' disinclination to mandate WUI wildfire mitigation in vulnerable neighborhoods in its aftermath, contributed to the California Legislature's decision to take matters into its own hands. The "Bates Bill" it adopted in 1993 established mandatory statewide standards for WUI wildfire mitigation on all private property over which the state has fire control authority and responsibility, and placed on local governments the burden of proof of showing why they should not adopt state standards at the local level. The legislature had decided to do what local governments would not: assert moral authority in using the police powers to protect public health and safety in the WUI when local governments would not.

This is not necessarily to assert that Berkeley and Oakland were failing to fulfill their moral obligations to their constituents by failing to mandate strict wildfire mitigation in existing hill-top neighborhoods – only that they obviously had a different sense of what the nature of that obligation actually is. And to better understand this divergence in views and value structures (between the state and local governments) on the use of power, we need a language that better explicates those value structures.

Jurisprudential theorist Philip Selznick recommended just such a framework in his 1992 opus, *The Moral Commonwealth* (Selznick, 1992). In it, he identified seven core values the institutions of any political community needed to simultaneously honor at some threshold level in order to be seen as fulfilling its moral obligations to its constituents. Morally grounded community, he held, is recognizable by its simultaneous honoring of certain key values at some threshold level: historicity, identity, mutuality, plurality, autonomy, participation, and integration.

Historicity is both an understanding of and respect for a community's shared history as an important basis for wise decision making about its future. *Identity* derives from shared history (as well as from family lineage, ethnicity, religion, profession, or common purpose); this is the means by which one defines oneself in relation to community.

Mutuality connotes reciprocal obligation; it is the duty of care we owe to each other by virtue of community membership, as well as the community's medium for the expression of common purpose (including the making of public policy). *Plurality* refers to "intermediate associations" in the larger community within which individuals can more immediately experience connection with others who hold shared views, interests, and purpose. Without these, the community becomes nothing more than the relationship between a collection of individuals and one central authority.

When the values of either mutuality or plurality are coercively enforced, it is nearly always at the expense of personal *autonomy* and liberty. The importance of respect for personal autonomy within community – in both theory and practice – is what most clearly distinguishes Selznick's "liberal communitarianism" from the earlier formative principles of a somewhat more conservative view of communitarianism put forth by theorists such as Etzioni and Glendon.

Regarding the value of *participation*, Robert Putnam and others' "social capital" and civic engagement are every bit as crucial to Selznick's concept of community as they are to that of either Putnam (2000) or Bellah et al. (1985). Personal, voluntary investment in the enterprise of community is ultimately what makes it possible. While autonomy respects the right to be left alone, participation respects equally the right of those who wish to participate to have the opportunity to do so.

Finally, *integration* refers to the "supportive institutions, norms, beliefs, and practices" required to actualize the foregoing values – to ensure that they are all honored simultaneously to some recognizable degree. In Selznick's view, the first six values and the community's ability to hold them all in balance via the seventh, comprise a metric: "the moral quality of a community is measured by its ability to defend all the chief values at stake, to hold them in tension as necessary, and to encourage their refinement and elaboration" (Selznick, 1992, p. 364).

The Case of WUI Wildfire Mitigation in the U.S. Mountain West

Like California, the wildlands–urban interfaces in other mountain states of the American West are the areas fastest growing in population in those states; and catastrophic fires there account for the greatest losses of both human life and property to fire. Unlike California, however, most of the other states leave it up to local governments to decide whether and to what extent they want to compel residents to engage in preventive wildfire mitigation.

Given these increasing dangers associated with living in the WUI and the scattershot responses of state government, in 2012 I led a class research effort, the purpose of which was to do a comparative analysis of WUI wildfire mitigation laws in seven western states (Burton, 2013). We categorized results along two parameters: locus of authority and form of authority. Locus of authority refers to the level of government from which WUI wildfire mitigation regulations (if there are any) emanate. Form of authority further distinguishes government standards using the "soft law/hard law" distinction; that is, are WUI wildfire mitigation standards advisory or mandatory?

Integrating these two dimensions, we categorized the states in the study into three groups. *Common standard* states (California and Oregon) have statewide mandatory standards enforceable at every level of government. The *local option* states (Arizona, Colorado, and New Mexico), have no statewide standards, but empower local governments to adopt them if they wish to do so. *Hybrid* states (Nevada and Utah) have statewide advisory standards and empower local governments to implement and enforce them as mandatory.

Applying Selznick's typology to these forms of regulation, what we see is that due to variations in regional political culture, the laws in these states bespeak variations in the hierarchical ordering of the values Selznick posits. Thus, the common standard states the *mutuality* value (the mutual obligations we owe to each other, as well as the obligation of government to protect communal health and welfare) presence of place, and therefore subordinates the values of *autonomy* (private property rights), *pluralism* (variations in regulatory approach among local governments), and direct *participation* (community control).

In the local option states, just the reverse is true. Deference to individual autonomy, local control, and community-based participation take precedence over the mutuality value, which local communities are free to either emphasize or ignore. The hybrid states fall into that category for two reasons. Utah has strongly recommended statewide standards, and provides programmatic assistance to local jurisdictions to help their residents comply and then to monitor compliance. For local jurisdictions (e.g., counties) who choose not to implement the statewide standard, however, if a fire breaks out on state land, the local jurisdiction can be held liable for maintaining dangerous conditions on its lands.

Nevada has voluntary statewide standards, except in two regions: Lake Tahoe (astride the California/Nevada border) and Lake Meade (behind Boulder Dam), both of which are areas managed under the auspices of interstate compacts. In both of these joint management areas, California's common standard approach applies.

The growing number of injuries and fatalities among WUI residents and firefighters is very much tied to the increasing numbers of people moving into the WUI and the increasing dangers of living there. The 19 wildland firefighters immolated in the Yarnell Hill fire in Arizona in 2013 lost their lives trying to defend a town that was not subject to mandatory wildfire mitigation and whose residents had done little to protect themselves: Arizona is a local option state. The WUI residents who died in Colorado's 2012 and 2013 wildfire seasons also lived in communities with either uneven or no mandatory regulations; Colorado is also a local option state. And some of its residents paid for that distinction with their lives.

As both Birkland and Diamond emphasize, political value structures are not fixed and immutable forces of nature. Resilient political cultures reexamine and re-order the relationship of their core values as changing circumstances seem to require; that adaptability is what makes them resilient. Those that lack that capacity prove out George Santayana's adage of being doomed to repeat history from which they cannot learn. They have failed the test of historicity – one of Philip Selznick's hallmarks of moral community.

REFERENCES

Agee, J. (1998). Forward to the paperback edition. In H. Biswell (Ed.), *Prescribed burning in California wildlands vegetation management*. Berkeley, CA: University of California Press.

Bellah, R., Madsen, R., Sullivan, W., Swindler, A., & Tipton., S. (1985). *Habits of the heart*. Berkeley, CA: University of California Press.

Biswell, H. (1989). *Prescribed burning in California wildlands vegetation management*. Berkeley, CA: University of California Press.

Bok, S. (1983). *Secrets*. New York, NY: Random House.

Burton, L. (2013). *Wildfire mitigation law in the mountain states of the American West: A comparative assessment*. Working paper series. School of Public Affairs, University of Colorado Denver. Retrieved from http://www.ucdenver.edu/academics/colleges/SPA/Research/EAWG/Research/wildfires/Pages/default.aspx

Butler, D. (2007). Focusing events in the early 20th century. In C. Rubin, (Ed.), *Emergency management: The American experience* (pp. 1900–2005). Fairfax, VA: Public Entity Risk Institute.

Davis, M. (1998). *Ecology of fear: Los Angeles and the imagination of disaster*. New York, NY: Holt.

Diamond, J. (2005). *Collapse*. New York, NY: Penguin Books.

Egan, T. (2006). *The worst hard time*. New York, NY: Houghton Mifflin.

Egan, T. (2009). *The big burn*. Boston, MA: Houghton-Mifflin.

Fraser, C. (2013). Megadrought in the U.S. Southwest: A bad omen for forests globally. Yale University School of Forestry and Environmental Studies, Hartford, CT. Environment 360. Retrieved from http://blog.smu.edu/research/2012/05/15/ancient-tree-ring-records-from-the-southwest-u-s-suggest-todays-megafires-are-atypical/. Accessed on July 11, 2013.

Geschwind, C. (2001). *California earthquakes: Science, risk, and the politics of hazard mitigation*. Baltimore, MD: Johns Hopkins University Press.

Hansen, G., & Condon, E. (1989). *Denial of Disaster*. San Francisco, CA: Cameron.

Headwaters Economics. (2009). *Solutions to the rising cost of fighting fires in the wildlands-urban interface*. Bozeman, MT: Headwaters Economics. Retrieved from http://headwaterseconomics.org/wphw/wp-content/uploads/HeadwatersFireCosts.pdf

Hoffer, P. (2006). *Seven fires: the Urban Infernos that reshaped America*. New York, NY: Perseus Books Group.

Putnam, R. (2000). *Bowling alone*. New York, NY: Simon and Schuster.

Pyne, S. (2004). *Tending fire*. Washington, DC: Island Press.

Selznick, P. (1992). *The moral commonwealth*. Berkeley, CA: University of California Press.

Smith, C. (2006). "What San Francisco Didn't Learn From the '06 Quake". San Francisco Chronicle. Retrieved from http://www.sfgate.com/homeandgarden/article/What-San-Francisco-didn-t-learn-from-the-06-quake-2520018.php. Accessed on Mar. 24, 2014.

Steinberg, T. (2000). *Acts of God: The unnatural history of natural disasters in America*. New York, NY: Oxford Press.

SYMBOLIC, COGNITIVE, AND STRUCTURAL OBSTACLES TO FORMULATING DISASTER POLICY

Justin Pidot

ABSTRACT

This chapter identifies and analyzes three systemic obstacles to American public policy addressing natural disasters: symbolic obstacles, cognitive obstacles, and structural obstacles. The way we talk about natural disaster, the way we think about the risks of building in hazardous places, and structural aspects of American political institutions all favor development over restraint. These forces have such strength that in the wake of most disasters society automatically and thoughtlessly responds by rebuilding what was damaged or destroyed, even if reconstruction perpetuates disaster vulnerability. Only by addressing each of the obstacles identified are reform efforts likely to succeed.

Keywords: Disaster mitigation obstacles; symbolic; structural; cognitive

Special Issue: Cassandra's Curse: The Law and Foreseeable Future Disasters
Studies in Law, Politics, and Society, Volume 68, 33–64

ISSN: 1059-4337/doi:10.1108/S1059-433720150000068016

INTRODUCTION

The chapters in this book contribute to a long tradition of scholarship calling attention to the role humans play in transforming natural events into natural disasters. As Phil O'Keefe, Ken Westgate, and Ben Wisner wrote in a 1976 path-breaking article in the journal *Nature*, "[w]ithout people there is no disaster" (p. 566). That realization has profound consequences. The choices we make facilitate and even create natural disasters and we have the potential to make better choices. Unfortunately, society does a remarkably poor job accounting for its starring role in the genesis of natural disaster. Despite repeated calls for reform, development continues at an explosive pace in areas of extreme hazard.

Florida, for example, a state facing hurricane risk so severe that private insurance companies have largely refused to issue policies covering wind damage, has also experienced one of the highest growth rates in the country (Kunreuther & Michel-Kerjan, 2006; Pidot, 2007). Within Florida, development is concentrated in counties facing particularly acute hurricane risks. The National Oceanic and Atmospheric Administration estimates that St. Lucie County will be struck by a hurricane an average of once every eight years and a major hurricane an average of once every 19 years (NOAA, 2012a, 2012b).[1] Yet the population in St. Lucie County increased by more than 40 percent between 2000 and 2010, as did the number of housing units.[2] The same is true of development subject to other natural hazards. As Lloyd Burton's chapter discusses, living along the boundary between urban areas and wild lands has become increasingly popular, despite the high risk posed by wildfire. The Department of Agriculture predicts that by 2030 more than 2.2 million homes will be located at the fire-prone, wildland–urban interface in the Rocky Mountains, a 40 percent increase from 2006 (United States Department of Agriculture, Office of Inspector General, 2006, p. 6).

In this chapter, I attempt to systematically examine the reasons we remain blind to the dangers of natural disasters and identify three categories of obstacles that impede the adoption of thoughtful, proactive policies to guide development in hazardous areas. These categories – symbolic, cognitive, and structural – reinforce one another, collectively causing society to make bad decisions both before disaster strikes and in its wake. So, for example, the symbolic importance attached to reconstruction in the wake of disaster may reinforce cognitive mechanisms that distort perceptions of risk. In turn, these cognitive mechanisms may amplify policy distortions created by structural aspects of government.

The purpose of this chapter is diagnostic, rather than prescriptive. Better understanding the reasons for these collective failures may help illuminate a path forward. Better understanding the obstacles facing proactive disaster policy will enable society to respond to natural hazards more appropriately. Each type of obstacle lends itself to different responses. Symbolic obstacles generally require a discursive remedy. Cognitive obstacles require strategies to correct or avoid systematic errors of cognition. Finally, structural obstacles require new arrangements for political institutions. A comprehensive policy that harnesses multiple strategies to address all three obstacles is most likely to result in a successful and sustained effort to reduce vulnerability to natural disaster. I leave a comprehensive consideration of specific mechanisms policy makers could deploy to overcome the obstacles identified in this Chapter for another day. Instead, the conclusion of this chapter offers only a brief, preliminary, and illustrative discussion of solutions as a means of demonstrating that the analysis offered could become the foundation for policy reform.

SYMBOLIC OBSTACLES

The language used to describe natural disasters shapes the cultural understanding of those events and affects response. Take this remark Vermont Governor Peter Shumlin made after he traveled the state taking stock of the damage from Hurricane Irene: "I kind of felt like I was coming out of a war zone" (Hallenbeck, 2011, p. 1A). Or this description of New York City in the aftermath of Superstorm Sandy by Mayor Michael Bloomberg: "To describe it as looking like pictures we have seen at the end of World War II is not overstating it" (Barron, 2012, p. A1). Describing the sites of natural disasters as war zones is commonplace (Adkins, 2011; Milwaukee Journal Sentinel, 2012; Scherer, 2011), and this imagery taps into a prevailing cultural framework that posits natural disaster as an armed assault by nature on society. Invoking this war metaphor infuses disaster response with powerful symbolism and triggers maladaptive responses. Rebuilding in the wake of disaster becomes an imperative. To do otherwise concedes defeat.

There are obvious similarities between war and natural disaster – conditions in Vermont following Hurricane Irene did resemble those found in a war zone. Flooding had caused widespread damage to public infrastructure, houses, and businesses. The governor and other government officials toured the state by helicopter because travel over land was impossible in some areas, and thousands of members of the National Guard, dressed in camouflage and operating military vehicles, descended on the state to aid with response.

But only certain aspects of natural disasters resemble war. Nature does not attack strategically or with malice like human foes, and responsibility for the damage caused by natural events lies in no small part with individuals who build in areas subject to natural hazards and the policymakers that facilitate this activity. In the words of Professor Richard Lazarus, "Mother Nature is not humankind's enemy. Nor is Mother Nature invariably our friend ... Mother Nature simply is" (Lazarus, 2007, p. 1021).

Metaphor, like the metaphor of war used to describe natural disasters, plays an important part in framing a social understanding of events that transpire in the world and can play a particularly important role in shaping popular understanding of difficult-to-grasp scientific concepts. The philosopher Kenneth Burke defines metaphor as "a device for seeing something in terms of something else" (Burke, 1989, p. 247). Metaphor, then, enables transference of understanding and insight from one conceptual arena to another.

But at the same time, metaphor risks causing misunderstanding and distortion. Understanding natural disasters by reference to the metaphor of armed conflict holds powerful allure because of the social resonance of war and because the metaphor accords with cultural mythology that identifies nature as the perpetrator of natural disasters. Seen through this lens, domestic natural disasters become an attack on the American homeland. It is no coincidence, perhaps, that the Federal Emergency Management Agency, charged with managing the federal response to natural disasters, is now housed within the Department of Homeland Security (Department of Homeland Security, Office of the Inspector General, 2009).

I am not the first to suggest that language and mythology shape perceptions of disaster policy. Bates and Peacock (1987) have argued, for example, that using the single term "disaster" to describe tragic events across multiple scales – personal, familial, neighborhood-level, and societal – confuses our understanding of these phenomena, which often have little in common other than the human suffering involved.[3] By extension, Bates and Peacock's analysis may suggest that identifying natural events, terrorist attacks, and large-scale accidents as "disasters," as is commonly done, may imply a false equivalency between the causes of these events.

Lisa Grow Sun's chapter in this book, along with her work elsewhere (2011), examines the effect that mythology about natural disaster has on short-term government response, rather than the longer-term, society-wide responses addressed in this chapter. Professor Sun's analysis focuses on a commonly held belief that disaster breeds civil disorder, and she argues that media outlets play a central role in perpetuating that belief even in the face of contrary evidence. As she explains, this error has "important implications for disaster law and policy" (pp. 1135–1136), leading the government to overemphasize law enforcement at the expense of humanitarian efforts.[4]

The metaphor of natural disaster as conflict resonates with significant cultural history. Historical views on natural disasters equivocated as to whether they were agents of good or evil. Take for example, alternate explanations of earthquakes in fifteenth-century Egypt. Prominent Islamic intellectuals of the time recognized two possible explanations for earthquakes. At times, earthquakes were viewed as a divine act necessary to punish a sinful world. At other times, earthquakes were attributed to evil. According to one belief, the world balanced on a large fish. The devil would, on occasion, flatter the fish and it would swell up with pride, shaking the world. God would calm the fish, restoring order (Akasoy, 2007). Parallel understandings of natural disaster have also long been a feature of the Judeo-Christian tradition, including a view of natural disaster generally as divine retribution or the work of infernal forces (Chester & Duncan, 2010).

Natural disasters continue to be described in a language that hearkens back to this religious history. For example, the phrase "act of God" is routinely used in the law to describe natural disaster.[5] Despite this legal reference to God, secular understandings of natural disaster dominate the contemporary discourse in the United States. As Ted Steinberg (2000) has richly detailed, by the end of the nineteenth century, religious understandings of natural disasters had fallen out of favor with the nation's elite, in no small part because such a perspective was viewed as undermining economic recovery. Steinberg suggests that natural disasters were rewritten, drained of moral meaning, and dressed up in the clothing of nature, rather than supernatural forces. But this transformation did not fully embrace scientific conceptions of natural events. Rather, powerful economic and social forces mobilized to downplay the importance of disasters. This mobilization led to, among other things, news reports by dishonest reporters influenced by financers with stakes in perpetuating booming development. Following the 1906 San Francisco earthquake, for example, reporters recast the event as an out-of-control fire, transforming a disaster arising out of the geological setting of the city into one that could occur anywhere. Similar efforts to deemphasize natural disaster followed the 1926 hurricane that struck Miami. The editor of the Miami Herald purportedly directed his staff to divide damage assessments by ten in their reporting to minimize concern about the dangers of living in the hurricane-prone city. Steinberg describes these efforts and many more as the "politics of forgetfulness" (p. 201), whereby economic and political leaders systematically attempted to distract from natural disaster to facilitate development in hazard-prone areas.

Steinberg captures a sensibility that dominated much of the twentieth century. Projecting safety and calm in the wake of disaster allowed cities to continue with rapid development, and, indeed, the desire to minimize the effects of disaster was so great that cities would turn down offers of financial assistance. Recent decades, however, have witnessed a return to sensationalized accounts of natural disasters, perhaps as a result of increasingly available information, which has made concealing natural hazards difficult, and a belief that the federal treasury provides a seemingly inexhaustible supply of recovery dollars (Moss, 1999).[6]

The contemporary incarnation of the disaster narrative continues to be predominantly secular. That is not to say that the religious narrative has died out altogether. A 2011 survey conducted by the Public Religion Research Institute found (2011) that a significant minority of Americans believes that natural disasters are of divine origin. The majority of Americans, however, view disasters as natural events. But even within this frame, disasters are often described as "acts of nature" rather than occurrences, imbuing agency to natural forces and maintaining the sense, even if not specifically voiced, that nature and humans are involved in a conflict in which nature is an enemy that must be resisted.

This cultural approach to disaster is reflected in and reinforced by the mass media's approach to natural disaster, which relies routinely on the metaphor of armed conflict as a source of evocative language and catchy headlines. Powerful storms "assault" and "attack" (Borenstein, Melvin, & Gibson, 1992; Burdeau & Kunzelman, 2012; Cauchon, McCoy, Keen, & Schmit, 2012; Schneyer & Gebrekidan, 2012; Yamanouchi, 2012). Nature acts with violence, terrorizing, and wreaking havoc on the human world, leaving in its wake areas resembling a "post-apocalyptic warzone" or "looking like they ha[ve] been hit by a bomb" (Action News at 11, 2011).[7] In the wake of Hurricane Katrina, New Orleans was consistently described by on-the-ground observers as a "war zone" (Tierney, Bevc, & Kuligowski, 2006, p. 71). In this war metaphor, nature is personified and made the enemy. Thus, the damage done to human development by natural events is an expression of nature's "fury" or "capricious wrath" (Alexander, 2012; Bastardi, 2012; Lake, 2012).

Similar narratives of the almost-intelligent malevolence of nature play themselves out in popular culture, particularly through disaster movies like *Dante's Peak*, *Twister*, and *The Day After Tomorrow*. Indeed, the history of the disaster-film genre suggests that the narrative parallels it exhibits with war movies are hardly coincidental. Rather, as public popularity for war stories dwindled due, in part, to shifting attitudes about the Vietnam War, Hollywood turned to stories about humans versus nature as "a generic surrogate for war films" (Mauch, 2009).

The narrative of armed conflict has become even more resonant in the wake of the 9/11 terrorist attacks. Indeed, 9/11 has become something of a benchmark against which other disasters are measured. Consider, for example, a column by New York Times columnist Paul Krugman (2005) explaining that "the failed response to Katrina shows that we are less ready to cope with a terrorist attack today than we were four years ago" (p. A21).[8] Or this, by columnist Frank Rich (2005):

> [W]e cannot allow ourselves to forget the real history surrounding 9/11; it is the Rosetta stone for what is happening now. If we are to pull ourselves out of the disasters of Katrina and Iraq alike, we must live in the real world, not the fantasyland of the administration's faith-based propaganda (p. 10).[9]

A newspaper article running in the Chicago Tribune explained that "even if the death toll from Katrina exceeds the roughly 3,000 fatalities from the 9/11 attacks, the obvious difference, initially, was how frightening and ominous 9/11 felt from border to border and coast to coast" (Zorn, 2005, p. Metro 1). Alternatively, consider this article in the New York Times (Feuer, 2005, § 14 p.1) describing sympathy expressed by those that lost a loved one in 9/11 for the victims of Hurricane Katrina:

> There is suffering, and there is suffering. There is private pain, and then there is the sort of pain that suddenly goes public, that is broadcast to the nation … It's a select group. The 9/11 families belong to it, of course, as do those who lost a loved one in the 1995 Oklahoma City bombing. Now the victims of Katrina, too, belong.

A column in the Savannah Morning News following Superstorm Sandy sums up the sentiment, explaining that "Mother Nature can be a terrorist like no other" (Hubbard, 2012).

The power of the conflict imagery has not been lost on advocacy groups. For example, an advertisement calling for a federal program for wind insurance read, "How do you deal with an enemy that has no government, no money trail and no qualms about killing women and children? The enemy is Mother Nature" (New York Times, 2011). This advertisement primes associations between natural disaster and armed conflict, evoking events like war and terrorism, with the obvious purpose of triggering a social response of resistance to enemy incursion. Military advertising may further strengthen these associations. National Guard recruitment efforts often mix images of disaster response with images of armed conflict (3 Doors Down, 2007; National Guard, 2009).

Political leaders draw on this language too. Consider this statement by the mayor of Atlantic City following Superstorm Sandy: "When Mother Nature sends her wrath your way, we're at her mercy" (Wilson, 2012, para. 7). Or these statements made by President Barack Obama and Mayor of New Orleans Mitch Landrieu in the hours before Hurricane Isaac made landfall in Louisiana in August 2012. Mayor Landrieu expressed the urgency of the situation by explaining, "We are officially into the fight, and the city of New Orleans is now on the front lines" (Schwartz & Robertson, 2012, p. A1). New Orleans, however, was prepared. "We are battle-ready," reported the Mayor (Hennessy-Fiske & Zucchino, 2012, p. A7). President Obama used similar language of conflict to invoke national unity, stating, "[W]hen disaster strikes, we're not Democrats or Republicans first, we are Americans first" (Schwartz & Robertson, 2012, p. A1).[10] Similar rhetoric was used in the wake of Hurricane Katrina. Testifying before the U.S. House of Representatives, Louisiana Governor Kathleen Blanco (2005) explicitly invoked feelings of patriotism tied up in armed conflict in discussing Hurricane Katrina: "After World War II our decision to rebuild Europe was farsighted and courageous. History will treat us well if we exhibit the same kind of political courage now." And in the wake of Hurricane Andrew, a local government official in Florida posed the question as television cameras rolled: "Where in the hell is the cavalry?" (Washington, 2007, p. B9).

The metaphor of natural event as attack is reinforced by the fact that the domestic response to natural disaster closely parallels responses to military action. While the notion of waiting for the "cavalry" evokes images of battlefields and weary soldiers desperate for reinforcements, local communities struck by natural disasters actually await military aid. For example, members of the New York National Guard's 101st Cavalry were activated to assist areas damaged by Superstorm Sandy (Goldenberg, 2012). The military also has a prominent role in engineering efforts to stave off disaster. The Army Corps of Engineers is primarily charged with construction and maintenance of structural defenses to natural hazards (U.S. Army Corps of Engineers, 2012). And emergency management agencies evolved out of civilian defense groups designed to address threats of air raid during times of armed conflict (Quarantelli, Lagadec, & Boin, 2006). The vivid image of military convoys rushing to disaster sites only reinforces the sense that we are, indeed, at war with nature.

All of this talk of war, assault, and attack perpetuates vulnerability to natural hazards by framing reconstruction as necessary. In the aftermath of 9/11, the phrase "these colors don't run" became a popular means of communicating America's resolve (Grand Rapids Press, 2011, p. A16). Retaliation and reconstruction were seen as the only available response to the terrorist attacks, else the terrorists would have secured a victory over the American psyche. Natural disasters trigger a similar response, a "knee-jerk reaction … to rebuild the same roads and bridges that existed before and bigger, more expensive homes" (Spinner, 2012, p. B1). Where a foreign agent – be it a foreign power or an overly proud fish – causes harm to the homeland, we respond using a militaristic frame in which we must defend ourselves and ultimately defeat the other. Such responses may be appropriate in the case of terrorist attack or armed conflict, but they have no value in the face of hurricanes, tornados, and earthquakes that pay no heed to society's actions. Natural events do not *intend* to cause destruction and terror. Proudly demonstrating a commitment to rebuild in the same hazard-prone locations will not deter future events. The rhetoric of conflict forecloses, or at least renders more difficult, decisions to rebuild in more sensible, more safe locations because, in the narrative of armed conflict, such response represents capitulation and retreat.

COGNITIVE OBSTACLES

The symbolic obstacles to reform discussed above interact with, and are magnified by, aspects of human cognition that systematically skew public perception of disaster risk.[11] Even when science provides a reasonably certain prediction about the likelihood of disaster, the human brain may unreasonably discount that risk. The perception that reconstruction isn't risky reinforces the intuition that rebuilding is a symbolic necessity. Here, I explore cognitive errors that may skew perceptions of natural hazards and thereby directly affect not only policymakers' interest in reducing vulnerability but also the public demand for such action.

In recent decades, psychologists have uncovered numerous ways that cognition leads to seemingly irrational decision making.[12] Processes of so-called "bounded rationality" lead to systematic skew in thinking that can have profound implications for law (Jolls, Sunstein, & Thaler, 1998, pp. 1477–1478). The human brain has trouble conceptualizing probabilistic events, particularly those with low frequency and high severity. This problem becomes extreme as probabilities approach zero. As a form of mental shortcut, in some circumstances the mind perceives very low probabilities as impossibilities. So, for example, scholars investigating insurance markets have suggested that this mental shortcut may account for widespread underinvestment in insurance to protect against very-low-probability events, particularly natural disasters (Kunreuther & Pauly, 2004; Kunreuther, Novemsky, & Kahneman, 2001; Slovic, Fischhoff, Lichtenstein, Corrigen, and Combs (1977)). Similarly, viewing low risks as zero risks may lead individuals to make economically irrational decisions about where and how to build.

Consider how this cognitive error could affect someone owning property in a 500-year flood plain. Such a risk might be sufficiently low that decisions about development will be made with no thought to flood risk, even if construction is economically marginal and would not be cost justified if the risk of loss were taken into account. This error may also infect government decisions, which are often made with little consideration for low likelihood events. Flood-control dams are rarely built to withstand 500-year flood events and the NFIP does not include any minimum design standards for buildings subject to such risks (GAO, 1995).[13] In some circumstances, of course, these decisions are economically rational based on the risks, but in others, risks may simply be neglected. This is true despite the fact that a flood that occurs on average every 500 years has a 1 percent chance to occur every five years, and a 10 percent chance to occur every 50 years. Such floods have done significant harm, as the residents of Duluth, Minnesota, discovered in June of 2012, where a 500-year flood caused more than $100 million in damage (Brooks, 2012). Because individuals and policymakers perceive risks likely to actualize an average of once every five hundred years as risk-free, they may overlook cost-justified mitigation efforts.

Other cognitive processes distort perceptions of natural hazards even when they are perceived. These rare events may be subject to two competing cognitive errors that lead to systematic devaluation of risk. The first, the gambler's fallacy, depresses estimation of risks in the immediate aftermath of disaster. The gambler's fallacy causes people to believe that an unlikely event that has recently occurred is less likely to recur in the near future. The gambler's fallacy is basically the belief that lightning doesn't strike the same place twice.[14] The gambler's fallacy, then, leads individuals and government entities to overinvest in reconstruction in the wake of disaster based on a mistaken assumption that a period of repose and relative safety will follow.

Interviews with those struck by multiple disasters bear out the operation of the gambler's fallacy. In upstate New York, a business executive for a company that had built a large commercial facility in a floodplain damaged in Hurricane Irene explained that since flooding had recently occurred, "[w]e thought we had a hundred years" (Semple, 2011, p. A13). Similarly, a Louisiana property owner explained his decision to rebuild saying "something like [Hurricane] Katrina happens only once in a hundred years. ... By that time, I'll be dead" (Whoriskey, 2007, p. A1). As a Florida resident explained, "I never had a problem. Then came [a hurricane]. Afterward, I said it wouldn't happen twice" (Bridges, 2000, p. B2). Similarly, in repeated flooding of the Susquehanna River in 2006 and 2011, one local resident explained that he believed the 2006 event had been a "once-in-a-lifetime flood" and another emphasized that "you don't expect it two times in five years" (Hall, Legere, & Mrozinski, 2011, para. 38, 45). This type of thinking can lead people to invest heavily in the wake of disaster. This behavior is particularly destructive because past experience with flood events may have little predictive value in an era in which climate change substantially alters patterns of weather, precipitation, and storm surge.

The gambler's fallacy affects estimation of risk in the immediate aftermath of disaster, but as time passes and memories of the aftermath fade, a second cognitive error may kick in and continue to skew risk perceptions. Specifically, the availability heuristic may replace the gambler's fallacy, leading to a similar result. The availability heuristic leads people to assess the likelihood that something will occur based on the ease with which an example of it comes to mind. Over time, the experience of disaster will come to mind less easily, leading to assumptions of relative safety and causing people to make decisions as though the natural hazards no longer existed. When disaster strikes again, people express surprise and shock at the ending of a long period of calm. As an experienced insurance adjuster put it, "Wherever it's been a long time since the last hurricane ... people become complacent" (Honeyman, 2012, p. 66).

Another version of the availability heuristic may also be at work. People typically believe that others make rational decisions, and observing others living and working in hazard-prone areas may lead to assumptions about safety (Kuran & Sunstein, 1999). In other words, observing others living and working in hazard-prone areas provides readily available examples that appear to suggest that risks are low. Similarly, people often overestimate the effectiveness of mitigation measures.[15] Because cognition depends in part on observation of the behavior of others, cognitive errors can compound, causing whole communities to adopt false understandings of disaster risk based on assumptions about the beliefs of others.

This dynamic can be particularly strong when public-works projects designed to reduce hazards are involved.[16] For example, people overestimate the protection afforded by dikes designed to protect against floods, and this is particularly so when others live and work in the shadow of those projects. This hard lesson has been taught repeatedly. The Central Valley of California is a particularly dramatic example. Before the construction of dams, the valley was subject to dramatic flooding (Department of Water Resources, 2007). After dams were constructed, residential and commercial development swiftly dominated the landscape to such an extent that "new homeowners have little notion that they live in a floodplain" (Diringer & McLeod, 1997, p. A1). But dams can only contain so much water, and in 1997 more than 185 homes were flooded when the Tuolumne River jumped its heavily engineered banks. Hurricane Katrina also taught the lesson of engineering increasing vulnerability in an even more dramatic fashion (American Society of Civil Engineers Hurricane Katrina External Review Panel, 2007; Burby, 2006).

The cognitive errors this chapter has been discussing skew perceptions of risk at both the individual and socio-political levels. This occurs because these errors influence policymakers individually and also shape the public's appetite for regulation. Where the electorate believes development is relatively risk free, they are likely to oppose regulation that will increase the cost of development.

Moreover, sophisticated parties can harness cognitive phenomena to advance their political agenda. Timur Kuran and Cass Sunstein have identified "availability entrepreneurs" leveraging cognitive errors in the context of political debates about technological risks (Kuran & Sunstein, 1999, p. 710-12). Kuran and Sunstein identify circumstances where advocates for restrictive policies have highlighted or even invented risks to trigger the availability heuristic. Similarly, availability entrepreneurs with vested interests in relaxed development policies may emphasize, as part of their advocacy, examples of development in hazard-prone areas that have not experienced catastrophic losses. In so doing, examples of "safe" development may more easily come to mind, causing people to overestimate safety.

In addition to the cognitive phenomena discussed above, the very fact that people perceive natural disasters as natural may lead to an underappreciation of risk. In experimental settings, individuals express a substantially greater degree of concern about artificial risks than natural risks, even when the risks are of the same magnitude (Viscusi, 1995). So, people assume they are relatively safe in the face of flood risk, even as they demand swift political action in response to artificial hazardous substances like those detected at Love Canal.

A final cognitive error that may affect risk perceptions is known as the "affect heuristic," which causes emotion to influence cognition, and particularly judgments about risk. The operation of the affect heuristic skews risk perception based on emotional attachment. So, for example, people tend to perceive things they like as being low risk and things they don't like as being high risk. This may lead to erroneous correlation of risks and benefits, whereby that which is beneficial is perceived as being safe and vice versa. The problem is, of course, that risks and benefits are not always correlated, and this may be particularly true in the context of development. Property subject to high natural hazards may also have amenities that make it particularly attractive for residential or commercial development. For example, ocean front property is highly desired both for its aesthetic attributes and also high risk. The affect heuristic may lead people to discount risks when they have emotional attachment to a particular piece of property. To make that concrete, a potential homebuyer who forms a rapid emotional attachment to a house will be susceptible to overestimating the house's safety.

The symbolism of reconstruction may itself activate the affect heuristic. The rhetoric of armed conflict creates social pressure to rebuild as a symbol of resistance and resolve and to avoid the appearance of surrender. Thus, policies favoring swift reconstruction activate positive emotions, while those disfavoring such activities activate negative emotions. Through the affect heuristic, these emotional responses become part of the public perception of natural hazard risk. Redevelopment, then, is not only culturally imperative but is also perceived as a relatively safe decision.

Assessment of redevelopment in the wake of disaster is, therefore, vulnerable to a range of cognitive errors. Coupled with the symbolic factors affecting risk perception, these factors often militate in favor of development even where such development is "irrational" in the market sense that risks outweigh benefits. This does not mean, of course, that all decisions to build in the face of natural hazards are irrational. Indeed, as we shall see, the structure of American political institutions separates the costs of disaster from the benefits of development and consequently creates a situation where, from the private landowner's or local government official's perspective, overinvestment in development is often highly advantageous.

STRUCTURAL OBSTACLES

So far, I have explained that the cultural and cognitive context of disaster policy is hostile to restrictive development policies. As a result of that context, people invest more heavily in hazard-prone areas than common sense or economic reality supports and government officials resist regulation. Effective disaster policy also faces obstacles from the very structure of the government institutions charged with its promulgation and effectuation. Some of these problems arise from relationships unique to the American constitutional experience and the principles of federalism it embodies. Others are inherent in the democratic structures of government more generally. These obstacles create substantial incentives for private individuals and government officials to facilitate development in hazard-prone areas.

The first structural obstacle arises from vertical relationships between local, state, and federal governments and their respective responsibilities for a natural disaster policy (Depoorter, 2006).[17] To understand those relationships, consider Brattleboro, Vermont, a town that lies at the confluence of the West River and the much larger Connecticut River. Based on flood maps prepared in 1977, the town contains approximately 1,000 acres in 100-year floodplains (Brattleboro, Vermont Town Plan Map Series, 2012; Brattleboro, 2004).[18] The Brattleboro zoning laws largely control land use and development within the town, and to a large extent, the town's policies dictate the extent of its vulnerability to flooding. Brattleboro's zoning code generally prohibits construction within stream channels themselves, but allows new development in floodplains so long as minimum building standards are met.[19] These standards, while locally adopted and enforced, largely reflect the minimum standards that the federal government requires for NFIP eligibility (Federal Emergency Management Agency [FEMA], 2011).

This is a pretty typical arrangement. Land-use planning and regulation of property have long been viewed as central functions of local government. That allocation has been consistently endorsed by the Supreme Court and featured in an 1868 Supreme Court decision, *Swift v. Tyson.*[20] *Swift* famously held that federal courts could generally interpret the common law without regard to decisions of state courts. *Swift* concomitantly held that the federal courts had no independent authority over the "rights and titles to things having a permanent locality, such as the rights and titles to real estate, and other matters immovable and intra-territorial in their nature and character."[21] The commitment to generally – although not absolutely – entrust land-use decisions to state and local governments has persisted. In 2008, a plurality decision of the Supreme Court echoed the views expressed in *Swift*. As Justice Antonin Scalia wrote, "[r]egulation of land use … is a quintessential state and local power."[22]

The federal government tinkers with land-use planning at the margins through the NFIP and laws like the Coastal Zone Management Act and Coastal Barrier Resources Act, which create incentives for local governments to restrict or at least regulate development.[23] On its face, Section 404 of the Clean Water Act also appears to have substantial implications for flood risk by requiring parties seeking to fill wetlands to secure permits from the federal government.[24] But regulations that implement the act render this tool ineffective because they require the Army Corps of Engineers to defer to land-use and zoning decisions made by state and local government.[25] The Corps implementation of those regulations has been even more favorable to local views. As Oliver Houck (2007) has explained, for example, robust political opposition in Louisiana to any effort to limit wetlands development resulted in a culture at the Corps that automatically approved virtually every request for a permit to fill wetlands.

The local government, then, decides whether to allow development to occur in high-hazard areas, a decision that may significantly increase the severity of the natural hazard itself. Local governments also exert substantial control over how development occurs through building codes, which can require construction practices designed to protect against hazards.[26]

Problems arise because local governments have significant incentives to underregulate, allowing development to occur where it should not and using insufficiently protective practices. Local governments typically receive much or all of their funding from property taxes, meaning that more development means more tax dollars and the ability to provide more services to residents. Increasingly, local governments fund public projects based on sophisticated financing instruments that turn projected increases in tax revenue into present dollars (Lefcoe, 2011).[27] This practice, called "tax increment financing," only increases the pressure on local governments to maximize development.

On the other side of the ledger, local governments pay relatively little of the costs of disaster, which are largely displaced to the federal government. The federal government has long been in the business of providing financial and technical assistance in the wake of disasters, and this role has only increased over time (GAO, 2012). Once a federal disaster is declared, which occurs with increasing frequency, the Stafford Act authorizes payment from the federal treasury to reimburse 75 percent or more of the costs local governments pay to rebuild public infrastructure (Frank, 2011).[28]

This is precisely what occurred in Vermont following Hurricane Irene. FEMA authorized reimbursement of 90 percent of the cost of repairs and reported providing $18 million to the state of Vermont and its municipalities by the end of 2011 (FEMA, 2011, 2012a). On top of the federal funding, the state agreed to reimburse local governments for all remaining costs that exceeded the revenue that would be generated by a three-cent tax increase (Minter, 2012). For Brattleboro, a town that has an annual revenue of over $14 million and that sustained substantial damage, this translated into a maximum direct cost to the town of about $340,000 (Brattleboro, 2011).[29]

The finances of local governments are, of course, influenced by more than just direct outlays for repair of public infrastructure. Property values may fall in the wake of a natural disaster, particularly if residents or business owners incur high recovery costs themselves. The financial well-being of those residing within a jurisdiction also affects overall economic health. And, of course, democratically elected leaders must be responsive to local concerns.

Local governments receive only mute forms of those signals, however, because individuals suffering losses from disaster also receive substantial subsidies. The federal government provides direct financial assistance in the form of individual grants and loans and block grants provided to state and local governments for recovery projects. In the wake of Irene, the federal government provided $22.7 million in grants and $17.6 million in low-interest loans to homeowners and renters, $19 million in loans to businesses, and over $20 million in such community development block grants (FEMA, 2012b; Ring, 2012; Southeastern Vermont Irene Long Term Recovery Committee [SVILTRC], 2011; The US Department of Housing and Urban Development, 2012). All told, the federal government is expected to pick up 75 percent of the total $733 million cost of recovering from Irene (Ring, 2012).

Natural disasters also generate substantial charitable donations, making additional funds available to those that live and work in areas affected by natural disasters. This charity comes in many forms, from large-scale organizational efforts to celebrity concerts (Audette, 2012; Burlington Free Press, 2011a; Burlington Free Press, 2011b; Hallenbeck, 2011). These funds are, in part, used to provide services to displaced individuals, but money is often made available to rebuild homes and businesses (Drelich, 2012). This, in turn, further reduces the amount of the cost of recovery borne directly either by the individuals living and working in areas subject to natural hazards or the local governments that govern these areas.

Even where property tax revenue shrinks, local governments may not feel the economic pinch. The state of Vermont, for example, offered to reimburse towns that received reduced property taxes in the wake of Irene and also agreed to pay certain costs of infrastructure repairs not covered by the federal government (Hirschfeld, 2012a, 2012b; Vermont, 2012).

All of these sources of funding substantially dampen financial signals to local governments to responsibly manage development in areas subject to natural hazards. Local government officials have the luxury of adhering to the view that the "free market" should drive development because neither the local government, nor its residents, will face the full costs of making foolish choices (Helgeson, 2006).

That natural disaster aid distorts public policy is not to suggest that it should be stopped altogether. Social policy should encourage an ethic of helping others who have lost their homes and businesses in natural disasters. Catastrophic moments can also build international goodwill and feelings of unity that benefit society. While engaged in response activities in Vermont following Hurricane Irene, one National Guard veteran said, "This is the proudest I've been [about] anything I've been involved in – being able to help out our neighbors in a time of need" (Hallenbeck, 2011, p. 1A).

At the same time, it is worth considering the reasons why social and charitable resources are channeled to those afflicted by events that we term "natural" disasters rather than more generally to those in need. That society chooses to provide financial compensation to those harmed by floods, hurricanes, and other natural events, but is generally more reluctant to aid those harmed by events perceived as human caused, may largely be a result of the social construction of natural disasters as being caused by nature.[30] Moreover, the fact that a natural disaster is an *event* may distract attention away from the desperate poverty and needs that many of our most vulnerable citizens experience on an ongoing basis.

In addition to distortions caused by vertical divisions of authority between local, state, and federal governments, the relationship between neighboring local jurisdiction impedes sensible development. This horizontal allocation of a natural disaster policy vests land-use decisions in local governments whose borders do not neatly map onto geographic features that dictate natural hazards. Because natural boundaries often span political boundaries, the benefits and costs of one jurisdiction's development policies may be displaced onto neighboring jurisdictions.

Flood risk is a quintessential example. Development within a watershed influences the likelihood and severity of flooding by increasing runoff and reducing the natural capacity to absorb high water. One town's decision to allow disturbance of natural floodplains within its borders may well lead to increased flooding within the borders of lower elevation towns. Moreover, towns in close proximity to each other often compete for commercial and residential development in an effort to channel funding streams into their jurisdiction. This dynamic has the potential to lead to a classic regulatory race to the bottom. Local governments may feel pressure to allow land to remain deregulated to attract business, particularly because they fear that the decisions of neighboring towns may undo any effort to curb vulnerability that they attempt. This concern is not just hypothetical. For example, during deliberations by the Brattleboro Selectboard on a proposal to limit new impermeable surfaces within floodplains, the concern was raised that surrounding towns would authorize tree cutting within the floodplain that would exacerbate the risk of flooding, thereby undermining any effort Brattleboro made to reduce flood risk through a new zoning policy (Brattleboro Selectboard, 2007a, 2007b).

Misalignment of political and natural boundaries extends beyond just the relationship of towns. Many natural systems span state and national boundaries, further complicating the policy picture. For example, the Connecticut River, which flooded along significant portions of its length in Hurricane Irene, finds its source in Fourth Connecticut Lake in New Hampshire, flows south along the border between Vermont and New Hampshire, and enters Massachusetts and eventually Connecticut. Its watershed also extends well into Canada. The policy choices of each state and neighboring Canadian provinces work in combination to affect flood risks along the river's entire length.

Both the vertical and horizontal dynamics described arise roughly from economic externalities. The policy choices of local governments resulting in increased vulnerability to natural hazards impose considerable costs, but neither the local governments themselves, nor their constituents, fully bear those costs. Instead, these costs are displaced onto state and federal taxpayers, donors, and the residents of neighboring jurisdictions. Put another way, the decision of local government officials to enact sensible policies to control development in areas subject to natural hazards creates some benefits felt beyond their borders, benefits that local government officials cannot capture and, therefore, have little incentive to pursue.

Beyond these problems, which we might consider economic in nature, disaster policy also presents a prime opportunity for government capture by special interests. That is because the cost of bad policy is both broadly distributed (to federal taxpayers, for example) and unpredictable, while the benefits of bad policy are highly concentrated in a few highly organized and well-funded industries. Public choice theory suggests that in such circumstances, policymakers disproportionately favor the interests of the few, even if doing so undermines social welfare (Depoorter, 2006; Farber & Frickey, 1987; Verchick, 2010). This means that even where ample information about disaster risk exists, there may be "no politically powerful constituency ready to support legislators and agency officials" advocating for policies to reduce disaster vulnerability (Lazarus, 2007, p. 1045). Moreover, disaster policy may be particularly subject to government capture because of the symbolic and cognitive obstacles discussed above. The public misperceives risk and overvalues reconstruction as a signal of societal resolve. As a result, even where regulation would enhance social welfare, the public may provide little or no counterbalance to the significant influence wielded by the development community.

Return again to the debate in Brattleboro about restricting development in floodplains. The public debate consistently referenced concerns about restricting development, and the development community generated opposition (Audette, 2010; Baird, 2011; Grunwald, 2000; Hunt, 2006). This same dynamic plays itself out around the country and on the national stage. In California, for example, the development community has fiercely opposed development restrictions in floodplains in the central valley, where more than 750,000 people already live in floodplains (Diringer & McLeod, 1997). In Birmingham, Alabama, soon after forming an advocacy organization, business and development interests successfully scuttled plans to substantially curtail development in the floodplain of Five Mile Creek, which had flooded in 2003 causing a billion dollars in damage (Hansen, 2006). And in Brevard County, Florida, a large development company lobbied for looser development restrictions within the 10-year floodplain (Florida Today, 2010). Indeed, developers have even opposed requirements to notify potential buyers that the property lies within a 25-year floodplain (Haas, 2002). The political advocacy of the development industry makes sense since building in areas subject to natural hazards and, indeed, responding to natural events generates substantial revenue.[31] Economic losses, on the other hand, are paid out by the federal treasury and, therefore, policies to reduce those losses lack a concentrated constituency.

Other political dynamics also impede an effective disaster policy. Natural hazards are probabilistic and require long planning horizons, while elected officials tend to have a short-time horizon calibrated to achieve reelection. From the perspective of an elected official, gains likely to occur during their term in office are more valuable than losses that will accrue outside of that time period. So, for example, politicians may be more sensitive to an immediate influx of tax dollars than to the greater social costs that may not actualize until decades in the future. Disaster policy may also fail to get on the agenda of policymakers because other issues, such as school funding, law enforcement, and unemployment, have more immediate effects.

INTERACTIONS AND SOLUTIONS

I have focused on obstacles to sensible disaster policy, and they present something of a grim picture. The language we use, the political systems we rely upon, and even the way that we think thwart efforts to regulate behavior in response to natural hazards and result in ever-increasing vulnerability. And these obstacles often interact, creating a policy landscape particularly hostile to reform.

The interactions between and among the three obstacles take many forms. The discourse of disaster causes people to view positively efforts to rebuild because within the metaphor of armed conflict, rebuilding means defying the efforts of the enemy and failing to rebuild means retreat. The positive emotion this symbolism vests in reconstruction may, in turn, trigger the affect heuristic, resulting in an exaggerated belief about the safety of rebuilding in hazardous locations.

Cognitive errors simultaneously feed back into the symbolic value placed on rebuilding in the wake of disaster. People systematically underappreciate the degree of risk of building in areas subject to natural hazards, making reconstruction appear relatively risk free. In other words, people perceive victory over nature as relatively easy to achieve because cognitive biases make natural hazards appear less dangerous. Where victory appears cheap, courses of action that lead to perceived defeat will be treated as particularly suspect.

These cognitive and symbolic obstacles reinforce the perverse incentives created by the allocation of governmental authority over disaster policy. Local government officials not only have political incentives not to restrict development, but those incentives are buttressed by their own cognition and the skepticism of the public driven by the cognitive and symbolic dimensions of natural disaster. And, as we have seen, government officials often draw on the armed conflict metaphor, reinforcing the symbolic value attached to reconstruction in the wake of natural disaster.

Recent history bears out the power of these dynamics. Economic losses attributed to natural disasters double every decade, and there is no end in sight (Farber, Chen, Verchick, & Sun, 2010). Transforming coastlines, riverbanks, and mountain forests into houses and storefronts also disturbs fragile and important ecosystems, which once provided natural protection against disaster.

Still, hope remains. The enormity of economic loss is becoming too big to ignore, particularly at a time of increasing scrutiny on government spending. The time may finally be ripe for reform. But enacting, implementing, and persisting with sensible approaches to natural disasters will require a coordinated approach that takes account of the suite of obstacles discussed in this chapter.

None of these obstacles, nor their effects in combination, is insurmountable. Developing a menu of comprehensive solutions lies beyond the scope of this Chapter, and policies that prove successful may vary. Here, I offer a few preliminary thoughts about solutions to suggest possible paths that may be worth further exploration.

In some circumstances, new institutional arrangements can realign regulatory authority and financial responsibility, ameliorating the adverse consequences of existing vertical and horizontal diffusion of authority. This could take the form of increasing federal responsibility for land-use decisions in hazardous areas. The Army Corps of Engineers could play this role, at least in part, through existing authority under the Clean Water Act. The Army Corps could administer the Section 404 permitting regime of the Clean Water Act so as to prevent or mitigate the effects of development in floodplains that also contain wetlands. This would inject the Corps into what have traditionally been local land use decisions, but doing so would acknowledge the substantial role the federal government plays in footing the bill for the consequences of developing in flood-prone areas. Alternatively, local governments could assume increasing financial responsibility for recovery. Forcing local governments to pay the costs of disasters would create incentives for better land-use regulation. Local governments could also enter into collaborative partnerships with one another to better coordinate development across jurisdictional lines. Or states could step in, playing a larger role in both planning for natural disasters and paying their price.

Law that generates public information about disaster risk – by, for example, providing updated, publicly available, and highly visible flood maps or requiring sellers to disclose natural hazard risks to would-be purchasers of property – may debias, at least to some extent, perceptions of risk. In some circumstances, insurance premiums that correctly reflect risk may serve this role. The cost of insurance can focus the mind, making concrete probabilistic risks that might otherwise be overlooked. At the same time, insurance markets do not provide a panacea because they are subject to many of the same dynamics this chapter has discussed. During the debate surrounding reauthorization of the NFIP, virtually everyone agreed that premiums offered through the program should be "actuarial." But as often, proponents of government insurance programs call for "affordability," and actuarially sound rates for buildings subject to high risks will often be unaffordable (Pidot, 2007). In 2012, Congress passed a law to update the NFIP and phase out explicit subsidies. (Grannis, 2012). Two years later, Congress revisited the issue and substantially undercut the 2012 reforms. (Knowles, 2014). In the future, the program could be further modified to front-load payments so that developers themselves feel the squeeze. For example, the NFIP could impose a one-time fee on developers to render new development in flood plains eligible for insurance. This could more effectively calibrate development decisions to the risk of natural hazards.

Political leaders should also consider the language they use in discussing disaster. Invoking the metaphor of war can prime a demand for reckless reconstruction without regard for the likelihood of future losses. When such rhetoric surfaces, political leaders can also intervene by emphasizing the multifarious ways in which natural disasters differ from armed conflict. Moreover, emphasizing the human role in creating circumstances in which natural events can lead to devastation may facilitate more rational development policy.

For decades, America has pursued a reckless path of building in areas threatened by severe risks from inevitable natural disasters. When disaster has struck, America has rebuilt, setting itself up for another round of destruction. As the president of a real estate firm in New York explained in the wake of Superstorm Sandy, "[I]f history teaches us anything, people always rebuild and they always come back" (Ariosto, 2012). But fortunately, some government officials and private individuals are beginning to ask the right questions. After Superstorm Sandy, the opinion pages of leading newspapers broadcast the message that the time has come to rethink our approach to building – and rebuilding – in hazard-prone places (Fraser, Karpanty, & Catlin, 2012; Lewis, 2012; Hartley, 2012; Psuty, 2012). In the wake of Hurricane Irene, for example, a report published by the Vermont Agency of Natural Resources posed similar questions:

"[W]hat will we learn from Irene's impacts, knowing that severe flooding may continue to become more common? How can we rebuild intelligently, incorporating greater flood resiliency in our communities while protecting our natural environment?" (Pealer, 2012, p. 6). Such inquiry is far from the norm, and the suite of obstacles discussed in this chapter confronting disaster policy has historically overcome common sense. But if the nation can successfully grapple with these questions and overcome the obstacles to progressive and proactive disaster policy, the next hurricane may simply be a notable weather event and not a "natural" disaster.

NOTES

1. This information about direct strikes underestimates risks to development because it does not include indirect strikes or tropical storms.
2. According to the 2000 census, there were 192,695 people and 91,262 housing units in St. Lucie County. The 2010 census reports 277,789 people and 137,029 housing units (U.S. Census 2010).
3. At one time, scholars of disaster suggested distinguishing between natural disasters and technological disasters but the distinction has not gained traction (Quarantelli et al., 2006). Grouping "disasters" intentionally caused by human agents with those resulting from natural events reinforces the armed conflict metaphor. In the rubric of disaster, terrorism and hurricane are equivalent. The intuition that society should respond to each in a similar fashion is an unintended consequence of this equivalency.
4. In related work, Professor Sun and Professor RonNell Anderson Jones examine the way that blending discourse about natural disasters with that related to war and terrorism results in government policies and practices that restrict the flow of information and limit transparency (Sun & Jones, 2013).
5. See, for example, 42 U.S.C. § 9607(b)(1) (2006) (Comprehensive Environmental Response, Compensation, and Liability Act); 33 U.S.C. § 1321 (2006) (Clean Water Act); 15 U.S.C. § 1693h (Consumer Credit Protection Act); 19 U.S.C. § 1315 (Tariff Act of 1930). Reinforcing the connection between divine interpretations of natural disasters and armed conflict, federal statutes often address acts of God and acts of war together. See, e.g., 16 U.S.C. § 19jj-1 (limiting liability of individuals damaging national parks where the damage "was caused solely by an act of God or an act of war); 33 U.S.C. § 2702 (limiting oil-pollution liability if caused by an act of God or an act of war).
6. The federal government's extensive expenditures on disaster relief likely fuel this belief. Between 2004 and 2011, the federal disaster relief fund, through which the Federal Emergency Management Administration provides recovery assistance to state and local governments, spent an average of approximately $10 billion a year (GAO, 2012).
7. Others have used similar language (Barron, 2012; Kassab, 2008; Quirk, McGrath, and Harris, McGrath, and Harris, 2011; Williams, 2009; Wood, 2007).

8. To give Krugman his due, after setting up an equivalency between 9/11 and Hurricane Katrina, Krugman does note the crucial difference, stating that "disasters must be coped with, even if they aren't caused by evildoers. Now we have another deadly lesson in why we need an effective government, and why dedicated public servants deserve our respect. Will we listen?" (2005, p. A21).

9. Doward, English, and Townsend described it this way: "[T]he disaster in New Orleans coming a week ahead of the fourth anniversary of 9/11, has a far wider national meaning than simply the Katrina catastrophe itself. Crucially it calls into doubt Bush's electoral promise that he was the best candidate to protect the nation from a terrorist attack" (2005, p. 15).

10. President Obama offered similar comments in the wake of Superstorm Sandy: "[W]hen disaster strikes, we see America at its best" (Bruce, 2012).

11. This section focuses on the ways that cognition skews perceptions of probabilities that risks will manifest. I do not mean to suggest, however, that public perceptions of the nature of particular risks are unimportant to public policy. As Slovic (1987) explained, "'riskiness' means more to people than 'expected number of fatalities'" (p. 285). Scientific estimates of the probabilities of floods, blizzards, earthquakes, and the like are also subject to a degree of social construction because, in most cases, the data require interpretation (Horlick-Jones, 1998). But in the context of natural disasters at least, predictions about periodicity have a real-world check because, over time, a certain number of disasters will strike any particular area.

12. Jolls and Sunstein (2006) provide an excellent general discussion of the cognitive errors discussed in this chapter. These errors are also discussed by Jolls, Sunstein, and Thaler (1998), Finucane, Alhakami, Slovic, and Johnson (2000), and Stitch and Nisbett (1980) and in volumes edited by Gilovch, Griffin, and Kahneman (2002), and Kahneman, Slovic, and Tversky (1982).

13. See, e.g., Exec. Order No. 11,988, 42 Fed. Reg. 26,951 § 6(b) (May 24, 1977).

14. The idiom fails even to accurately describe the behavior of lightning (MythBusters, 2011).

15. The National Hurricane Center, for example, instructs people not to tape their windows before a hurricane because it "leads to a false sense of security" (Schneider, 2012). As Ropeik (2012) aptly described in the Washington Post following Superstorm Sandy, "The more control over a risk you think you have, the less worrisome it feels, no matter how false that sense of control might be."

16. Raymond Burby has termed this the "safe development paradox," whereby efforts to enhance safety result in increased vulnerability to natural hazards (Burby, 2006, p. 173).

17. Dispersal of authority across federal, state, and local governments also has substantial ramifications for rescue efforts, law enforcement, and humanitarian response in the wake of natural disaster (Griffin, 2006).

18. Flood maps of this vintage are common but recognized to substantially underestimate risks.

19. See Town of Brattleboro, VT., Zoning Ordinance art. III, §§ 3210, 2357(d), 3255 (July 3, 2007).

20. 41 U.S. 1, 8 – 9 (1842), *overruled by* Erie R.R. Co. v. Tompkins, 304 U.S. 64, 79–80 (1938). Even before *Erie* largely ended the project of federal common law, federal courts had already recognized exclusive state control over the law of property, including land use.

21. *Id.* at 18.
22. Rapanos v. United States, 547 U.S. 715, 738 (2006) (plurality opinion).
23. Coastal Zone Management Act (2006); Coastal Barrier Resources Act (2006).
24. 33 U.S.C. § 1344 (2006).
25. See 33 C.F.R. § 320.4(j)(2) (2011).
26. See, e.g., New York City Building Code, Appendix G § G303.7(1) (2011) (prohibiting grading and fill in flood hazard areas "[u]nless such fill is placed, compacted and sloped to minimize shifting, slumping and erosion during the rise and fall of flood water and, as applicable, wave action"), available at http://publicecodes.cyberregs.com/st/ny/ci-nyc/b200v08/index.htm?bu=YC-P-2008-000006; City of South Pasedena Florida Building Code § 108-18(A) ("All new construction and substantial improvements shall be anchored to prevent flotation, collapse or lateral movement of the structure."), available at http://www.ecode360.com/7147993.
27. Lisa Grow Sun provides a careful description of the redevelopment of the Portland, Oregon, waterfront as an example of public funds, including over a hundred million in tax increment financing, increasing hazard risk (Sun, 2011). If serious flooding destroys or severely damages the new development, Portland would have considerable incentive to secure state or federal disaster assistance to enable reconstruction to minimize shortfalls in projected tax revenue already dedicated to future bond payments.
28. See Robert T. Stafford Disaster Relief and Emergency Assistance Act, 42 U.S.C. §§ 5121–5207 (2006).
29. A report produced by the U.S. Department of Commerce estimates that Windham County, which contains Brattleboro, will eventually receive $35 million in public assistance (U.S. Department of Commerce, 2012).
30. As Professor Michelle Landis Dauber has argued, differentiation between losses due to "natural" causes and human causes makes little sense from the perspective of those suffering losses (Landis, 1998). In a vivid example of this from early in American history, Dauber contrasts the dramatic losses suffered by a sea captain whose valor led to the capture and criminal trial of would-be pirates with those of individuals whose homes burned in a city-wide fire in Arlington, Virginia.
31. Insurance companies are an interesting case. They make money by providing a hedge against risk but also face steep losses when natural disasters strike. This dichotomy incentivizes the company to reduce vulnerability – either by declining to offer insurance or reducing the risks faced by the properties they insure – or find other sources of financing to lay off some of their risk. In recent years, the federal treasury has been an attractive target and there has been a concerted, although as of yet unsuccessful, effort to secure passage of legislation to create federal multiperil insurance (Pidot, 2007; Taylor, 2008). The business of transacting insurance claims has its own constituency (Grantham, 2011).

ACKNOWLEDGMENTS

A version of this Chapter previously appeared in the Brigham Young University Law Review under the title *Deconstructing Disaster*, 2013

B.Y.U. LAW REV. 213 (2013). I would like to thank Federico Cheever, Brigham Daniels, John Echeverria, Nancy Leong, Justin Marceau, Peter Byrne, Michael Wara, and Annecoos Wiersema for their thoughtful comments. I would also like to thank Elizabeth Hutchinson, Courtney Mcvean, and Stephanie Pham for their outstanding work as my research assistants.

REFERENCES

3 Doors Down. (2007, November 23). Citizen Soldier. *YouTube*. Music video. Retrieved from http://www.youtube.com/watch?v=emm4VFvn2Jg

Action News at 11. ABC television broadcast. *Action News at 11*, December 1.

Adkins, C. (2011, August 31). Town un-common. *The Daily Southerner*. Retrieved from http://dailysoutherner.com/x803539061/TOWN-UN-COMMON

Akasoy, A. (2007). Islamic attitudes to disasters in the middle ages: A comparison of earthquakes and plagues. *Medieval History Journal*, *10*, 392.

Alexander, S. (2012). Simulating nature's wrath, when it comes to calculating disasters, computer simulations aim to measure the "possible risk of ruin." *The Star Tribune*, July 8, p. D3.

American Society of Civil Engineers Hurricane Katrina External Review Panel. (2007). *The New Orleans hurricane protection system: What went wrong and why*, 63. Retrieved from http://www.asce.org/uploadedFiles/Publications/ASCE_News/2009/04_April/ERP report.pdf

Ariosto, D. (2012). First Irene, then Sandy: Jersey city recovers, again. *CNN Wire*, November 14.

Audette, B. (2010). Board nixes erosion hazard regulation. *Brattleboro Reformer*, January 20.

Audette, B. (2012, July 21). More Irene money coming to Windham county. Classic hits 92.7 WKVT. Retrieved from http://wkvt.com/2012/07/20/More-Irene-money-coming-to-Windham-County/13777730

Baird, J. (2011). Brook's rage cuts off Brattleboro residents. *Burlington Free Press*, August 30, p. B4.

Barron, J. (2012). After the devastation, a daunting recovery. *The New York Times*, October 30, p. A1.

Barron, L. (2012). Together through any storm. *Beauregard Daily News*, June 16, p. 1.

Bastardi, J. (2012). Natural cycles trigger extremes. *USA Today*, August 1, p. A6.

Bates, F., & Peacock, W. (1987). Disaster and social change. In R. Dynes, et al. (Eds.) *Sociology of disasters: Contribution of sociology to disaster research* (pp. 291–330). Italy: International Sociological Association.

Blanco, Governor Kathleen. (2005). Hurricane Katrina: Preparedness and response by the state of Louisiana. Hearing before the select bipartisan committee to investigate the preparation for and response to Hurricane Katrina. 109th Congress.

Borenstein, S., Melvin, D., & Gibson, W. (1992). Powerful Andrew launches assault on Louisiana's coast. *South Florida Sun-Sentinel*, August 26, p. A1.

Brattleboro Selectboard. (2007a). *April 17 Meeting minutes 2*. Retrieved from http://bit.ly/BrattleboroMinutes%20Brattleboro%20Selectboard%20April%2017th%20Minutes%202%20(2007b). Retrieved from http://www.brattleboro.org/vertical/Sites/%207BF60

A5D5E-AC5C-4F97-891A-615C172A5783%207D/uploads/%207B04A5BE4C-AAFC-4E5E-8512-4790A373738B%7D.PDF

Brattleboro Selectboard. (2007b). *April 17 Meeting minutes 2.* Retrieved from http://bit.ly/BrattleboroMinutes%20Brattleboro%20Selectboard. April 17th Minutes 2 (2007b), Retrieved from http://www.brattleboro.org/vertical/Sites/%207BF60A5D5E-AC5C-4F97-891A-615C172A5783%207D/uploads/%207B04A5BE4C-AAFC-4E5E-8512-4790A373738B%7D.PDF

Brattleboro.org. (2012, October 27). *Brattleboro, Vermont town plan map series: Flood hazard areas.* Retrieved from http://www.brattleboro.org/vertical/sites/%207BF60A5D5E-AC5C-4F97-891A-615C172A5783%207D/uploads/%207BDC196E51-1FDA-4CD9-B71A-4A4FDFC0F03D%207D.PDF

B 2000). Victims are stunned by ferocity of storm. *Miami Herald*, October 6, p. B2.

Brooks, J. (2012, July 12). Special session set for August on flood relief, *Minneapolis star tribune.* Retrieved from http://www.startribune.com/politics/statelocal/%20162147585.html?refer=y

Bruce, M. (2012, November 1). Obama Invokes Superstorm Sandy on the Campaign Trail. *ABC News.* Retrieved from http://abcnews.go.com/blogs/politics/2012/11/obama-invokes-superstorm-sandy-on-the-campaign-trail/

Burby, R. (2006). Hurricane Katrina and the paradoxes of government disaster policy: Bringing about wise governmental decisions for hazardous areas. *Annals American Academy of Politics and Social Science*, *604*, 181.

Burdeau, C., & Kunzelman, M. (2012). Gulf Coast takes beating from slow-moving Isaac. *The Denver Post*, August 30, p. 19A.

Burke, K. (1989). *On symbols and society*. Chicago, IL: University of Chicago Free Press.

Burlington Free Press. (2011a). Grace Potter concerts raise $300,000 for flood relief. *Burlington Free Press*, October 22, p. W7.

Burlington Free Press. (2011b). Students hold penny drive to save covered bridges. *Burlington Free Press*, October 22, p. W12.

Cauchon, D., McCoy, K., Keen, J., & Schmit, J. (2012). Big deals of 13: Problems we welcome and those we'd rather leave behind. *USA Today*, December 31, p. 1A.

Chester, D. & Duncan, A. (2010). Responding to disasters within the Christian tradition, with reference to volcanic eruptions and earthquakes. *Religion*, *40*, 87.

Coastal Barrier Resources Act. 16 U.S.C. §§ 3501–3510 (2006).

Coastal Zone Management Act. 16 U.S.C. §§ 1451–1464 (2006).

Department of Homeland Security, Office of the Inspector General. (2009). FEMA: in or out? (OIG-09-25).

Department of Water Resources. (2007). State of California, a California challenge—flooding in the Central Valley iii. Retrieved from http://www.water.ca.gov/news/%20newsreleases/2008/101507challenge.pdf

Depoorter, B. (2006). Horizontal political externalities: The supply and demand of disaster management. *Duke Law Journal*, *56*, 104.

Diringer, E., & McLeod, R. (1997). Floods warn valley of worse to come / storms, growth expose region's rising risk. *San Francisco Chronicle*, March 3, p. A1.

Doward, J., English, S., & Townsend, M. (2005). Aftermath of the hurricane: America's ordeal. *The Observer*, September 4, p. 15.

Drelich, K. (2012). Kellogg raises $50,000 for marine businesses harmed by sandy. *The Day*, December 29. Retrieved from http://www.theday.com/article/20121229/NWS01/312299976/-1/zip06

Farber, D., Chen, J., Verchick, R., & Sun, L. (2010). *Disaster law and policy* 3. New York, NY: Aspen Publishers.

Farber, D., & Frickey, P. (1987). The jurisprudence of public choice. *Texas Law Review*, *65*, 892.

Federal Emergency Management Agency. (2011a).National flood insurance program community enrollment and eligibility handbook (enr-3). Retrieved from http://www.floods.org/ace-files/documentlibrary/State_Local%20Resources%20and%20Tools/3.4_FEMA_553_EligibilityHandbook_01-2011.pdf

Federal Emergency Management Agency. (2011b). More than $72 million in disaster aid supplied to Vermont in 2011 (No. 4022–072). Retrieved from http://www.fema.gov/news-release/more-72-million-disaster-aid-supplied-vermont-2011

Federal Emergency Management Agency. (2012a). FEMA will give Vermont 90 percent funding for Irene repair work (No. 4022–080). Retrieved from http://www.fema.gov/news-release/fema-will-give-vermont-90-percent-funding-irene-repair-work

Federal Emergency Management Agency. (2012b). Federal aid for Irene, spring 2011 flooding tops $100 million in Vermont (No. 4022–073). Retrieved from http://www.fema.gov/%20news-release/federal-aid-irene-spring-2011-flooding-tops-100-million-vermont

Feuer, A. (2005). A fellowship of suffering, ever expanding. *The New York Times*. September 4, § 14 p. 1.

Finucane, M., Alhakami, A., Slovic, P., & Johnson, S. (2000). The affect heuristic in judgments of risks and benefits. *Journal of Behavioral Decision Making*, *13*, 13.

Florida Today. (2010). County delays wetlands changes, p. B1.

Frank, T. (2011). 'Disasters' strain FEMA's resources. *USA Today*, October 24, p. A1.

Fraser, J., Karpanty, S., & Catlin, D. (2012). Too close to the shore. *The Washington Pos*t, November 23, p. A23.

Gilovch, T., Griffin, D., & Kahneman, D. (Eds.). (2002). *Heuristics and biases: The psychology of intuitive judgment*. Cambridge, MA: Cambridge University Press.

Goldenberg, R. (2012). N.Y mobilizes more than 2,300 guardsmen to battle Hurricane Sandy aftermath. Defense Department Documents.

Grand Rapids Press. (2011). Glory gave comfort to a wounded nation, often waved in dissent or disagreement, it gave us unity after attacks, p. A16.

Grannis, J. (2012, August 2). Analysis of How the Flood Insurance Reform Act of 2012 (H.R. 4348) may affect state and local adaptation efforts. Georgetown Climate Center. Retrieved from http://www.georgetownclimate.org/sites/default/files/%20Analysis%20of%20the%20Flood%20Insurance%20Reform%20Act%20of%202012.pdf

Grantham, R. (2011). Hitting the road after catastrophe. *Atlanta Journal-Constitution*, September 4, D1.

Griffin, S. (2006). Stop federalism before it kills again: Reflections on Hurricane Katrina. *St. John's Journal*, *21*, 527.

Grunwald, M. (2000). Wetlands protection rules due; Army Corps would slow development. *The Washington Post*, March 3, p. A1.

Haas, B. (2002). New homes plan passes. *Bradenton Herald*, August 9, p. C1.

Hall, S., Legere, L., & Mrozinski, J. (2011). Flood victims recount their experiences. *Times-Tribune*, September 10.. Retrieved from http://thetimes-tribune.com/news/flood-victims-recount-their-experiences-1.1201023

Hallenbeck, T. (2011). The chief cheerleader. *Burlington Free Press*, December 27, p. 1A.

Hansen, J. (2006). New business alliance flexes its muscles to get its way; Foes accuse BARD of putting its desires above community's. *Birmingham News*, December 10, p. 1.

Hartley, M. (2012). Effects of Sandy should impel us to try to tread carefully. *Daily Gazette*, November 4, p. E10.

Helgeson, B. (2006). Risky rebuilding. *Tampa Tribune*, November 5, p. 1.

Hennessy-Fiske, M., & Zucchino, D. (2012). Nervous Gulf residents brace for gathering storm. *Orlando Sentinel*, August 28, p. A7.

Hirschfeld, P. (2012a). Winners and losers as legislature closes session. *Vermont Today,* May 6. Retrieved from http://www.vermonttoday.com/apps/pbcs.dll/article?AID=/%20120506/NEWS03/705069821/-1/NEBJ

Hirschfeld, P. (2012b). House approves tax relief for Irene-ravage towns and cities. *Vermont Press Bureau,* January 5. Retrieved from http://www.vermontpressbureau.com/house-approves-tax-relief-for-irene-ravage-towns-and-cities

Honeyman, S. (2012). When Uncommon Storms Make a Surprise Visit. *Rough Notes, 66*, May 1. Retrieved from http://www.roughnotes.com/rnmagazine/2012/may2012/%2012_05p066.html

Horlick-Jones, T. (1998). Meaning and contextualization in risk assessment. *Engineering and Systems Safety*, *59*, 81.

Houck, O. (2007). Retaking the exam: How environmental law failed New Orleans and the Gulf Coast South and how it might yet succeed. *Tulsa Law Review*, *81*, 1076.

Hubbard, C. (2012). The new year. *Savannah Morning News,* December 20. Retrieved from http://m.savannahnow.com/bryan-county-now/2012-12-20/new-year

Hunt, S. (2006). Groups object to Big Darby plan; Builders and landowners tell state that proposed protections go too far. *Columbus Dispatch*, March 22. C1.

Jolls, C., & Sunstein, C. (2006). Debiasing through law. *Journal of Legal Studies*, *35*, 209.

Jolls, C., Sunstein, C., & Thaler, R. (1998). A behavioral approach to law and economics. *Stanford Law Review*, *50*, 1478.

Kahneman, D., Slovic, P., & Tversky, A. (Eds.). (1982). *Judgment under uncertainty: Heuristics and biases.* Cambridge, MA: Cambridge University Press.

Kassab, B. (2008). Any economic bump could be blown away. *Orlando Sentinel*, August 19, p. C1.

Knowles, S. (2014). *Flood Zone Foolishness, Politicians from disaster-prone states lead fight against disaster reform.* Slate.

Krugman, P. (2005). Killed by contempt. *The New York Times*, September 5, p. A21.

Kunreuther, H., & Michel-Kerjan, E. (2006). Climate change, insurability of large-scale disasters, and the emerging liability challenge. *University of Pennsylvania Law Review*, *155*, 1810.

Kunreuther, H., Novemsky, N., & Kahneman, D. (2001). Making low probabilities useful. *Journal of Risk and Uncertainty*, *23*, 103.

Kunreuther, H., & Pauly, M. (2004). Neglecting disaster: Why don't people insure against large losses? *Journal of Risk and Uncertainty*, *28*, 7.

Kuran, T., & Sunstein, C. (1999). Availability cascades and risk regulation. *Stanford Law Review*, *51*, 712.

Lake, H. (2012). Preparing for the worst: Windham eyes emergency micro-grid program. *The Chronicle*, May 21, p. 1.

Landis, M. (1998). "Let me next time be 'tried by fire'": Disaster relief and the origins of the American welfare state. *Northwestern University Law Review*, *92*, 995.

Lazarus, R. (2007). Environmental law after Katrina: Reforming environmental law by reforming environmental lawmaking. *Tulsa Law Review*, *81*, 1019.

Lefcoe, G. (2011). Competing for the next hundred million Americans: The uses and abuses of tax increment financing. *Urban Law*, *43*, 427.
Lewis, R. (2012). Heeding the cruel housing lessons of Hurricane Sandy. *The Washington Post*, November 17, p. E3.
Mauch, C. (2009). Introduction. In Christof Mauch & C. Pfister (Eds.), *Natural disasters, cultural responses: Case studies toward a global environmental history* (pp. 1–16). Plymouth, UK: Lexington Books.
Milwaukee Journal Sentinel. (2012). Deadly Joplin tornado was one year ago, p. C8.
Minter, S. (2012, July 11). Memorandum from Sue Minter, Irene recovery officer, to municipal officials involved in Irene recovery. Retrieved from http://www.trorc.org/pdf/irene/%FEMA%20updates%20for%20PA%20July%202012.pdf
Moss, D. (1999). Courting disaster? The transformation of federal disaster policy since 1803. In K. Froot (Ed.), *The financing of catastrophe risk* (pp. 307–355). Chicago, IL: University of Chicago Press.
MythBusters: Lightning Strikes Twice. (2011, April 5). Discovery Channel television broadcast. Retrieved from http://dsc.discovery.com/tv-shows/mythbusters/videos/lightning-strikes-twice-minimyth.html
National Guard. (2009, November 12). At This Moment. *YouTube*. Video. Retrieved from http://www.youtube.com/watch?v=AbfPj00pTNY
NOAA. (2012a, September 11). *Return period hurricane*. Retrieved from http://www.nhc.noaa.gov/climo/images/return_hurr.%20jpg
NOAA. (2012b, September 11). *Return period major hurricane*. Retrieved from http://www.nhc.noaa.%gov/climo/images/return_mjrhurr.jpg
O'Keefe, P., Westgate, K., & Wisner, B. (1976). Taking the naturalness out of natural disasters. *Nature*, *260*, 566.
Pealer, S. (2012, January 4). Lessons from Irene: Building resiliency as we rebuild. Vermont Agency of Natural Resources. Retrieved from http://www.anr.state.vt.us/anr/%20climatechange/Pubs/Irene_Facts.pdf
Pidot, J. (2007). *Coastal disaster insurance in the era of global warming: The case for relying on the private market*. Washington, DC: Georgetown Environmental Law and Policy Institute.
Psuty, N. (2012). The data is in. Now we need action. *The New York Times*, November 27.
Public Religion Research Institute. (2011, March 24). Few Americans see earthquakes, floods, and other natural disasters a sign from God. Retrieved from http://publicreligion.org/%20research/2011/03/few-americans-see-earthquakes-floods-and-other-natural-disasters-a-sign-from-god-2/
Quarantelli, E., Lagadec, P., & Boin, A. (2006). A heuristic approach to future disasters and crises: New, old, and in-between types. In H. Rodriguez, et al. (Eds.), *Handbook of disaster research* (pp. 16–41). New York City, NY: Springer.
Quirk, J., McGrath, M., & Harris, C. (2011). Flood victims fed up. *The New Jersey Record*, October 9, p. A1.
Rich, F. (2005). Fallujah floods the superdome. *The New York Times*, September 4, § 4 p. 10.
Ring, W. (2012). Vermont Irene recovery bill at $733M, more work to do. *Vermont Today*, June 15. Retrieved from http://vermonttoday.com/apps/pbcs.dll/article?AID=/%20120615/NEWS03/706159860
Ropeik, D. (2012). Did D.C. Overreact to Sandy? *The Washington Post*, November 4, p. B2.

Scherer, R. (2011). After the snowstorm: Power outages mean no heat, no trick-or-treating. *The Christian Science Monitor*, October 31.

Schneider, M. (2012). Don't tape your windows before a hurricane, officials say. *The Virginian-Pilot*, March 28, p. A3.

Schneyer, J., & Gebrekidan, S. (2012). Insight: Sandy gives New York oil supply lesson. *Reuters*, November 27.

Schwartz, J., & Robertson, C. (2012). Hurricane gains power and hits Louisiana coast. *The New York Times*, August 29, p. A1.

Semple, K. (2011). A dilemma, a promise, a voice: After the storm: On flood plain, pondering wisdom of rebuilding anew. *The New York Times*, September 5, p. A13.

Slovic, P. (1987). Perception of risk. *Science*, *236*, 285.

Slovic, P., Fischhoff, B., Lichtenstein, S., Corrigan, B., & Combs, B. (1977). Preference for insuring against probable small losses: Insurance implications. *Journal of Risk and Insurance*, *44*, 237.

Southeastern Vermont Irene Long Term Recovery Committee. (2011, November 15). *Windham county Vermont status information*. Retrieved from http://www.windhamstatus.org/%2011/11/15/southeastern-vermont-irene-long-term-recovery-committee

Spinner, K. (2012). Girding nation for weather extremes. *Sarasota Herald-Tribune*, November 15, p. B1.

Steinberg, T. (2000). *Acts of God*. Cary, NC: Oxford University Press.

Stitch, S., & Nisbett, R. (1980). Justification and the psychology of human reasoning. *Philosophy of Science*, *47*, 193.

Sun, L. (2011). Disaster mythology and the law. *Cornell Law Review*, *96*, 1131.

Sun, L. (2011). Smart growth in dumb places: Sustainability, disaster, and the future of the American city. *Brigham Young Law Review*, *2011*, 2157.

Sun, L., & Jones, R. (2013). Disaggregating disasters. *UCLA Law Review*, *60*, 884.

Taylor, G. (2008). Federal insurance reform after Katrina. *Mississippi Law Journal*, *77*, 790.

The New York Times. (2011). Advertisement, August 29, p. A11.

The US Department of Housing and Urban Development (HUD) Community Development Block Grant Disaster Recovery Funding (CDBG-DR). (2012). I am Vermont strong. Retrieved from *http://vtstrong.vermont.gov/Home/StateRecovery/%20HUDCommunityDevelopmentBlockGrant.aspx*

Tierney, K., Bevc, C., & Kuligowski, E. (2006). Metaphors matter: Disaster myths, media frames, and their consequences in Hurricane Katrina. *Annals American Academy Politics & Social Science*, *604*, 76.

Town of Brattleboro. (2004). *Brattleboro town plan 121*. Retrieved from http://www.brattleboro.org/vertical/sites/%207BFABA8FB3-EBD9-4E2C-91F9-C74DE6CECDFD%207D/uploads/Ch_10_Natural_Resources.pdf

Town of Brattleboro. (2011). *2011 annual report 65*. Retrieved from http://brattleborovtrebuild.govoffice.com/vertical/Sites/%207BFABA8FB3-EBD9-4E2C-91F9-C74DE6CECDFD%7D/uploads/Town_Report_2011_FINAL1(1).pdf

U.S. Army Corps of Engineers. (2012, November 1). *About us*. Retrieved from http://www.usace.army.mil/About.aspx

U.S. General Accounting Office. (1995). Midwest flood: Information on the performance, effects, and control of levees 2-3 (GAO/RCED-95-125).

U.S. Department of Agriculture, Office of Inspector General, Western Region. (2006). Audit report: Forest service large fire suppression costs (No. 08601-44-SF).

U.S. Department of Commerce. (2012). Economic impact assessment 7 (Vermont DR-4022). Retrieved from http://vtstrong.vermont.gov/Portals/0/Documents/%20Vermont_Econ_Impact_Final%20-%2042312.pdf

U.S. Government Accountability Office. (2012). Federal disaster assistance: Improved criteria needed to assess a jurisdiction's capability to respond and recover on its own, 14. Retrieved from http://gao.gov/assets/650/648162.pdf

Verchick, R. (2010). *Facing Catastrophe: Environmental Action for a Post-Katrina World* (2nd ed.). Cambridge, MA: Harvard University Press.

Vermont. (2012, May 5). Irene and jobs, a record of results. Retrieved from http://governor.vermont.gov/newsroom-irene-and-jobs-a-record-of-results

Viscusi, W. (1995). Carcinogen regulation: Risk characteristics and the synthetic risk bias. *American Economic Review*, *85*, 54.

Washington, W. (2007). Can FEMA handle S.C. hurricane? Candidates vary on if agency should stay part of Homeland Security. *Columbia St.*, August 26, p. B9.

Whoriskey, P. (2007). New Orleans repeats mistakes as it rebuilds: Many houses built in areas Katrina flooded are not on raised foundations. *The Washington Post*, January 4, p. A1.

Williams, M. (2009). Utilities no match for hurricanes. *Press-Register*, January 7, p. F3.

Wilson, J. (2012, November 1). Victims fall to superstorm's wrath. CNN. Retrieved from http://www.cnn.com/2012/10/31/us/superstorm-sandy-victims-profiles/index.html.

Wood, A. (2007). Weather or not: A history-making hurricane year (Yes, this one). *Philadelphia Inquirer*, November 1, p. D1.

Yamanouchi, K. (2012). Gas prices; Storm plays role as fuel costs rise. *Atlanta Journal-Constitution*, August 30, p. 1A.

Zorn, E. (2005). Katrina shows we're not ready for catastrophe. *Chicago Tribune*, September 4, p. Metro 1.

FORESEEABLE DISASTER MISMANAGEMENT IN A CHANGING CLIMATE

Lisa Grow Sun and Sabrina McCormick

ABSTRACT

The intensifying effects of climate change and the growing concentration of population in hazardous locations mean that, for many communities, disasters are increasingly becoming not only foreseeable, but inevitable. While much attention is, and should be, focused on what these foreseeable disasters require in terms of disaster planning and mitigation, attention should also be focused on a related and equally pressing phenomena: mismanagement of disaster response, particularly as climate proves an increasing stressor. Like disasters themselves, disaster mismanagement – while not entirely predictable – may exhibit some predictable patterns. This chapter explores past disaster management failures, considers how climate change may alter or exacerbate certain response pathologies, and evaluates some potential remedies that might mitigate these challenges.

Keywords: Foreseeable disaster response mismanagement; climate change

Special Issue: Cassandra's Curse: The Law and Foreseeable Future Disasters
Studies in Law, Politics, and Society, Volume 68, 65–93

ISSN: 1059-4337/doi:10.1108/S1059-433720150000068003

Disasters are revelatory. They may tell us more than we want to know about our inability to protect ourselves from foreseeable harm, whether it be the hubris of building a seaside nuclear reactor in the historical path of tsunamis Fukushima, 2011, or leaving the neediest and most vulnerable among us to fend for themselves in the midst of calamitous weather events Hurricane Katrina, 2005.

When disaster strikes, the most attention-getting stories tend to be the most photogenic ones, usually about failed infrastructure. The collapsed bridges and buildings after an earthquake or flood and the charred ruins of a mountain subdivision after a wildfire tell a tale of planning unequal to the natural forces we have set ourselves against. And as often as not, a parallel story is that of failed *administrative* infrastructure: of the denial or downplaying of risk (illustrated in Lloyd Burton and Justin Pidot's chapters in this volume), inadequate preparation, uncoordinated and inadequate response, or misapplication of government authority.

What seems to be less newsworthy is when things go right: when bridges and buildings *don't* collapse, or when evacuations are orderly and those displaced are well cared for. When both structural and administrative infrastructure are resilient and perform as planned, it's good news, and therefore not news. And in many disaster situations, this is just the case.

These, however, are not the stories told in this chapter. While fully acknowledging the great strides that have been made in the field of disaster management, both as practiced and as a subject of research, a great deal can nonetheless be learned from case studies in which disaster management goes terribly awry and administrative infrastructure fails.

The intensifying effects of climate change and the growing concentration of population in hazardous locations in the United States and worldwide mean that, for many communities, disasters are increasingly becoming not only foreseeable, but inevitable. While much attention is, and should be, focused on what these foreseeable disasters require in terms of disaster planning and mitigation, attention should also be focused on a related and equally pressing phenomena: mismanagement of disaster response, particularly as climate proves an increasing stressor. In fact, analyzing mismanagement can help identify how disaster planning might proceed more effectively. Given that disasters themselves are on the rise, disaster mismanagement is becoming critically important. And, like disasters themselves, disaster mismanagement – while not entirely predictable – may exhibit some predictable patterns. This chapter explores past disaster management failures, considers how climate change may alter or exacerbate certain response pathologies, and evaluates some potential remedies – particularly, legal remedies – that might mitigate these challenges. Our particular focus on legal solutions develops the book's larger theme: the role of law in mitigating foreseeable future disasters.

Any locality in the throes of disaster faces innumerable challenges. Restoring critical life-systems, such as water, power, and medical care, requires managing a complex and interdependent web of public, quasi-public, and private systems, each of which can depend on the others for its functioning and restoration. Even when confronting less acute crises, prioritizing the deployment of limited resources in the face of uncertainty and incomplete information presents difficult challenges. Balancing public expectations and demands for public voice in disaster decision-making against the apparent need for quick, decisive actions presents its own complexities. Densely populated urban areas also face particularly difficult quandaries in the run-up to disaster, as city officials are increasingly required to make critical decisions about evacuation and resource deployment while there is still great uncertainty about, for instance, the path that a particular hurricane will take (Boin & Egan, 2012; Travis, 2011).

There are, of course, many scholarly and practical prisms through which to view these disaster response challenges. A growing focus on resiliency in both theory and practice suggests new ways for managing disaster risk. Normal Accident Theory, with its emphasis on the inevitability and inherent unpredictability of accidents in highly complex, tightly coupled systems (Perrow, 1994) has clashed with High Reliability Organization Theory, with its more optimistic assessment of the potential to manage for safety in complex systems. This debate has provided rich fodder for scholarly discussion about potential changes in organizational behavior that can minimize disaster disruptions (LaPorte & Consolini, 1991).

Yet, public decision-making during and in the immediate aftermath of disasters, particularly the kind of so-called "natural" disasters with which this book is primarily concerned, does not always fit neatly within the scope of much of this ongoing debate. While emergency management departments at all levels of government may have much to learn from the safety culture of high reliability organizations, the breadth of the issues confronting government decision-makers, combined with the primacy of political pressures and constituent demands, can make translating and implementing these lessons difficult. In addition, the increasing frequency and severity of disasters in a world experiencing climate change may alter which past lessons are relevant for the future. Moreover, these existing theories have little to say about the darker side of disaster management and the ways in which politicians can exploit disasters to increase their own power and subvert normal democratic processes and norms of openness, transparency, and participation. Countering these temptations is often the particular province of law and a task to which law is generally better suited than changing safety culture.

This chapter thus explores four kinds of foreseeable disaster mismanagement based on some notable management failures in the past, and situates those failures in the relevant sociological and legal literature to help explain why we see these patterns of problematic disaster response. We also attempt to evaluate how climate change may affect these types of mismanagement. Finally, we consider some potential remedies that might help prevent some of these typical response failures in the future.

Our focus here is on foreseeable mismanagement in the disaster response phase, even though the mitigation and planning phases of disaster risk management are obviously closely tied to disaster response. We focus on four common forms of disaster response mismanagement: (1) poor assessment and prioritization of risks; (2) marginalization of public participation and civic engagement in managing and responding to those risks; (3) unwarranted extension of emergency measures and emergency powers beyond the immediate emergency that justified them; and (4) neglect of vulnerable populations.[1]

Even for the response phase, we do not purport to create a comprehensive review of disaster mismanagement, but instead identify and focus on some of the most pressing and troubling patterns of disaster mismanagement we have experienced in the past. In this sense, we suggest that at least some of the pitfalls of public decision-making in the face of natural disasters are not akin to "normal accidents," accidents that are both in some sense inevitable and unlikely to be replicated in future disasters. That is not to say, of course, that the past is always prologue or that each of the kinds of disaster mismanagement we explore is likely to surface in any given disaster. Nonetheless, the foreseeability of these types of mismanagement suggests both the need for structural reforms to minimize their occurrence, as well as a possible role for tort liability in incentivizing government actors to recognize and eliminate some of these potential disaster response pitfalls.

AN EXPLORATION OF DISASTER MISMANAGEMENT

Poor Government Assessment and Prioritization of Risks During the Response Phase

One common and foreseeable form of disaster response mismanagement occurs when government decision-makers poorly assess and prioritize risks and thus misallocate scarce disaster response resources. Assessing damage and needs in the aftermath of a major disaster and prioritizing attention to ongoing and unfolding risks are undeniably difficult tasks. Poor governmental risk assessment, then, can be driven by a number of different factors, including limited information, communications failures, and inadequate situational awareness.

In the midst of such uncertainty, flawed government assessment of disaster response risks is hardly a surprise. Moreover, public officials, like individual citizens, are susceptible to resorting to heuristics – swapping out hard questions about the wisdom of risk management strategies for easier ones – in order to render decision-making in the face of risk and uncertainty more manageable. In particular, poor risk assessments often follow predictable paths informed by common misconceptions ("disaster myths") about typical human behavior in the aftermath of disasters. These narratives of post-disaster human behavior may exert a particularly powerful sway over public decision-making when information is limited and clear direction is otherwise lacking.

One common disaster myth is that the typical human response to disaster is characterized primarily by antisocial behavior, such as looting and violence (Quarantelli & Dynes, 1972). This tendency to overemphasize the risk of disaster criminality is prevalent, not only in the way that the public at large conceives of post-disaster behavior, but also in official perceptions of likely disaster responses by the public. Indeed, in the aftermath of Hurricane Katrina, it was often public officials – including both the New Orleans police chief and mayor – who perpetuated and fed overblown and exaggerated narratives of violence and looting on New Orleans' streets. New Orleans Mayor Ray Nagin, for example, painted a dramatic but misleading picture of post-Katrina New Orleans when, on the Oprah Winfrey show, he asserted that New Orleans' residents had deteriorated to an "almost animalistic state" after days of "watching hooligans killing people, raping people" (Thevenot, 2006).

Some sociologists suggest that public officials may be particularly prone to indulge negative stereotypes and fears about their constituents' likely response to disaster, as disaster may threaten the status quo, as well as established and entrenched power structures. The potential for such "elite panic" (Clarke & Chess, 2008) means that public officials may be more likely than the public at large to prioritize security concerns over other public safety matters, including the distribution of much needed humanitarian aid.

This misprioritization of the risks in disaster's aftermath can translate into the misallocation of limited disaster response resources. For example, in the aftermath of Hurricane Katrina, in response to largely unsubstantiated rumors about widespread looting, violence, and chaos on New Orleans' streets, New Orleans mayor Ray Nagin redeployed 1,500 police officers, who had been engaged in search and rescue, to search out, intercept, and arrest alleged looters (New Orleans, 2005). Similarly, overblown concerns about the security situation inside shelters of last resort, such as the Superdome, led to substantial delays in the delivery of essential supplies, including food and water, while living conditions for those sheltering there deteriorated rapidly (New Orleans, 2005). Even in less catastrophic disasters, fears of looting and unrest may substantially delay residents' return to their homes, as officials seek to limit access to deter looting, and may also encourage imposition of strict curfews once residents are allowed to return (Sun, 2011). Indeed, one survey of emergency managers found that 39 percent of them believed that residents of disaster stricken communities were likely to engage in looting (Fischer, 2008). That belief may be even more widely held among public officials who lack emergency management training and experience.

Another possible casualty of poor risk prioritization in disaster response is the flow of information from the government to the public. Government provision of available, accurate information to citizens has the potential to help them make the best protective decisions for themselves and their families. Public decision-makers, however, may sometimes withhold information, fearing that citizens will "panic" and behave in unreasoned, "frenzied" ways that only increase the danger to themselves (Sun & Jones, 2013, p. 926, and sources cited therein).

In the aftermath of the Fukushima disaster, for example, the Japanese government withheld modeling data about the predicted path of the radioactive fallout plume because of concern that the data would cause the public to panic (Onishi & Fackler, 2011; Osnos, 2011). After some local residents evacuated directly into the predicted (and actual) path of the plume, "one local mayor ... accuse[d] the government of murder" (Osnos, 2011, p. 59). In other disasters, officials have delayed calling for evacuations because of similar fears that the evacuation order would trigger public panic (Fischer, 2008; Scanlon, 2007; Sorenson & Mileti, 1987).

The inclination of public officials to delay transmission of information to the public to prevent public panic typically reflects a poor weighing of risks by the government decision-maker. Withholding information from the public may compromise the ability of individual citizens to make decisions to protect themselves and their families (Sun & Jones, 2013). Of course, individual decision-making may be influenced both by common heuristics and disaster mythology, but official decision-making is also subject to many of these same failings (Sun & Jones, 2013). Moreover, denying the public information about ongoing risks as a disaster unfolds also risks undermining any trust that public officials hope to engender in official recommendations (Sun & Jones, 2013).

In contrast, there is broad consensus among disaster sociologists that the risk of public panic is actually quite small in most disasters. Indeed, researchers have identified the misconception that the public is prone to panic during disasters as another prevalent disaster myth (Clarke & Chess, 2008; Quarantelli & Dynes, 1972; Sun & Jones, 2013). As Clarke and Chess have explained, "Regardless of whether the hazard is dramatic or mundane, whether there is a low or high body-count, or whether the threat is acute or chronic, social scientists agree that 'panic' explains little that is important about how people, in collectivities, respond to disaster" (2008, p. 993).

In other instances, poor risk assessment is driven less by government reliance on heuristics and the mistaken assumptions embedded in disaster myths than by a lack of adequate situational awareness. In contrast to the problems created by reliance on disaster mythology and heuristics, most emergency managers are well aware of the need for greater awareness of the facts on the ground – and the concomitant need to get that information from their own staff (and maybe citizens), rather than relying primarily on news media.

Marginalization of Public Participation and Civil Engagement

Another common type of disaster response failure is the marginalization of public participation and civil engagement in the development and implementation of response measures. Although scholars have broadly argued that empowering civil society to respond to crisis results in the most effective crisis management (Glass & Schoch-Spana, 2002), others have argued recently that there is little room for civil society to engage in response during these moments (Flynn, 2007). These moments, as a result, may disempower citizens while empowering some institutions. Klein (2008), for example, claims that capitalism as a global system has depended heavily on moments of disasters or traumas in order to assert free market economic control over citizens.

Some have argued that the formal triggering of a disaster situation is used to justify the marginalization of public engagement. In fact, understanding who benefits from the declaration of an emergency or crisis helps explain why they are declared. Research on moral panics (Goode & Ben-Yahuda, 1994) sheds light on who wins and who loses when crisis is invoked. In these instances, a "moral threat" is generated by the perception of danger, the responsibility for which is generally attached to a particular group and results in the demonization of that group by a more powerful set of social actors (Cohen, 1980). Similarly, government officials may frame disasters as wars, which likewise encourages "enemy construction" – the creation of disaster enemies, who may be blamed for the disaster itself, its social consequences, or both (Sun & Jones, 2013). When these disasters enemies are treated as akin to the "thinking enemies" of war and terrorism, government officials may point to the existence of these constructed enemies to legitimize both withholding information from the public and imposing measures of social control on those identified as enemies of the public good (Sun & Jones, 2013). This may occur, for instance, when officials are fearful of a panicked public response.

By labeling a situation or event an emergency, crisis, or pending disaster, government agencies generate justifications for circumventing public participation in policymaking, while simultaneously gaining access to new resources, including authority to act in particular, potentially oppressive ways that undermine community efforts (Chamlee-Wright & Rothschild, 2007). While the marginalization of the public is not always intentional, the need for resources is often such that triggering an emergency, which results in federal provision of funds, is attractive. Once an emergency is triggered, there is a need to justify its existence. Moreover, these newfound justifications and powers are heightened when the invocation of disaster is linked, as it often is, to war both through the rhetoric of disaster response and the legal categorizations of emergency power (Sun & Jones, 2013).

In states of emergency – and, perhaps to an even greater extent, in states of war – government officials (and particularly executive branch leaders) have an enhanced capacity to invoke control measures outside of the bounds of norms without incurring rebellion or contestation, and, indeed, sometimes do so within the written authority of the governing body itself. Agamben (2005) conceptualizes this "state of exception" as the ambiguous power suggested by constitutional law that allows for the suspension of law, a space generally created in response to equally ambiguous crises and always with ramifications for civil liberties. Public officials sometimes view disasters as creating such a state of exception. In the aftermath of Hurricane Katrina, for instance, "both New Orleans Mayor Ray Nagin and Jefferson Parrish President Aaron Broussard reportedly purported to declare martial law in their jurisdictions" (Sun, 2011, p. 1179), even though state law neither authorized nor defined martial law.

There is a family resemblance between the "state of exception" and a FEMA-type "state of emergency," whether a declared disaster or a declared emergency (McCormick & Whitney, 2012). Declared disasters and emergencies may require quick and decisive government response – the kind of response for which the Executive is best suited, as the Executive can initiate response without first achieving broad consensus or invoking complicated and time-consuming procedures.

However, in the United States, at least, the Executive usually need not act without some form of prior authorization by the legislative branch. The perceived exigencies of disaster have led legislators to confer, in advance, broad emergency authority on the Executive to react to a wide variety of disasters that might occur. Thus, the President has considerable discretion to craft emergency response measures for natural (and some non-natural) disasters, discretion that is conferred and endorsed by Congress itself. The President's authority is accordingly much clearer than if he were acting in Justice Jackson's "twilight zone" of presidential inherent authority – the ill-defined space where the President acts neither in conflict with Congress nor in accordance with its dictates.[2] The major federal disaster management act, the Stafford Act, gives the President substantial (and likely unreviewable) discretion to determine whether the conditions for declaring a disaster or emergency are met. Once the President has made the requisite declaration, the President then has substantial discretion to redirect federal government resources to meet pressing needs.[3] Accordingly, the democratically accountable Congress has already made some important decisions about disaster powers before the disaster even occurs, and the democratically accountable President makes additional decisions once the disaster is underway.

Nonetheless, invoking the label and rhetoric of states of exception or states of war should not obscure the important, ongoing moral and ethical questions at stake in response to crises, nor the concomitant need for civic engagement and public participation in the resolution of those issues. Indeed, "crises may force citizens to confront profound moral questions – questions central to individuals' conception of their selves and notions of the so-called 'good life' – such as the extent to which they are willing to prioritize small risks to their own safety over much greater risks to others" (Sun & Jones, 2013). Thus, citizens might be required to decide, for example, whether to obey a government instruction to "shelter-in-place" in order to keep the roads clear to allow individuals closer to a disaster site to evacuate more quickly. To fully confront and grapple with these difficult decisions, citizens need a free flow of information from their government (Sun & Jones, 2013).

Similarly, public officials confront many unresolved and difficult choices in their formulation and implementation of appropriate response measures. Nonet and Selznick (2001) argue, for example, that some situations may actually require a form of repressive action in order to save lives. In health-related emergencies, important questions arise about "the meaning of fairness in allocating moral attention and health resources; and implications for ethics of links forged into medicine, public health, law enforcement, and private industry in emergency assessment, response, and preparation" (Eckenwiler, 2003, p. 112). Disasters that affect health are particularly potent as opportunities for social control (McCormick & Whitney, 2012). Examining, measuring the body against a standard, and diagnosing illnesses that are the root of a Public Health Emergency (PHE) are central to "disciplining" the body, as Foucault (1977) termed it. This process consequently brings the body into a new form of visibility, one with names and diagnoses attached to it. As communicable illnesses are detected, emergency measures can be put in place by authoritative government institutions, possibly against the will of the individual or community, to protect the larger population. Quarantine is possibly the most controversial emergency health power and is granted to states in relatively new Model State Health Emergencies Act laws passed by the majority of states in the United States. This type of "governmentality," as again coined by Foucault, brings to light the importance of political institutions in producing citizens who can be governed and, in particular, the role of practices and techniques that are critical to this process. These biopolitics, or the ways in which the modern state subjugates its constituents through bodily control, are critical to these powers of the state. State measures that involve the measuring and regulation of human health and well-being, such as risks to human health or racial identity, are examples of biopolitics.

Surveillance is central to biopower because it is based on a criterion established and managed by credible experts often embedded in or guiding the state. Hacking (1999) argues that such standards and the individuals to whom they are applied are mutually constitutive. The ways that people and diseases are classified open possibilities for and impose limits on actions. That is, the actions available to people are both created and constrained by the available categories.

Recent policy developments like the Model State Health Emergencies Act proposed in response to the 9/11 terrorist attacks implicate these kinds of questions, raising issues regarding the meaning of due process in the context of emergencies and the state's power over potentially exposed or infected individuals. The Act also raises questions about the power of federal agencies over state representatives, the provision of resources, and the proper approach to phenomena that cross state boundaries (Greenberger, 2005). For example, when is it appropriate to invoke quarantine measures? Which agencies have the authority to impose quarantine? How can rapidly expanding risks be managed across geographic boundaries? What kinds of agreements are in place to do so?

Other instances, like the emergence of West Nile Virus, demonstrate the mechanics of public disenfranchisement during emergencies, especially in the absence of formal policy measures. In the original instance of West Nile Virus emergence in New York City, authorities ubiquitously sprayed the city with pesticides despite the lack of scientific evidence that this intervention would be effective (McCormick & Whitney, 2012). Affected communities, aggrieved that they had no formal power or role in the decision-making process, launched a lawsuit against the City to prevent that practice from being repeated in the future. The parties negotiated a settlement that allowed plaintiffs to participate in developing the pesticide spraying plans for future events, but the communities ultimately felt that their concerns were only minimally addressed. This example reflects the lack of formal mechanisms through which affected communities may exercise decision-making power or influence in planning disaster responses. While there is a public comment mechanism in many instances, it is often *pro forma* and does not influence decision-making. Whether or not the government's ultimate decision is wise, this framework for engagement engenders contention and mistrust between officials and the public. The absence of formal policy guidance suggests that difficult policy choices are likely to be made under cover of "emergency" on an ad hoc basis, as questions arise, largely outside of processes subject to public scrutiny. When a public health emergency is declared, there is blanket power given to local and/or state governing bodies.

Despite (or perhaps in some cases, because of) the importance of the many policy questions that arise in disaster response – and the difficulty of the many trade-offs that will inevitably be required – public officials may be inclined to limit public participation in disaster decision-making and shield their own decisions from public review. A recent survey of state sunshine laws, including open meeting and open records law designed to ensure transparency in government actions, reveals that many such laws have exceptions that can be invoked to close official meetings on important disaster issues and to prevent public disclosure of disaster information (Sun & Jones, 2013).

These exceptions may provide legal cover for officials who wish to limit transparency and openness in disasters. The possibility that emergency exceptions to state sunshine laws, developed primarily to prevent terrorists from exploiting disaster information, will be invoked to shield decision-making for other disasters from public scrutiny is particularly problematic given the absence in these disasters of "thinking enemies" determined to exploit information to do others harm (Sun & Jones, 2013). Curtailing government transparency during disaster can also undermine official accountability for disaster decision-making and threaten the functioning of political checks that might otherwise constrain executive officials from exploiting the broad discretion granted to them by disaster response laws in ways that promote private interests, rather than the public good (Sun & Jones, 2013). Government secrecy thus delegitimizes the exercise of emergency powers. Allowing officials to clamp down on information during disasters also implicates concerns that control over information may ultimately facilitate control over people.

Perpetuation of "Emergency" Measures Beyond the "Emergency"

One of the longstanding debates in the emergency powers literature is the extent to which procedures and policies, developed quickly in response to an immediate crisis, become entrenched in laws, policies, and institutional behavior and thus are perpetuated beyond the contours of the emergency that spurred their creation. In the terrorism context, for instance, Ackerman has argued that public fear occasioned by terrorist attacks is likely to result in oppressive emergency measures that will persist beyond the emergency itself, unless specific measures are taken to contain their reach (2006). In a similar vein, Gross has argued that, when governments confront "violent crises," the line between "normalcy" and "emergency" is "constantly blurred" (2003, p. 1070). Temporary emergency measures "tend[] to become entrenched over time and thus normalized and made routine" (Gross, 2003, p. 1090), resulting in the "normalization of the extraordinary" (Gross, 2003, p. 1089).

In contrast, Posner and Vermeule critique the idea – which they label the "emergency ratchet" – that a series of emergencies necessarily tends to push toward "*unidirectional* and *irreversible* change in some legal variable" (Posner & Vermeule, 2005, p. 58). Posner and Vermeule note that the common suggestion is that emergencies "produce a *statist ratchet*: an irreversible trend toward increased state power and official suppression of civil liberties, free speech, and political association" (Posner & Vermeule, 2007, p. 132). However, Posner and Vermeule vigorously contest both the notion that emergencies tend to push state power irrevocably in one direction and the related notion that emergency measures necessarily persist and become more and more oppressive over time (Posner & Vermeule, 2005, 2007).

So far, most of this ongoing debate has occurred in the context of emergency measures implemented in response to terrorism or war emergencies as part of a larger debate about whether emergencies should be dealt with in accordance with, or outside, normal constitutional and legal norms. We do not attempt here to make a wide-ranging empirical analysis of the frequency at which emergency measures persist beyond the initial emergency that precipitated their enactment, nor do we attempt to discern whether emergency measures significantly affect the long-term trajectory of personal or political freedoms.

Nonetheless, observations of emergency measures enacted in response to natural disasters suggest that disaster events are not self-contained events. Rather, the responses on both the institutional and individual levels that occur when one event takes place can recur in subsequent events that are similar either in type of risk, geographic location, or in other ways.

Accordingly, foreseeing disasters involves tracking "bleed" outside of the specific contours of an event. Short-term practices generated within fleeting moments of disasters may become embedded in institutions and practices. The events within a disaster or crisis are a particularly black box not only theoretically, but also empirically. In such moments, fear and urgency can result in the abrogation of pre-existing rules and procedures, resulting in less credible evidence on which to base decision-making and, simultaneously, fewer conflicting narratives with which decision-makers must contend.

One recent disaster in which emergency measures arguably persisted beyond the scope of the immediate emergency is Superstorm Sandy. After Sandy struck the eastern seaboard of the United States on October 29, 2012, numerous affected communities imposed states of emergency and mandatory curfews to prevent looting and ensure citizen safety. Almost three months later, in January 2013, many communities still remained in a declared state of emergency, often subject to strict curfews, with residents forbidden "from walking outside after 6 p.m." (Zernike, 2013). Checkpoints continued to dot local roads, which required local residents to produce "special permit[s]" and permitted travel "only to and from their homes" (Zernike, 2013). Indeed, some communities remain "under an evacuation order from the governor" and have not permitted residents to return home at all (Zernike, 2013).

While the devastating consequences of Sandy persist, and rebuilding has been slow, by January, residents were beginning to take the issue with the emergency measures, which at times suggested a "demilitarized zone" rather "than a seaside haven" (Zernike, 2013). One resident of Ortley Beach, where residents were still forbidden from entering their own homes, explained that "[i]n the beginning" the restrictions "ma[de her] feel safe," but that "[n]ow it feels like Big Brother watching" (Zernike, 2013). Local public officials declined to "give … a specific timeline" for lifting the state of emergency, unsure whether the restrictions would be removed by the Memorial Day benchmark set by state officials (Zernike, 2013). This example underscores how the boundaries of any given emergency are both highly malleable and contestable.

The experience of these residents also suggests that unnecessarily prolonging states of emergency can generate substantial uncertainty for local residents and businesses, which in turn can undercut recovery efforts and community morale. These protracted states of emergency can likewise prolong public feelings of disempowerment and dependency, and undermine any personal or community sense of responsibility for the restoration of community life. Ultimately, this administrative over-reaching favors continued bureaucratic empowerment at the expense of community empowerment and may thwart full community engagement in the recovery process.

Another interesting example of the bleed of emergency measures beyond the geographic and temporal contours of the immediate emergency occurred in the response to West Nile Virus. The initial declaration of a Public Health Emergency, only the second in U.S. history, was repeated in a wide range of states wherein the illness appeared (McCormick & Whitney, 2012). This occurred despite the lack of clear criteria for declaring such an emergency. Some claimed that this declaration was meant to garner resources for otherwise under-resourced departments of public health that did not have the facilities to respond to a widespread vector-borne disease. There were few other pathways through which planes and pesticides used for spraying could be gained.

Neglect of Vulnerable Populations in Disaster Response

Certain populations are more vulnerable to disaster than others, as determined by many contextual factors like social environment, age, gender, pre-existing health conditions, and built environment (Cutter, Boruff, & Shirley, 2003). The disaster literature shows how individual-level factors that are unaccounted for in planning can exacerbate disaster impacts, yet often remain unaddressed in planning for the next event (Cutter, 1996). For example, older persons have a number of physiological and social risk factors that place them at elevated risk during heat waves. These include a decreased ability to thermoregulate (control internal body temperature) and inability to adjust to high outdoor temperatures. Pre-existing chronic disease, more common in the elderly, also impairs compensatory responses to high, sustained temperatures and other disaster events. Many older persons may also be more likely than younger persons to be isolated and living alone, leaving them with fewer means of alerting others to their plight.

Many subpopulations are vulnerable to disaster impacts. Areas with high crime rates, low social capital, and socially isolated individuals experience increased vulnerability during disasters, such as in the Chicago heat wave of 1995 (Klinenberg, 2002). People living in socioeconomically disadvantaged areas are generally at a higher risk of a variety of disasters, and structural factors, such as appropriate infrastructure, existence of green space, and distance from risks like flood zones, represent some of the central contextual factors that shape this risk (Cutter, Mitchell, & Scott, 2000; Schmidtlein, Deutsch, Piegorsch, & Cutter, 2008). Minorities and communities of low socioeconomic status are more frequently situated in vulnerable neighborhoods (Harlan, Brazel, Prashad, Stefanov, & Larsen, 2006). Disasters can compromise the infrastructure necessary to deal with impacts to medical care or energy distribution systems. For example, increases in emergency medical dispatch calls during periods of elevated Heat Index place increased pressure on multiple financial and human resources (Golden, Hartz, Brazel, Luber, & Phelan, 2008). Because of greater strain on more limited resources in these areas, power grids have failed secondary to strain from high electricity demand. Areas with lower margins face increased risk of disruptions to generating resources and transmission under excessive heat events (North American Electric Reliability Council, 2006).

Another example is the transport of vulnerable, immobile populations from nursing homes, hospitals, and even residential homes during a multitude of disaster events. Floods, earthquakes, and hurricanes often necessitate the movement of populations from one place to another for short- or long-term periods. However, research has documented the lack of resources for these groups and the critical nature of assistance with evacuation. Often, resource constraints in low-income communities, in combination with emerging, high-pressure situations, mean that the vulnerable are unable to get access to the support they need, leaving them in harm's way.

THE IMPLICATIONS OF CLIMATE CHANGE FOR DISASTER MISMANAGEMENT

The proposition that climate change is increasing risk for disasters, catastrophes, and illness is now widely accepted; it is a recurrent theme throughout the chapters in this book. Most recently, the United States government has acknowledged that climate change has already affected the country by exacerbating extreme weather events. Climate change has happened slowly over time, although sudden changes are predicted (NRC, 2004), with indirect but immediate impacts on human populations (Campbell-Lendrum, Pruss-Ustun, & Corvalan, 2003). Some climate-related events may be minor but have extreme impacts due to vulnerabilities. Weather and climate-related extremes include a range of events, such as glacial lake outbursts, typhoons, droughts, hurricanes, heat waves, and others (Niepold, Herring, & McConville, 2008).

In addition to increasing the potential frequency and severity of weather-related disasters, climate change may have important implications for the disaster response failures that we have articulated in this chapter (Cutter et al., 2012). Climate change is likely to affect each of these facets of disasters in unique ways. Generally, we suggest that (1) the rapidly manifesting and possibly surprising impacts of climate change may increase the difficulty of assessing and prioritizing risks; (2) the increased frequency (temporal compression) of disasters may result in both the increased marginalization of civic engagement in the formulation of response measures and the increased bleed of such emergency measurers across specific events; and (3) climate change impacts may expand the scope of vulnerable populations, likely creating new types of unexpected vulnerabilities. While these hypothesized outcomes may or may not ensue, they deserve consideration as we try to foresee future vulnerabilities in disaster response.

Climate change may have interesting implications for government assessment and prioritization or risks in shaping its response efforts. Some risks introduced by climate change are unexpected, novel risks for the affected population – such as the spread of an unusual disease to regions in which it has not previously been seen (Asnis, Conetta, Teixeira, Waldman, & Sampson, 2000). One might thus expect that both the public and public officials will have some very strong reactions (arguably "overreactions") to those risks, as compared to more familiar, commonplace risks (Sunstein, 2005). More generally, the unpredictable and unexpected nature of some climate-change impacts may present real challenges for appropriate assessment of ongoing risks during the response phase.

Another potential implication of climate change for disaster response failures is that as disasters occur more frequently, one might expect a growing temptation to capitalize on these events to enhance executive authority at the expense of public engagement. In particular, public officials may exploit the discretion that disaster declarations authorize to consolidate executive power and marginalize public participation in the development and implementation of response measures. Yet the increased frequency of disaster will engender an increased need for a democratized disaster response, rather than a hardened one. Responses are more likely to be effective in the short- and long-term when they engage, rather than marginalize, the affected population, and the success of disaster response and recovery will become all the more critical as the pace of disasters accelerates and the timeframe for recovery shrinks.

The temporal compression of disaster events might result in increased "bleed" of emergency measures adopted in response to one emergency into subsequent emergencies. Alternatively, temporal compression may increase attempts to cite back-to-back emergencies as justification for leaving emergency measures in place permanently, or at least indefinitely. The entrenchment of emergency measures adopted outside of normal channels and without adherence to normal procedures would be particularly problematic. Of course, a long series of emergencies might increase public attention to emergency measures and prompt, instead, a broader and more deliberative consideration of the appropriateness of both particular emergency measures and their extension beyond that specific emergency context.

In addition, climate change may have important consequences for the oft-noted failure to provide effectively for the disaster needs of vulnerable populations. Climate change threatens to create newly vulnerable populations by expanding the reach of disasters. Since climate-related disasters are often a surprise and therefore unplanned for, they may induce novel effects. For example, as noted previously, during heat waves, high emergency medical dispatch volumes related to heat stress are greatest at the same time as maximum demand for electricity, which increases strain on an aging power grid and increases vulnerability to heat stress (Berry, McBean, & Séguin, 2008; California Energy Commission, 2007).

As demand for electricity increases, brown-outs and blackouts may also expand, preventing those who have a medical need for air conditioning from having access to it, even though they might otherwise have had access. Accordingly, the number of elderly and ill who are particularly vulnerable to heat waves may multiply outside the areas typically most affected by heat waves as the effects of climate change and the concomitant demand for increased power for air conditioning push our electricity infrastructure beyond its capacity.

Moreover, as the effects of climate change increase, one would expect climate change mitigation efforts, including a price on carbon, to gain more traction. Potential resulting increases in the price of electricity will likely aid in climate change mitigation, but will also likely increase the number of heat-vulnerable individuals who cannot afford air conditioning during climate-change induced heat waves, calling perhaps for some form of need-based aid in paying utility bills. These examples suggest that both climate change itself and potential mitigation efforts may expand the size and nature of at-risk populations for whom disaster planning must carefully account.

POTENTIAL REMEDIES FOR TYPICAL DISASTER RESPONSE FAILURES

Remedies to minimize the risk of the kind of disaster response failures discussed here will require an integrated approach spanning all phases of the disaster management cycle. They will also necessitate a broader acknowledgment of climate change as a stressor for many types of disasters. Of course, not all disaster response failures are predictable – and the types of failures we identify do not occur in every disaster – but many response missteps follow predictable, well-traveled paths. The foreseeability of these types of disaster response mismanagement suggests a moral, if not legal, duty to mitigate these predictable failures, keeping in mind the ways climate change might alter or exacerbate these typical failures.

Accordingly, disaster planning, preparation, and mitigation should focus not only on reducing the direct risks posed by a hazard event itself, but also on mitigating associated response failures of the kinds exemplified by, and identified in, this article. Recognizing that these typical governmental response failures require their own preparation and mitigation strategies is an important first step in countering foreseeable disaster response mismanagement. Further work should focus on identifying other typical disaster response failures that also need to be remedied, as well as identifying and implementing measures to correct these flaws in disaster response. Moreover, while we focus primarily on failures in government disaster management, a parallel exploration could also be undertaken for private disaster mismanagement, and the risk of those response failures, too, should be considered and mitigated throughout the emergency management cycle, whether the private actors are ordinary citizens, corporate resilience planners, or private owners of critical infrastructure.

One important approach to minimizing disaster response failures will be implementation of structural changes or regulatory measures in advance of any particular disaster during the mitigation and preparation phases of disaster management. Many of these structural changes may require amending existing federal, state, and local disaster laws and policies. For example, structural changes focused on poor governmental risk prioritization during disasters could include predisaster legislative or administrative guidance prioritizing particular risks to be addressed during the emergency response phase. To address the tendency to overemphasize security risks based on unfounded assumptions about survivor looting and violence, for instance, the guidance could make clear that life-saving measures are always to be prioritized over property protection measures such as antilooting patrols (Sun, 2011, p. 1136).

Legislation could also create presumptive guidelines about resource allocation and priorities that can be overcome during the disaster itself only upon a strong showing of need. In the context of overblown looting fears, for instance, disaster legislation could impose greater evidentiary thresholds that must be met before concerns about looting or other security risks could be invoked to delay humanitarian aid to devastated areas (Sun, 2011). For example, state and local disaster provisions could require "credible, reliable, verified evidence" of looting or violence before diverting first responders from search-and-rescue roles to law enforcement (Sun, 2011).

More broadly, predisaster planning focused on how resources will be allocated, prioritized, and distributed during disasters may also be helpful, even though sufficient flexibility must be built in to ensure that unexpected needs can be accounted for and accommodated. Whether such predisaster legislation would actually mitigate poor risk prioritization during disaster response depends, of course, on a number of factors. These factors include the extent to which predisaster risk assessments are less prone to false assumptions grounded in disaster myths and other heuristics than those assessments made during the heat of the moment while the disaster is actually underway, as well as the extent to which predisaster risk prioritization could be encapsulated in rules or guidance that would actually be enforced or adhered to during the disaster event.

Other structural, legal reforms could help mitigate other typical response failures by changing the background legal norms against which emergency measures are enacted and implemented. For example, the tendency of emergency response measures to "bleed" beyond the emergency could perhaps be countered by overarching legislation imposing either automatic sunset provisions for emergency response measures or periodic reauthorization requirements. Ackerman has argued that potentially repressive response measures adopted in response to highly visible terrorist attacks should automatically expire after a relatively short period of time unless reauthorized by "escalating ... supermajorities" of Congress (Ackerman, 2006, p. 80). While the terrorism context differs from the kinds of disasters we are discussing in important and vital ways (Sun & Jones, 2013) and the disaster measures in question are more likely to be local in scope than terrorism response, predisaster decision-making about how long emergency measures should persist may well make sense for the broader range of disasters we address here.[4]

Such automatic sunset provisions would be particularly appropriate for measures adopted outside of normal political processes or pursuant to emergency exceptions to public hearing, participation, or disclosure requirements. Ensuring that emergency measures adopted without the standard procedural safeguards and without opportunities for public participation are time-limited may incentivize public officials to follow preexisting channels whenever possible. Time limits would thus mitigate the tendency to curb public engagement, particularly if the automatic sunset provisions provide for quicker expiration of emergency measures adopted under emergency procedures that limit public input. Moreover, if automatic sunset provisions apply only to measures adopted once the disaster has begun, those provisions might incentivize public officials to engage in more predisaster planning, when opportunities for full public disclosure and full public participation in deliberation are more likely to be available.

Official attempts to limit public access to disaster information may also be countered by carefully evaluating the continued need for emergency exceptions to public sunshine laws and by ensuring that disasters that lack "thinking enemies" who might exploit public information are not reflexively grouped with terrorism and war emergencies for purposes of public information disclosure rules (Sun & Jones, 2013).

Other structural solutions may be less legal in nature. For example, the lack of situational awareness that contributes to poor risk assessment and prioritization during disaster's aftermath may be mitigated somewhat in future disasters by data crowdsourcing and social media, which allow disaster survivors to play a much more interactive role in the generation of on-the-ground information about disaster effects. However, many obstacles may prevent emergency managers from utilizing social media and crowdsourcing data. Such obstacles include concerns about "data verification, security of information, liability, and information subjectivity" (McCormick, 2013).

Problems plaguing vulnerable populations also necessitate structural, medical, and social measures to address vulnerability. Because threats to vulnerable populations are known, planning to avoid them can be effective. For example, transportation barriers for wheelchair-bound seniors were a major obstacle to reducing the impacts of Hurricane Katrina. An appropriate infrastructure for disabled people could accommodate vulnerable groups. Heat waves clearly affect people living in denser urban "heat island" environments without sufficient greenspace (Harlan et al., 2006). Therefore, planting trees and planning parks in these areas can serve as preventive measures for the worst mortality outcomes. Social circumstance and interventions meant to address vulnerable populations have affected the outcomes of many disasters.

Sometimes structural solutions to disasters will span legal, technological, and social realms. Verchick (2012), for example, has suggested a number of important structural mechanisms for addressing the needs of the vulnerable in disaster, which – working together – may help ensure just treatment of the vulnerable in disaster's aftermath. Verchick's solutions include a "proposed ... federal 'Executive Order on Disaster Justice'" and a "nationally consistent disaster-justice mapping tool" that would help communities identify and plan for vulnerable populations (2012, p. 68).

Just as many of the structural changes that prevent response failures must occur during the planning and preparation phases of emergency management, lawsuits intended to deter disaster response mismanagement will also often be most effective when focused on planning and preparation actions taken before the disaster actually occurs. Foreseeability is often an important touchstone of tort liability: if harm is foreseeable and a reasonable actor would take precautions to avoid it, then tort liability may be appropriate (assuming that all the elements of a given tort action, including causation and damages, are satisfied). Foreseeable disaster response mismanagement thus seems like a potential basis for tort liability.

However, lawsuits against federal, state, and local disaster response entities and officials often are barred by governmental immunities. These immunities exist not just in the disaster context, but for governmental action more broadly, particularly action that is discretionary or policy-making in nature (Rosenthal, 2007). In addition, many disaster-specific immunities also exist, which make holding government entities liable for disaster mismanagement particularly difficult. For example, the Stafford Act, under which most major federal disaster mitigation and response efforts are conducted, has a specific immunity provision stating that "[t]he Federal Government shall not be liable for any claim based upon the exercise or performance of or the failure to exercise or perform a discretionary function or duty on the part of a Federal Agency or an employee of the Federal Government in carrying out the provisions of the Act."[5]

In post-Katrina litigation, the Fifth Circuit Court of Appeals applied this Stafford Act immunity provision to bar a lawsuit by plaintiffs who alleged that the federal government had been negligent in the "provision of food, water, shelter, medical assistance, and transport [to shelters of last resort]" in accordance with procedures outlined in the federal National Response Plan. In particular, the court held that the immunity provision barred liability because the Plan did not impose nondiscretionary duties on federal officials.[6]

Broad disaster immunities of this variety make suits against the government for disaster response failures difficult, even if those suits can be premised on the planning stage, unless there are clear, nondiscretionary mandates to undertake certain planning. Where those mandates exist, however, and where they require that certain factors be properly considered, immunities may sometimes be overcome. In a related context, for example, a federal district court held that FEMA was not immune from a post-Katrina suit alleging that the agency imposed improper eligibility criteria for the Short-Term Lodging Program it administers.[7] The court noted that FEMA had immunity only as to discretionary acts and that the court could thus review "any actions that are mandated by statute," as well as any alleged constitutional violations.[8]

Additionally, some state disaster-specific immunities are focused more narrowly on creating immunities for actions taken during the emergency itself.[9] Thus, depending on how these disaster-specific immunities are interpreted in relation to broader existing immunities in state law (i.e., whether the more specific disaster immunity is intended to displace any broader existing immunities in state law that might otherwise apply to predisaster actions), there may be more opportunities to challenge predisaster action than specific actions taken (or not taken) during the disaster itself.

Moreover, beyond questions of immunity, other features of tort law may make challenging predisaster government decisions easier than challenging decisions made in the heat of the emergency itself, as state tort law may take disaster conditions into account in determining whether particular decisions were reasonable. In effect, this approach may create a lower emergency standard of care because of the time pressures of the crisis (Hoffman, 2008).

Accordingly, lawsuits based on a government entity's failure to accommodate the needs of vulnerable populations are typically more likely to be successful in galvanizing change if they are focused on failures in the planning process rather than on specific response decisions made once the disaster is underway.[10] For example, one recent case – filed in the immediate aftermath of Hurricane Irene – alleged that New York City failed to properly account for the needs of the disabled in the city's emergency planning.[11] In particular, the plaintiffs alleged, among other failings, that most of the emergency shelters the city opened during Hurricane Irene were not accessible to the disabled, that emergency broadcasts did not include American Sign Language interpretation, and that the evacuation transportation provided by the city did not adequately accommodate those with mobility disabilities.

Rather than premising liability on any of these specific Irene response failures, however, the gravitas of the plaintiffs' claim was that the city's "failure to plan" for "the unique needs of persons with disabilities during emergencies" puts the disabled "in unnecessary danger" during disasters.[12] The plaintiffs contended that these planning failures violate Title II of the Americans with Disabilities Act (ADA),[13] Section 504 of the Rehabilitation Act of 1973,[14] and the New York City Human Rights Law.[15] Moreover, rather than seeking damages, the plaintiffs sought injunctive and declaratory relief to require the City to comply with the statutory mandates in question.[16] In November 2013, the district court for the Southern District of New York agreed with the plaintiffs, holding that New York City violated the rights of the city's disabled by failing to plan for adequate and accessible emergency evacuation, transportation, shelters, and communication.[17]

A similar lawsuit filed against the city of Los Angeles, alleging that the city's failure to provide for the unique needs of the disabled in its emergency planning violated the ADA, Section 504, and California state law, resulted in summary judgment for the plaintiffs.[18] A subsequent settlement required the city to alter its emergency planning to account for the special needs of the disabled.[19] These types of poor-planning claims thus seem more likely to succeed than challenges to the particular missteps that occurred during the disaster itself, and the high-profile decisions in New York City and Los Angeles may motivate other jurisdictions to undertake more comprehensive planning for the needs of vulnerable populations during disaster response. While there is no doubt that, as the court suggested in the New York case, such planning is a "Herculean task," and there is always the danger that the resulting planning documents will be "fantasy documents" designed to appease rather than effect meaningful change (Clarke, 2001), the process of advance planning for the special needs of vulnerable populations may nonetheless result in better outcomes for the disabled than the ad hoc responses, formulated in the midst of crisis, on which cities have traditionally relied. As Boin & Egan argued, analyzing the "highly effective" evacuation of New Orleans on the eve of Hurricane Gustav, "detailed planning can work in spite of pessimistic overstatements to the contrary" (2012, p. 74).

CONCLUSIONS

At the beginning of this chapter we warned of the parade of horrors to come, in the form of case studies detailing disaster management gone terribly wrong. And we also cautioned against the tendency to use these worst-case scenarios as a basis for concluding that government mismanagement is the norm in every disaster.

However, the rising number and cost of disasters make it imperative that we examine how they can be best addressed. By understanding how disasters have sometimes been mismanaged in the past, we can begin to learn from mistakes and move beyond them. In this chapter, we have begun to articulate foreseeable disaster management issues, as well as the role that climate change may play in altering or exacerbating these typical response failures in the coming years. We have focused on four common forms of disaster response mismanagement: (1) poor assessment and prioritization of risks; (2) marginalization of public participation and civic engagement in managing and responding to those risks; (3) unwarranted extension of emergency measures and emergency powers beyond the immediate emergency that justified them; and (4) neglect of vulnerable populations.

Additionally, we argue that climate change may aggravate some of these phenomena by, for example, increasing the difficulty of assessing and prioritizing risks, further marginalizing civic engagement in the formulation of response measures, heightening the risk that such emergency measurers will bleed across specific events, expanding the scope of vulnerable populations, and introducing new, unexpected vulnerabilities.

In particular, we conclude that the foreseeability of these typical disaster response failures creates an imperative to plan for and mitigate these typical government missteps throughout all phases of the emergency management cycle, just as the direct risks posed by hazard events must be planned for and mitigated. Particularly as climate change threatens to exacerbate many of these existing response failures, recognizing that these response failures merit their own planning and mitigation strategies is a critical step in minimizing the harms of disaster response mismanagement.

Cassandra's voice of warning calls to us, through both the stories of past disasters and the vision of future disasters exacerbated by climate change, to address these patterns of failed disaster response. To begin to answer that call, we have argued that structural reforms – both legal and otherwise – as well as legal liability can play an important role in preventing disaster response mismanagement. Because climate change is likely to shift all of these outcomes, integrating both climate projections and adaptive capacity into planning for climate-specific disasters is also essential. Heeding the call to mitigate both the direct risks posed by natural hazards and the risks posed by inadequate and misguided government response is the best hope for minimizing the human suffering that Cassandra's warnings portend.

NOTES

1. This list is, of course, not fully comprehensive. Other issues that could be explored in subsequent work include interjurisdictional conflicts that arise in realms of overlapping state, federal, and local power, and the paralysis and shirking of responsibility that can result from unclear lines of authority, whether vertical or horizontal.

2. Youngstown Sheet and Tube Co. v. Sawyer (1952).

3. 42 U.S.C. §§ 5170, 5170a (2006).

4. In Texas, for example, when the governor declares a state of disaster under Texas state law, the "state of disaster may not continue for more than 30 days unless renewed by the governor." Texas Gov. Code §418.014(c). Moreover, the Texas state legislature "may terminate a state of disaster at any time." *Id.* These provisions may facilitate political checks on the length of a state of disaster and its concomitant emergency measures.

5. 42 U.S.C. §5148.
6. See Freeman v. United States (2009).
7. McWaters v. FEMA (2006).
8. *Id.* at 814.
9. See, for example, Cal. Civ. Code § 1714.5 (Deering, 2013) (stating that disaster service workers who are performing services during emergencies are not liable for injuries or deaths resulting from their acts or omissions, unless inflicted willfully); Mont. Code Ann. (2012) (creating immunity for any state, political subdivision, or their representatives from liability for any injuries, damages, or deaths for actions taken in response to disasters or emergencies).
10. One could, of course, imagine that a poorly managed disaster that inflicted serious harm on vulnerable populations might present sufficiently compelling circumstances to spur either changes in common law torts principles or legislative action to reduce obstacles to postdisaster suits based on specific disaster response failures.
11. Brooklyn Ctr. for Independence of the Disabled v. Bloomberg (2012) (certifying the class action).
12. *Id.*
13. 42 U.S.C. § 12131, et seq.
14. 29 U.S.C. § 794, et seq.
15. N.Y.C. Admin. Code. § 8-101, et seq.
16. In general, injunctive relief is far less likely to be barred by sovereign immunity, which, at least in practice, is implicated primarily by claims for monetary relief. See Ex Parte Young (1908) (holding that sovereign immunity does not bar claims for injunctive relief against state officials). Of course, cities, municipalities, and counties do not have sovereign immunity from suits based on federal law. *See, for example*, Lincoln County v. Luning (1890). Such local government entities can and often do, however, have immunities from state law claims as a matter of state law, particularly for discretionary decision-making and particularly against claims for money damages.
17. Brooklyn Ctr. for Independence of the Disabled v. Bloomberg, __F. Supp.2d. __, 2013 WL 5943995 (S.D.N.Y.).
18. *Communities Actively Living Independent and Free v. City of Los Angeles* (2011).
19. CALIF v. City of Los Angeles (2013).

REFERENCES

42 U.S.C. §§ 5170, 5170a (2006).

Ackerman, B. (2006). *Before the next attack: Preserving civil liberties in an age of terrorism.* New Haven, CT: Yale University Press.

Agamben, G. (2005). *State of exception.* Chicago, IL: University of Chicago Press.

Asnis, D., Conetta, R., Teixeira, A., Waldman, G., & Sampson, B. (2000). The West Nile Virus outbreak of 1999 in New York: The Flushing Hospital experience. *Clinical Infectious Diseases, 30*, 413–418.

Berry, P., McBean, G., & Séguin, J. (2008). Vulnerabilities to natural hazards and extreme weather. In J. Séguin (Ed.), *Human health in a changing climate: A Canadian assessment of vulnerabilities and adaptive capacity* (pp. 43–111). Ottawa, Ontario: Health Canada.

Boin, A., & Egan, J. (2012). Hurricane Gustav: The management of a transboundary crisis. In I. Helsloot, A. Boin, L. Comfort, & B. Jacobs (Eds.), *Mega-crises* (pp. 66–76). Springfield, MA: Charles Thomas.

Cal. Civ. Code § 1714.5 (Deering 2013).

CALIF v. City of Los Angeles. (2013). *The city and county of L.A. will include people with all types of disabilities in emergency planning*, Disability Rights Advocates. Retrieved from http://www.dralegal.org/impact/cases/communities-actively-living-independent-and-free-calif-et-al-v-city-of-los-angeles. Accessed on September 12, 2013.

California Energy Commission. (2007). *Final staff forecast for 2008 peak demand.* (CEC-200-2007-006SF). Sacramento, CA: California Energy Commission.

Campbell-Lendrum, D., Pruss-Ustun, A., & Corvalan, C. (2003). How much disease could climate change cause? In D. Campbell-Lendrum, C. Corvalan, K. Ebi, A. Githeko, & J. Scheraga (Eds.), *Climate change and health: Risks and responses* (pp. 133–158). Geneva: World Health Organization.

Chamlee-Wright, E., & Rothschild, D. M. (2007). *Disastrous uncertainty: How government disaster policy undermines community rebound.* (Mercatus Policy Series No. 9). Arlington, VA: Mercatus Center, George Mason University.

Clarke, L. (2001). *Mission improbable: Using fantasy documents to tame disaster.* Chicago, IL: University of Chicago Press.

Clarke, L., & Chess, C. (2008). Elites and panic: More to fear than fear itself. *Social Forces, 87*(2), 993–1014.

Cohen, S. (1980). *Folk devils and moral panics.* New York, NY: St. Martin's Press.

Communities Actively Living Independent and Free v. City of Los Angeles, No. CV 09-0287, 2011 U.S. Dist. LEXIS 118364 (C.D. Cal. Feb. 10, 2011).

Cutter, S., Osman-Elasha, B., Campbell, J., Cheong, S.-M., McCormick, S., Pulwarty, R., … Ziervogel, G. (2012). Managing the risks from climate extremes at the local level. In C. B. Field, V. Barros, T. F. Stocker, D. Qin, D. J. Dokken, K. L. Ebi, M. D. Mastrandrea, K. J. Mach, G.-K. Plattner, S. K. Allen, M. Tignor, & P. M. Midgley (Eds.), *Managing the risks of extreme events and disasters to advance climate change adaptation. A. Special report of working groups I and II of the Intergovernmental Panel on Climate Change (IPCC)*. Cambridge: Cambridge University Press.

Cutter, S. L. (1996). Societal responses to environmental hazards. *International Social Science Journal, 48*(4), 525–536.

Cutter, S. L., Boruff, B. J., & Shirley, W. L. (2003). Social vulnerability to environmental hazards. *Social Science Quarterly, 84*(2), 242–261.

Cutter, S. L., Mitchell, J. T., & Scott, M. S. (2000). Revealing the vulnerability of people and places: A case study of Georgetown County, South Carolina. *Annals of the Association of American Geographers, 90*(4), 713–737.

Disabled v. Bloomberg 287 F.R.D. 240 (S.D.N.Y. 2012).

Eckenwiler, L. A. (2003). Emergency health professionals and the ethics of crisis. In J. D. Moreno (Ed.), *The wake of terror* (pp. 111–131). Cambridge, MA: MIT Press.

Ex Parte Young, 209 U.S. 123 (1908).

Fischer III, H. W. (2008). *Response to disaster: Fact versus fiction and its perpetuation: The sociology of disaster* (3rd ed.). Lanham, MD: University Press of America.

Flynn, S. (2007). *The edge of disaster: Rebuilding a resilient nation*. New York, NY: Random House.

Foucault, M. (1977). *Discipline and punish: The birth of the prison*. New York, NY: Vintage Books.

Freeman v. United States. 556 F.3d 326, 337 (5th Cir. 2009).

Glass, T., & Schoch-Spana, M. (2002). Bioterrorism and the people: How to vaccinate a city against panic. *Clinical Infectious Diseases*, *34*, 217–223.

Golden, J., Hartz, D., Brazel, A., Luber, G., & Phelan, P. (2008). A biometeorology study of climate and heat-related morbidity in Phoenix from 2001 to 2006. *International Journal of Biometeorology*, *52*, 471–480.

Goode, E., & Ben-Yahuda, N. (1994). *Moral panics: The social construction of deviance*. New York, NY: Wiley.

Greenberger, M. (2005). *The role of the federal government in response to catastrophic health emergencies: Lessons learned from Hurricane Katrina*. University of Maryland Legal Studies Research Paper No. 2005-52.

Gross, O. (2003). Chaos and rules: Should response to violent crises always be constitutional? *Yale Law Journal*, *112*(5), 1011–1134.

Hacking, I. (1999). Making up people. In M. Biagioli (Ed.), *The science studies reader* (pp. 161–171). New York, NY: Routledge.

Harlan, S. B., Brazel, A. J., Prashad, L., Stefanov, W. L., & Larsen, L. (2006). Neighborhood microclimates and vulnerability to heat stress. *Social Science & Medicine*, *63*(11), 2847.

Hoffman, S. (2008). Responder's responsibility: Liability and immunity in public health emergencies. *Georgetown Law Journal*, *96*(6), 1926.

Klein, N. (2008). *The shock doctrine: The rise of disaster capitalism*. New York City: Knopf.

Klinenberg, E. (2002). *Heatwave: A social autopsy of disaster in Chicago*. Chicago, IL: University of Chicago Press.

LaPorte, T. R., & Consolini, P. (1991). Working in practice but not in theory: Theoretical challenges of high reliability organizations. Journal of Public Administration *and Theory*, *1*(Winter), 19–47.

Lincoln County v. Luning. 133 U.S. 529 (1890).

McCormick, S. (2013). *New tools for emergency managers: An assessment of obstacles to use and implementation*. Unpublished manuscript.

McCormick, S., & Whitney, K. (2012). The making of public health emergencies: West Nile virus in New York City. *Sociology of Health & Illness*, *35*(2), 268–279.

McWaters v. FEMA. 436 F. Supp. 2d 802, 811-12 (E.D. La. 2006).

Mont. Code Ann. § 10-3-11 (2012).

New Orleans Mayor Orders Looting Crackdown. (2005, September 1). *MSNBC*. Retrieved from http://www.msnbc.msn.com/id/9063708/

Niepold, F., Herring, D., & McConville, D. (2008). The role of narrative and geospatial visualization in fostering climate literate citizens. *Physical Geography*, *29*(6), 255–273.

Nonet, P., & Selznick, P. (2001). *Law and society in transition: Toward responsive law*. Piscataway, NJ: Transaction Publishers.

North American Electric Reliability Council. (2006). *2006 long-term reliability assessment. The reliability of the bulk power systems in North America*. Retrieved from http://www.nerc.com/files/summer2006.pdf

NRC. (2004). Abrupt climate change: Inevitable surprises. *Population and Development Review*, *30*(3), 563–568.

Onishi, N., & Fackler, M. (2011, August 9). Japan held nuclear data, leaving evacuees in peril. *The New York Times*. Retrieved from http://www.nytimes.com

Osnos, E. (2011, October 17). Letter from Fukushima: The Fallout: Seven Months Later: Japan's Nuclear Predicament. *New Yorker*. Retrieved from http://www.newyorker.com

Perrow, C. (1994). *Normal accidents: Living with high risk technologies*. New York, NY: Basic Books.

Posner, E. A., & Vermeule, A. (2005). Accommodating emergencies. In M. Tushnet (Ed.), *The constitution in wartime* (pp. 55–92). Durham, NC: Duke University Press.

Posner, E. A., & Vermeule, A. (2007). *Terror in the balance: Security, liberty, and the courts*. New York, NY: Oxford University Press.

Quarantelli, E. L., & Dynes, R. R. (1972). When disaster strikes (It isn't much like what you've heard and read about). *Psychology Today*, 5(February), 66–70.

Rosenthal, L. (2007). A theory of governmental damages liability: Torts, constitutional torts, and takings. *University of Pennsylvania Journal of Constitutional Law*, *9*(3), 797–870.

Scanlon, J. (2007). Unwelcome irritant or useful ally?: The mass media in emergencies. In H. Rodriguez, E. Quarantelli, & R. Dynes (Eds.), *The handbook of disaster research* (pp. 413–429). New York, NY: Springer.

Schmidtlein, M. C., Deutsch, R. C., Piegorsch, W. W., & Cutter, S. L. (2008). A sensitivity analysis of the social vulnerability index. *Risk Analysis*, *28*(4), 1099–1114.

Sorenson, J. H., & Mileti, D. S. (1987). Decision-making uncertainties in emergency warning system organizations. *International Journal of Mass Emergencies & Disasters*, *5*(1), 33–61.

Sun, L. G. (2011). Disaster mythology and the law. *Cornell Law Review*, *96*(5), 1131–1208.

Sun, L. G., & Jones, R. A. (2013). Disaggregating disasters. *UCLA Law Review*, *60*(4), 884–948.

Sunstein, C. R. (2005). *Laws of fear: Beyond the precautionary principle*. New York, NY: Cambridge University Press.

Thevenot, B. (2006). Myth-making in New Orleans. American Journalism Review, December 2005–January 2006.

Travis, W. (2011, August 29). A future of mass evacuations. *The New York Times*. Retrieved from http://www.nytimes.com

Verchick, R. R. M. (2012). Disaster justice: The geography of human capability. *Duke Environmental Law & Policy Forum*, *23*(1–2), 23–71.

Youngstown Sheet and Tube Co. v. Sawyer. 343 U.S. 579 (1952).

Zernike, K. (2013, January 14). Police barricades and curfews wear on Jersey shore nerves. *The New York Times*. Retrieved from http://www.nytimes.com

DISASTER ASSISTANCE AND LEGAL ACCOUNTABILITY: CARE AND SURVEILLANCE

Susan M. Sterett

ABSTRACT

Extreme events are the occasion for many people's encounters with climate change. Though causation is complex and no one event is directly attributable to climate change, when we consider Cassandra, we can consider what people encounter in assistance after an extreme event. This chapter takes the case of assistance to displaced people after Katrina to explore how care and surveillance were intertwined. Methods include analysis of government documents as well as interviews. When we consider assistance people receive, we often focus on the intended assistance and how it worked or did not. Evaluation is difficult, not least because criteria for determining what it means to work are uncertain. However, if we include the process of gaining assistance as part of the experience, we broaden concerns from the instrumental outcomes to the mixed messages people get in assistance. Assistance appears in a context, where the most vulnerable people have reasons to mistrust government and nonprofits, and where in the United States assistance has come intertwined with

Special Issue: Cassandra's Curse: The Law and Foreseeable Future Disasters
Studies in Law, Politics, and Society, Volume 68, 95–123

ISSN: 1059-4337/doi:10.1108/S1059-433720150000068004

supervisory rules, a focus on getting people to work, and a need to manage criminal histories. Trust in government may be limited, emergency care can operate outside ordinary legal frameworks when providers are new, and legal accountability for assistance may be experienced as confining, despite caregivers' intent.

Keywords: Disaster legal accountability; surveillance; displaced people

To me, one silly task is like another.
I bare the shambling tricks of lust and pride.
This flesh will never give a child its mother,—
Song, like a wing, tears through my breast, my side,
And madness chooses out my voice again,
Again: I am the chosen no hand saves:
The shrieking heaven lifted over men,
Not the dumb earth, wherein they set their graves.

(Cassandra, by Louise Bogan, http://www.poetryfoundation.org/poem/178040)

Cassandra needed salvation herself, and no one saved her. She was subject to Apollo's "tricks of lust and pride," and that's what led to her ability to prophecy. Both the ability to prophecy and her lack of persuasiveness were her curse. Her curse resulted from men's violence, beginning with Apollo's bitterness when she resisted his seduction. Had she yielded to him because of his powers, it would have been rape. In Cassandra's world, women's experiences of trickery are meaningless, and being ignored is enough to drive one mad. The madness chooses her; her lack of agency in either the harm done to her or her prophecies could not be plainer.

Cassandra requires that we incorporate her injuries as part of law, prophecy, and disaster; she is not outside what she sees. Her injuries were Apollo's curse: *both* foretelling the future *and* no one believing her. The model for disaster relief and mobilization has historically been war and civil defense (Rozario, 2007). The practices of humanitarian relief rely upon both military command structures and the militarization of relief (Fassin & Pandolfi, 2010; McFalls, 2010), distributing assistance through command rather than through aspiring to legality, or accountability through courts and rules. Relief, relief camps, and the military responsible for relief all bring to mind the importance of including sexual violence as part of the story of prophecy and disaster. Violence is one response to trauma, including the trauma of being displaced from home. The United States military is both on the forefront of climate change adaptation in the United States (National Research Council, 2010, 2013), and recently in the headlines for the pervasiveness of sexual assault within its ranks (Department of Defense Sexual Assault Prevention and Response Office, 2013). The caretakers can enact what Patrick Roberts, following Hannah Arendt, calls "administrative evil," harming both the people they are charged with caring for and their own colleagues (Roberts, 2013). By opening with a retelling of Cassandra, I invite us to remember the centrality of people and harm every stage of disaster, including adaptation, mitigation, or response, and how much we are a part of what we assess. The disasters come, Cassandra tells us, and adaptation to circumstances, mitigation of harm, and response to disaster prove crucial.[1]

For that reason, turning to the legal/political ground into which disaster falls can illuminate legal structures, in addition to cumulating information for each disaster. Legal structures are unlikely to be completely unsettled by disaster. Where a disaster puts new demands on courts, bureaucratic policymaking, rules, and voluntary agencies, they are likely to respond with more or less than the same concerns they have had in other fields. The 'state of exception' (Agamben, 2005) acts as an already existing state. While outlining some themes this approach leads us toward, the chapter that will draw on illustrations from displacement after Hurricane Katrina. Including the framework of law that already exists and drawing conclusions from that can be helpful as we look to the future. Sticking close to areas where we have substantial data makes foretelling the future a less unlikely business. Sticking close to what we know can also allow seeing points where it would be possible to intervene and improve.

This chapter relies upon interpretation of meanings by participants at multiple levels. The research site is not clearly delineated precisely because the field under examination is emergent and changeable (Yanow & Schwartz-Shea, 2014). The process of response to disaster is dynamic; the field within which disaster works is likely to remain more stable than any one response. The project contributes to building theory; whether the practice in a particular disaster will later generalize is not the point (Schwartz-Shea & Yanow, 2012). Without changing practices well beyond disaster, the basic issues concerning individual responsibility and surveillance are likely to persist.

INDIVIDUALIZATION, SURVEILLANCE, AND JURIDIFICATION

In interpreting a response to disaster by already existing legal institutions and practices, this chapter will focus on three elements in disaster response. First, individual responsibility and surveillance often accompany the care that response to disaster is to exemplify. Legal responses in much of law have called upon *individuals* to be responsible for themselves and their actions, and to be ready to respond to any problem, including in preparation for disaster (O'Malley, 2013; Silbey, 2005). Understanding problems as resting in individual action is a way of understanding a problem that is deeply embedded in American culture (Gusfield, 1981), including in the American legal system. Floods and earthquakes can make it impossible for state assistance to get in, lending support to the principle that Ready.gov teaches, that the "first seventy-two hours are on you," or the first three days after a disaster is the responsibility of the people themselves.

The focus on individual responsibility cuts off causal stories that could contribute to complex understandings of why things happen as they do, making individuals responsible for their own fate (Ewick & Silbey, 1995). Lawsuits after harms provide retrospective accountability, sometimes useful in the future. I will draw examples primarily front responses give by displaced people after Hurricane Katrina, focusing on coordination of voluntary and state assistance. Given the expectation of more displacement, we can expect similar problems will arise.

Focusing on assistance for displaced people can illuminate help well beyond the domestic disasters that are the focus on concern in this collection. After Hurricane Katrina, assistance relied on a model drawn from services for refugees (Sterett, 2012a, 2012b). The mixture of state and voluntary assistance will persist for refugees as well. In the absence of extensive legal aid, voluntary agencies also provide assistance to immigrants who might want to regularize their status. Knowing what voluntary agencies under stress can do illuminates the assistance voluntary agencies are increasingly called upon to provide as well (Bloemraad & Gleeson, 2012).

Next, juridification, or the use of legal rules and appeal to courts structures accountability. Courts and legal rules have been crucial in supervising response to disaster, and they are part of the story of what states do. Since courts are asked to allocate responsibility after something happens in common law countries, courts have been asked to respond to disaster. Courts are to bring legality to governing, including process and reasons.

Emergency means states govern in exception, and courts mean states are to govern through reflection and reason. What happens in working out that tension is an empirical question. Courts and rights are increasingly evoked in governing, both in supranational legal instruments such as the Guidelines on Internal Displacement (Kalin, 2008), and in high courts and supranational courts that are charged with implementing rights. Courts work backward when deciding compensation claims. They also decide other questions relevant to mitigation of harm and adaptation to hazards, including how national states regulate, how local governments make zoning decisions, and how insurance companies include or exclude claims.

This chapter will remind us of the tension in law as the articulated principle in the courts and as the practices used to implement accountability and reference to rules.

LAW AS PRACTICE

As law and society scholarship has long demonstrated, law works, at least, at two registers. First, upper-level courts in a hierarchy announce decisions that other organizations are then to follow. The Supreme Court in the United States, the European Court of Human Rights, the Supreme Court in Britain, the Supreme Court of Canada in Ottawa all state principles. They sometimes focus on what is right under the law, and they get press. Other times, they focus on processes, giving state administrators an opportunity to revise what they have done to comply with the law. In either case, when we do focus on law, it is how law is the articulation by those who are at the top of a hierarchy of final decisions. In that model of analyzing law, we can learn how those in the upper reaches of national policymaking state what must be done, who is right and wrong, and who is to be compensated when things go wrong and when disaster strikes. Courts articulate rules and provide exemptions from rules for national security. From this perspective, we see final decisions, losses, and victories. Appellate courts tell administrators what to do, and they declare some things right and other things wrong. They enable state power, including acting in disaster (Burton, 2008; Dauber, 2013).

At another level, organizations transform legal proclamations from the upper reaches of legal institutions into the law that people experience every day. People mobilize the law, bringing claims to court, using filings, documents, and information gathered from clients, to publicize claims and try to gain settlements, whatever the eventual pronouncements from upper level courts might be. People apply for benefits, decide what to do when officials tell them it would be wise to clear brush, get rid of standing water, fix a sidewalk, adopt solar power, or evacuate an area (Sarat, 1990; Shaw, Robbins, & Jones, 2010; Thaler & Sunstein, 2009; Valverde, 2011). Decisions from upper-level institutions are remade in a field of people and organizations who decide what to do with a decision. In this world of the "everyday state" (Painter, 2006) decisions seldom are final and organizations look for paths and support for what they do rather than following orders. High-level court decisions are most likely to translate into action when another branch of government is an ally, for example.

After Katrina, private law firms and public interest organizations sued for more federal money to support housing assistance for people who had been long displaced. Local governments had many displaced people who would still remain in their cities once the federal government stopped the money since rental housing, public housing, and housing in poorer areas where many were homeowners in New Orleans was not being rebuilt, and housing advocacy groups saw it as a way to address housing needs, however short term (Sterett, 2009). The local governments did not have programs to pay for housing, and more people were likely to remain homeless. They needed to extend the distribution of money from the federal government (Sterett, 2009). The confluence of these two levels – where people and organizations mobilize the law, ask for rulings from authoritative courts, and then take those rulings to where they might help distribute benefits or change administrative practices – make up the law people experience in disaster.

In this second register of law, where people and organizations make legal rules and decisions meaningful, decisions are part of a world in which response to disaster has a history that can evoke mistrust. The mistrust is a cautionary tale that could change the place of law and surveillance in adapting to changing conditions and responding to disaster. We can only know what those court decisions mean by tracing the law through legal and quasi-legal officials who act upon law. Therefore, bureaucratic practices, including efforts to develop fairness across cases, accountability, and care are all part of the law as well.

The Future and the Present: Modesty through Extending Where we Know

Cassandra's unusual ability to tell the future is a myth born out of her personal disaster. We might wish to avoid that curse. Yet our desire to tell the future persists, and warnings about how unlikely we are to be right and how fortunate we are not to have that ability have their spokespeople. As Charles Mackay said in 1841, human beings have been given the gift of NOT knowing the future most of the time, and everywhere people have not recognized that gift and instead "endeavoured to trace the events of unborn centuries" (Mackay, 1841). We have learned that we are most likely to be correct in modest claims about near future events, in areas in which we have extensive experience and a plethora of data, and recognizing that claims are probabilistic rather than a matter of certainty (Clarke, 1999; Silver, 2012; Tetlock, 2006). No one can anticipate a sudden intervention – an asteroid, a large earthquake, a huge volcanic explosion. Even if we could, or accurately anticipate when and where likely events will, precisely, strike, most of us have other things on our minds. People have families to care for daily, and that trumps worrying about potential, low-probability events. People have a hard time caring about events that are slow-moving rather than sudden. Individuals also have a hard time worrying too much about events that do not have a person easy to imagine as the wrongdoer (Roberts, 2009). We can, however, trace what happened in an event. For all these reasons, we can expect disaster to continue, making it particularly useful to trace what has happened as a way of understanding what might happen.

ASSISTANCE AND ACCOUNTABILITY FOR DISPLACED PEOPLE AFTER HURRICANE KATRINA

For the rest of the chapter, I will illustrate how people engage the law after a disaster by drawing from a project on legal accountability of state bureaucracies for people displaced after Hurricane Katrina (Sterett, 2009, 2012a, 2012b). The sudden spectacle of the event draws most of the public attention in disaster (Birkland, 1997); the events are horrifying and disrupt our daily routine. That draws most attention to where disasters happen: to the coasts, or to the site of a tornado. Those two points – attention to the sudden event, and to the site of disaster – lead us to neglect the long response to disaster, and to people who are out of place after disaster (Sapat & Esnard, 2013). Yet both are part of the disaster, as evidenced, for example, by the UN Guidelines on Internal Displacement (Kalin, 2008), and the recognition from around the world where millions of people are displaced after disaster. Even explaining return takes place as more central than the people who may remain scattered (Aldrich, 2010). People resettle by figuring out what family they can draw upon, as well as what they can do through rules; the law facilitates calling a place home and longing for it, or going back, or resettling. The Guidelines on Internal Displacement not only recognize that people are displaced; they affirm that states must allow people to choose where they live after disaster, whether to return to the home they left or to find a new place. Finally, focusing on people displaced after disaster allows us to see how law works when people and organizations are less stressed than they are at the site of disaster in the immediate moment.

For this project, we interviewed people who were displaced to Denver after Hurricane Katrina. We interviewed caseworkers and attended meetings with nongovernmental organizations and volunteers who were delivering services to those who were displaced. We interviewed in teams of two; interviewers were often young white women, and we were all strangers to those we interviewed. The response for displaced people was new to the people who came together in Denver, including those that provided and received services. It changed frequently, and people who did not work for FEMA were providing information about it to evacuees who had little reason to be certain FEMA and volunteers were not working together, and every reason to want to find a way to ensure they got the benefits they needed. We heard the stories that people wanted to tell in their uncertain, stressful circumstances.

We also gathered newspaper reports, both local and national, and we analyzed government documents and tracked lawsuits. More than 4,000 households were displaced to the metropolitan Denver area and even by May of 2006, more than 2,000 households were registered with FEMA in the Denver metropolitan area (Federal Emergency Management Agency, 2006). Colorado received federal funds that paid for emergency housing and rent, and the support of caseworkers paid for from a federal grant to the United Methodist Committee on Relief (Sterett, 2012b). FEMA changed policy housing while class action suits, that made their way through the federal courts; changes usually applied in Denver as well (Sterett, 2009). FEMA officials worked with voluntary agencies to help coordinate response, just as they did in other disasters. Some FEMA officials had experience in voluntary organizations in disaster. In other words, Colorado had experience with providing services to individuals, though not at the level of Katrina, yet helping did not strain local services as much as response in the Gulf Coast or in Houston did. This chapter will draw on interviews with caseworkers about the coordination of assistance and about the experience of collective emergency housing provided immediately after disaster.

Surveillance and Care Far from the Storm

The first task that emergency managers and volunteers took on in Denver after Katrina was setting up emergency housing for those who would come by government plane (Sterett, 2012a, 2012b). The hope for all was that the misery made evident in the news coverage in Katrina (Dawson, 2012) could be made better in a city far away with sympathetic volunteers, professionalized charities, and emergency managers, some who had once lived in New Orleans or had family there. As caseworkers began to help, they were to coordinate assistance through a casework system that allowed caseworkers from many agencies to share information.

Racial injustice grounds mistrust in the United States, including unequal access to resources after disaster (Tierney, 2006). Within the United States, medical experts, for example, have had a history of working in communities of color without informed consent, doing harm, and without compensation (Skloot, 2011). In the United States, the response to the Great Mississippi flood of 1927 was very racially discriminatory; the Red Cross provided relief differentially, African American people stranded on levees were starved and then press-ganged into providing relief for white people (Barry, 1998). Women have experienced disaster through responsibility for family, and men and women often have different interpretations of their responsibility and that of the state and charity in disaster (Fothergill, 2003). The rules operating through state bureaucracies now are to apply equally when distributing benefits. Gaining assistance requires knowing how to work the rules, which can contribute to ongoing inequality after disaster.

Trying to lessen mistrust in response to disaster, emergency managers work on inclusion of volunteers by demographic groups. When people were displaced after Katrina, churches with many African American members organized to help in Denver; the churches had not had a history of working in disaster. Differences in expectations about how organizations would work could make working together an ongoing challenge. Emergent organizations based in churches act from God's love, and believe in the importance of prayer and sharing that love (Sterett & Reich, 2007). Professional organizations are not as familiar with that language used at work, and the professionalized religious organizations have nondiscrimination rules regarding provision of services.

Protection also polices. Governments police in disaster, believing that victims of disaster must be contained for their own protection or because officials interpret the victims themselves are a threat to order. Drawing people together makes visible the victimization that in turn draws sympathy, donations, and support for assistance. However, containment also makes victimization central in a way that reduces people's lives to an event. Without the visibility that the event and the containment creates, the sympathy for assistance could be harder to mobilize. However, the containment also polices and places the focus on victimization. The containment that was most visible after Katrina was in New Orleans and in Houston. It is iconic in response to disaster; it *is* the disaster, and when the group of victims is less visible, so is the disaster.

After Katrina evacuees who came to Denver were housed in a college dormitory that was about to be repurposed. Its use as a home for evacuees would be its last use. Volunteers and businesses hurried over Labor Day weekend in 2005 to make the building warm and welcoming, and to ensure the plumbing worked. People painted, put together furniture, and put blankets on beds; a local company redid the plumbing. The dormitory had rooms that locked, and each room would be allocated to a family; the dorm provided much more privacy than the usual shelter in a school gymnasium, with rows of cots. Volunteers were proud of what they did. Evacuees were greeted by volunteers and state workers as they arrived on buses after they had been brought to a local air force base by government plane. They had come from the New Orleans airport or the Superdome and had had no change of clothing or access to bathing for days. They had also not been told where they were going. Some were pleased and relieved when they could guess, and others were outraged at having been moved with no information about where they were going. How they had been treated did not accord with international guidelines on displacement, which require consent; no one framed criticism in international human rights terms (Sterett, 2012b). Volunteers greeted people off the bus as they arrived at the dormitory from the air force base. A service center helped with FEMA registration, donations, and family services.

More people came in cars or via buses than had been sent without their consent. Because they were not all in one place and did not all come together, they did not exemplify all of the relief in local coverage as the people in the dorm did. Indeed, it was hard to capture people who came on their own at all in public imagery. A city in Colorado that did not house people in a dormitory did not get the same attention in the newspaper, though the service of getting people into housing that was not emergency shelter was just what managers aspired to. Because people kept moving, the numbers of FEMA registrants was actually higher in Denver in May 2006 than it was in February, both long after the dorm had closed. Over 2,000 households were registered with FEMA in the Denver metropolitan area in May 2006, with each registrant representing a household. By then, the press coverage was sparse. Coverage concerned individuals who were being cut off of assistance or who had improved their lives by getting off of assistance.

In the early period, the visibility of victims came with containment. A chain link fence went around the perimeter of the campus where people were first housed. Evacuees were given identification cards to show they were staying in the dorm. Voluntary organizations tried to put together a way of credentialing volunteers who could be admitted to the grounds. The guards were there to protect the evacuees from those who might want to prey on them, the press was told. There were many homeless people in the area who were not entitled to the housing after disaster, and they had to be kept out. Still, the photographs and the experience could evoke camps in public news commentary (Carman, *Denver Post*, Sept 7, 2005). According to the press at the time there had been rampant looting and personal violence and crime in post-Katrina New Orleans; protection overlapped with policing of people who were far from home. Indeed, pictures that became iconic in criticizing the press depicted the different portrayal of a white and a black person gathering goods in New Orleans in the immediate aftermath. Even volunteers worried that without supervision, the street crime that they saw as rampant in New Orleans would come to Denver via the nearby commercial street. The dormitory could not and did not house everyone who came to Denver after Katrina. One person captured the double meaning of care and imprisonment within a few short sentences. When asked what he thought of the dorm, John answered:

> It was a place where I could go in the close the door and get on my knees and thank God for bein' alive and pray for my family. It was like, we didn't have to stay on there, but I didn't know anywhere to go. They fed us what they wanted us to eat. Half the time it was good, half the time it wasn't. We had a certain time to eat. We was constantly guarded. It was like a prison camp per se, you know?... They always provided food, enough, it just didn't feel right. I felt like a prisoner. In prison, they provide enough food.

He could report being grateful for the place, and for the door that closed, a rarity in emergency disaster shelter. At the very same time, he could report that the dorm felt like a prison. The imprisonment so common in the United States might have been more on the minds of the evacuees than of the volunteers, aid workers, and government workers, making the emphasis on care and containment different. Another evacuee, Sarah, did not explain the food and service as imprisonment:

> The Lowry shelter was comforting, it was comforting, because you had breakfast, lunch, and dinner, and you could take a snack. They provided you with cold drinks and water. They acclimated you to the climate. They provided medical care if that's what you needed. In the cafeteria they had Social Security, food stamps, old age pension, all the social services was in one place. I had never seen anything like that. And then you had bus service to wherever you wanted to go. People was comin' to the community center, to the dorm, offerin' jobs, clothes, work, house.

Some eventually had to be "loved out the door" of the dormitory, as one volunteer put it, because the dormitory had to close after six weeks and moving was hard.

The dormitory and assistance center with its perimeter fence also made the disaster in Denver look like what the world has come to expect in the depiction of humanitarian disasters around the globe: people in camps, and restricted freedom of movement. The camp is the paradigm of both militarization and humanitarian assistance after disaster. Protection could be protection of or protection from, and survivors could look like perpetrators. The privacy people were afforded inside of the dormitory also made it more difficult to supervise than the usual Red Cross shelter, which relies on many cots in one large room. The Red Cross also believed that not only was it more difficult to supervise; the very comfort would make it very difficult to close.

Those who came later to Denver when there was no space in the dormitory reported being disappointed, and explained the failure of disaster assistance as a problem of not having moved quickly enough. The federal government had offered cash cards to help evacuees with immediate needs; not everyone got those cards for no very clear reason except that getting the cards out was part of the logistical challenges that met the federal government after Hurricane Katrina. Nevertheless, people who knew others had received things they had not ascribed their inability to get debit cards or other donations to not having been at the center when it was all on offer. As Mary, who came on her own after the dormitory had closed, put it:

> When I got here [the dormitory] was closed. I missed everything. And all the help, and I mean, I came directly from the shelter to here .... So far, I feel like – just like I missed [the dormitory], I missed it, if you came to Colorado after [the dormitory] closed, you missed out. You missed out on the same thing that you were promised. We were

> promised a lot of things that the damn folks never – I think if I would have gotten food the first week I was here inside this apartment, I would probably have been able to maintain. I got nothing. I make too much. I had to go to the food stamps office three days. Hell, I never been on food stamps. But you know, I mean, I didn't have any food. I had to go three days to listen to this lady talk about her kids not wanting to go to school. Every day I came in there, three days I went in there. "You need to bring this back." "You coulda told me that the first time." The second day I go in, "You didn't bring this. You need one more thing." She just wanted to get me the hell out. They didn't care whether I was from Hurricane Katrina or anything – after [the dormitory]. They didn't care.

After disaster, one can need law in a way not experienced before. To be forced into law when one has lost one's home brings new legal identities: as a victim, as a displaced person, as a supplicant before charities or the state.[2] Disaster and the requirement that one qualify for assistance by having been affected by the disaster reduces identities to that of a victim of disaster (Fassin & Rechtman, 2009), when people might have been thinking about moving anyway, or when the disaster is one part of a complex story about why one is in Denver with or without family members, with or without a job. People who fled the storm were not only disaster victims, nor was it all anyone wanted to be; the assistance and the interest in disaster kept people disaster victims who needed to choose where to live. Yet people did not believe they could ever return, especially those who rented. Whatever their previous stance had been, some people found themselves "against the law" (Ewick & Silbey, 1998) entangled in conflicting strands over which they felt they had little control.

Coming to law evokes both the protection of the state and being subject to surveillance in the benefits, not only in the imagery of housing for the displaced. People who had shared housing outside of state categories and without recognition suddenly could find that identity was a problem when trying to stay qualified for rental assistance. Early on FEMA smoothed out procedures to accommodate both that individuals had to be held responsible for spending money properly AND that few had received any instructions on how to spend emergency money that came to them shortly after the disaster. People were supposed to document that they had spent the first large checks they had received on housing. They hadn't necessarily, or they couldn't document it. FEMA allowed people to sign affirmations stating they had spent the money appropriately without showing receipts. The story of relief required deserving victims and bureaucratic accountability. Improving the story of bureaucratic accountability required making the stories of money received match the need for bureaucratic accountability.

Although we separate out forms of assistance, particularly because disaster assistance is temporary, people do not experience assistance that way. In bureaucratic legal terms, food stamps are not part of disaster assistance. For people who need both after displacement, they are entangled. Helping in disaster meant getting people all the assistance they needed, and that's how the one stop system was set up at the site in Denver. To Mary, the difficulty of making food stamps work for her was a problem of disaster assistance. People bring an understanding what the law means for them and whether it is something that could help them deal with trouble. What the law means could be general and about the law as a whole (Ewick & Silbey, 1998), or it could be specific to a field (Marshall & Barclay, 2003). People transfer what they learn from one field to another (Levitsky, 2008). Many people displaced by Hurricane Katrina had been on disability insurance or veterans' benefits. Not only did those benefits shape how easily people could resettle in a new area without a job. They also shaped people's understandings of the new individual assistance for which they were eligible.

The individual assistance itself was confusing because it did and did not look like other benefit programs. The money could only be spent on housing, and it ended when people used the maximum amount, not when they had reestablished themselves or gotten their homes back or did not need anything anymore. For people who were accustomed to work or benefits payments that did not end if there wasn't a comprehensible reason that had something to do with time or with what they had done, to have the program end when they still needed housing was difficult to explain. To people who had been homeless in Denver and not in the storm, suddenly new housing was available to people who seemed no more needy than they were. One could have been in New Orleans a brief time, or have been planning on moving and putting it off, and been entitled to housing assistance when local homeless people were not. To the press and to far-away housing policy advocates, the special status of people displaced from the Gulf Coast made sense. The special concern with disaster victims need not to a homeless person, who is in a shelter. Individualization of responsibility in law meant that the official story could not be that the money was confusing or that it is impossible not to take advantage of free money.

ACCOUNTABILITY AND SURVEILLANCE: IMPERFECT TECHNOLOGIES

The United States welfare state has developed technology to enforce individual accountability for clients of Temporary Assistance to Needy

Families (TANF), a program that is both most stigmatized and one of the least generous in the United States. Technology has allowed tracking of the money that people get (Gilliom, 2001). That is the field into which individual assistance for rent for evacuees entered. In addition, contracted caseworkers were responsible for tracking donations and ensuring their value did not duplicate state benefits. The Coordinated Assistance Network (CAN) was a large database that was to track all the donations that came in. It would allow people to find out the resources that were available – a donated car, perhaps some furniture after the initial donations were done – and, in turn, to ensure that people did not get duplicated benefits. If someone had bought a replacement vehicle with their state benefits they could not then get a donated one; anyone who had received a donated car could not then buy a replacement car with their state benefits. Statutory compensation is for replacement of uninsured lost goods. That means donations do not necessarily supplement lost goods, though neither states nor the federal government necessarily want donated goods back that may be owed because they were duplicated. Anyone who got a car should not get another one, an example that was easily cited because its necessity outstripped its availability. A car was much needed in a sprawling western city when people were settling everywhere. It was not often available.

However, CAN was difficult to work. As explained by one of the people responsible for developing case management:

> Right now, they tell me, in CAN, they've got about two million pieces of information in there. And so this thing has been stretched so bad since they started it, but it still – the concept is good, and the mechanism is working out bugs and glitches as it comes along. It's coming along, it really is. And so the concept is if you're here, and you're getting help, as you're getting help that's disaster related, and you decide to move back with family, you have more family support back in Tennessee, then the next agency that you come in contact there can pull it back up and see everything you got here. Or, by the way, you found out everything that you got on your way to get to Colorado. And what we try to do with the attorneys, and they're still arguing, we wanna download some of the basic FEMA information on what you were eligible for, if you got an offer of an SBA (Small Business Administration) loan. Or, the reason you got denied is you haven't sent back your SBA paperwork. The case manager, that would be helpful information they need to know. And so we're still working on that part. That's a legal part. The concept has been approved, but the attorneys being so nervous with the privacy act, we understand that, too. It's a big issue.

Even within a framework of care, private donations and state benefits and supervision of both were deeply entangled. The caseworkers were paid out of a private grant made by the federal government, and donations were private. The FEMA records were federal. So were SBA loans.

CAN required caseworkers or volunteers associated with them to do data entry, something no one enjoyed doing. It was not what volunteers had signed up for, yet it was the work that most needed doing. The need could continue as long as people were receiving benefits, yet interest in the disaster by the volunteers flagged as it moved its way off the national public agenda, which disasters always do rather rapidly. It required the computer system to coordinate well across agencies, which it did not. It required a clear wall between the federal government and the caseworkers, yet it would be helpful to import information FEMA could provide. It also required that it be possible to track the recipients of aid, and there was no way to get a list of people. When the Government Accountability Office evaluated casework after Katrina, it faulted the coordination of assistance and what the caseworkers had done (GAO, 2009). People had not tried hard enough.

The computer system aspired to be but was not a vast national connected system. Working it simply to make sure people did not get something twice required superhuman interest in bureaucratic accountability and policing people as well as a high tolerance for tracking donations, something few caseworkers or volunteers had. Furthermore, as the quotation above illustrates, privacy concerns meant it could not coordinate completely. Case workers and managers were aware of privacy concerns, and could be all the more nervous for that. These stories could readily spin into ones of legal accountability and lawsuits. The person quoted above went on:

> The federal privacy act is one of the most stringent ones, even more stringent than the state or – see, agencies also have a confidentiality agreement, and states usually do, too, but this federal one is written so strict, and there are some heavy duty payment. And if you violate it, I mean, you can't say you didn't. They can take you to court and sue you, you're gonna lose. And also, too, if you did, you could be charged with the misdemeanor crime of violating that, as well the fine that goes with – with every, probably 100 people, that's 100 times five, 500,000 dollar fine. And 500 – and so, that's what they're – that's probably a reason, too, we can't share some of this stuff.

Law could be feared as a surveillance mechanism for the caseworkers too, not by the bureaucracy but by clients imagined to be capable of bringing a lawsuit, or by the police.

What was available was never enough and it was easy for the wrong people to get goods. Also, how could anyone possibly know about every kind of help? No one could figure out how to solve that problem. Government information was separate from what the charities had, which meant there was no easy way to import citizens into the assistance database, nor would that make it easier to do the tangled tracking of both government payments and donations that was supposed to happen. The care that went with managing donations assumed donations greater than need, a ready match between donation and need, and a perfect technology that is simply not the experience of those who worked with the system (Reich, 2008).

Eventually, recipients were cut off for potentially being ineligible for funds, and sometimes investigated for fraud. FEMA could ask for benefits that had been paid incorrectly to be returned. It's hard to know how much they tried to do that. People did get cut off, sometimes for incomprehensible reasons that no one explained. Applying for benefits can bring to light previous legal problems; after disaster one was ineligible for assistance if one had other unpaid federal obligations, such as federal student loans, or if one could not document that one had lived in the flooded area. Since disaster is only one part of the reason people move, and people could have been in New Orleans temporarily, or thinking of moving anyway, it could be hard for other people who needed housing help to distinguish between themselves and evacuees. Yet one claimed assistance legally and one did not. People who had shared housing before the storm could find themselves out of help when one person in the household claimed the money first. Although FEMA was to pay to everyone who needed housing, even if households split up, that did not translate perfectly into practice. If one succeeded in making a claim, FEMA could later cut one off or pursue someone for fraud. Even once officials had corrected their practices and allowed rent for more than one member of a household, caseworkers reported that only one person could be paid for replacement of goods. The person who got the claim in first won.

What can we learn in this encounter with the protection/supervision interface? We have a particular image of what response to disaster looks like, and it includes mass housing. Mass emergency housing is visible, and draws the sympathy that Michele Dauber found to be crucial to the public relations campaign for assistance in the New Deal (Dauber, 2013). Need and assistance extend beyond the visible, yet tracking anything more than individual stories is difficult once the mass need is gone. Furthermore, the need of those who were not in the mass housing was easy to miss. Finally, supervision of caseworkers appealed to a fear of the law as something that made one's work impossible. Both caseworkers and those who might get too much would experience their faults as individual, not the result of a system that mandated both privacy and surveillance. Nor was fraud in claiming assistance by a homeless person a problem with demarcating disaster from every other tragic reason one might be homeless.

Responses to disaster happen in an already-existing legal field that organizes claims into the categories people and organizations understand. The surveillance that the press and some evacuees noticed – both in the event and in accounting for how individuals spent money – echoes the protection, surveillance, and criminalization in other disasters. The risk is it can be tied to individual responsibility and punishment. Anticipating mass shootings, for example, could bring a response focused on punishment, on harm reduction through managing guns, or one focused on mental health. The United States practice of mass incarceration makes punishment the available response to many problems. In the United States, protection in schools has brought a police presence that makes small infractions of the rules visible to state officials in a way that disrupts the supervision students otherwise do of each other (Kupchik, 2010; Monahan & Torres, 2010). Young men who write rap lyrics have been prosecuted and convicted for their threats (Nielsen & Kubrin, 2014). Threat assessment requires assessing how threatening an individual is, and threatening individuals in the United States are incarcerated.

When experts govern in disaster, they can respond as though the people in crisis need to be policed, and as though assistance has to emphasize order at least as much as it does care. Militaries deliver humanitarian assistance, making militarism and containment a likely framework for response. The need for assistance and the political need to provide it leads governments and nongovernmental organizations to act quickly, which means it is difficult to act consistently across cases, following rules that ensure like treatment.

The imperative to act quickly in disasters presents an empirical puzzle. We live in an increasingly juridified world, with the force of court decisions, rules, and the people who reference them exerting a strong enough gravitational pull to shape fields. States in disaster are supposed to cut through the red tape, and to help people immediately, and police people. When and where do people invoke rules? Or court decisions? Or international humanitarian guidelines? Since law is part of the world in which it acts, we could expect that it's likely to become intertwined with mandates to act.

I next turn Cassandra in the direction that legal accountability in compensation after disaster works: backwards. I will do so in the context of juridification, or the worldwide expansion of the use of judiciaries and legal frameworks in handling difficult problems (Bilchner & Molinder, 2008; Hirschl, 2004; Slaughter, 2004).

JURIDIFICATION

Judiciaries get invited into many different problems. When judiciaries make pronouncements at the elite level of law, they can do so to protect rights of groups and individuals. They can also act as agents of the central state, ensuring their policies are enforced to the extent that it is possible to tell what those policies are (Shapiro, 1986). Litigation reorganizes political fields and increases law as a reference point for politics (Silverstein, 2007). While many issues come before the courts, judiciaries in the United States have been more reluctant to make expensive, high profile orders, after federal district courts did just that with regard to prisons and schools (Cooper, 1988). Legal institutions are notably reluctant to make orders against central government policies, or orders that would be so costly as to damage an industry; in turn, political elites contain decisions via limiting them and taking time to apply them (Conant, 2002; Haines, 2009; Hirschl, 2004; Keck, 2007; Sterett, 1997).[3] Courts do not impose orders from outside the world they govern; judges gather information about what to order from what people and organizations are already doing, and they often make orders based on what industries explain are best practices (Edelman, Uggen, & Erlanger, 1999). Furthermore, cases take years to work their way through court as appeals courts reconsider not only lower courts but what they themselves have done on an issue (see e.g., In re Katrina Canal Breaches, 2012). Delay itself can make the prospect of compensation less than heartening.

At the same time, reference to courts and what lawyers will do with rules can be a central part of the process, even when orders are not final. A field can become *juridified*, that is with inclusion of courts and reference to rules in governing, and yet the rules may not change outcomes rather than the process of what central political authorities mean to do. Because decisions require follow-through, court decisions are seldom the final word on a problem. In law in practice, we seldom have final decisions. We just choose where to end the story.

The relatively advantaged "haves" come out ahead in litigation because institutional repeat players can choose which cases to settle, which to appeal, and how to resist decisions, a finding robust across policy domains, including that of disaster assistance (Fortun, 2004; Galanter, 1974). Sometimes the relative 'have nots' can come together as a group and litigate collective claims and pursue implementation. Then, we sometimes see instrumental change in the law (Epp, 1998). Litigation has more than instrumental effects; people use litigation to educate public, to tell stories, and to change conversations, and sometimes to change what legislatures do as well (Keck, 2009). Where people can use courts that way in disaster litigation, we see effects spiraling outward; those effects may not be, though, to compensate the victims of disaster.

Courts often keep their options open for decisions in the future, especially when they work with a system of precedent. If precedent is to bind courts for the future, and the future is unknowable, they had best ensure that they have not bound themselves to something that can turn out to be untenable (Shapiro, 1972). For example, after Hurricane Katrina, lawsuits in the federal courts were to hold the federal government accountable for how it was distributing individual assistance. The reasons FEMA gave for terminating people were opaque, they processed cases slowly, and they made incorrect decisions concerning the damage to homes in New Orleans. The federal courts held that FEMA could be sued, and it was not exempt under sovereign immunity. It could still escape liability for any particular decision (Sterett, 2009). The federal government was held not liable for causing the damage to New Orleans via having built the Mississippi River Gulf Outlet, which had channeled storm surge into the city, though the case dragged its way through the federal courts and brought newsworthy condemning language from judges along the way (In re Katrina Canal Breaches, 2012). Decisions to hold FEMA accountable for its decision-making processes in individual assistance were made moot when FEMA changed its policy by extending payments, or when decisions were appealed they were overturned or otherwise decided so that they would not set a precedent useful to those harmed by extreme weather events in the future (Sterett, 2009).

When courts allocate responsibility after an event, they do so by *looking backward* to what has already happened. Tracing disasters to broad scale changes in climate or harms to toxins is probabilistic. Poisons raise illnesses in an exposed group above the base rate before the exposure; that's a much more cautious statement than saying one thing caused another. As communities build in vulnerable areas, people are more exposed to extreme weather events, which in turn can cause more harm. Accountability after the fact in litigation has found probabilistic reasoning difficult to accommodate in litigation concerning responsibility for disasters from mass poisonings, whether through drugs or poisons governments or businesses use. Uneasiness with the ability to attribute causation of a particular event to policies has led courts to force settlement around the harms associated with the use of Agent Orange in Vietnam, for example (Schuck, 1987). We can expect something similar in climate change. Probabilistic reasoning is also difficult to accommodate in the individualization that courts often do in attributing responsibility.

What *has happened* is not a probability distribution; the event makes what the courts are doing different from what risk managers do. An event can be contested concerning who was harmed, how they were harmed, and how well states or corporations are taking responsibility for harm and compensating people (Cassels, 1993; Fortun, 2004). Still, some event *happened.* Courts have proven more likely to *think through individual stories and the choices individuals make* in assessing harms including employment discrimination and personal injury law (Engel & McCann, 2009; Haltom & McCann, 2004; Nelson & Bridges, 1999). Legal reasoning has often worked through a story one can tell, where one person or organization did something that caused a harm that courts can then remedy (Ewick & Silbey, 1995; Ewick & Silbey, 2003; Stryker, Docka-Filipek, & Wald, 2012). In law, the causal story told after industrial disasters is one of human error: someone forgot to make sure a door was unlocked, or forgot to follow a safety procedure (Fortun, 2004; Perrow, 1984). In complex systems, failure usually happens at multiple points. Human error is consistent with the story of individualizing responsibility discussed above.

The causal stories we tell, including in law, take the form of "hegemonic tales" or "subversive stories" (Ewick & Silbey, 1995). Patricia Ewick and Susan Silbey argue that hegemonic tales and subversive stories are alternative ways people interpret what has happened to them, and these alternative frameworks are embedded in law. "Hegemonic tales" cut off inquiry into causation that link the immediate problem to structures and multiagent, interlocking explanations of why harm came about (Ewick & Silbey, 1995). Causal storytelling is cut off long before the complex stories are told, and the responsibility is or is not placed in the lap of the agent who is before the law. In climate stories, the weather brought about a storm surge that flooded a city, not the interlocking, multiagent building out into marshlands and out into coastlines, the decision to build channels that allow storm surge to flood a city, or, in Manhattan, the long-ago depletion of oyster beds that had once moderated storm surges. The Mississippi River Outlet provided a perfect channel for storm surge from hurricanes to rush into New Orleans, flooding the city (Freudenberg, Gramling, Laska, & Erikson, 2009). Thinking through anecdotes and individual responsibility reinforces the temptation in disaster to ascribe problems to individual error. In the United States, the failure of state infrastructure that allowed levees to fail leads to exemption by way of sovereign immunity.

In governing what other state agencies have done, legal institutions in common law countries often focus on process: were the rules followed, did people receive notice of what was going to happen, and did they have a chance to produce evidence relevant to the decisions made about them. That is what the courts did concerning housing assistance for people displaced after Katrina (Sterett, 2009). To move from the elite level of law declaring legal principles to the law that comes to life, political alliances can make decisions about process effective. Local governments needed the federal money to continue to flow after Katrina, which meant the lawyers and advocacy groups were not trying to extract money from the federal government for poor people by themselves. Court decisions are sometimes an effort to hold administrative agencies accountable to following their own rules in a way that the political leaders would agree with; court can help the central government rather than fight it.

Court decisions that try to hold states accountable for how they provide relief can be vacated on appeal, or crafted to be limited to the individual disaster, particularly because disaster relief is so idiosyncratic. Some disasters bring temporary trailers in which people can live, others rental payments, and some replacement of goods for those without insurance. States claim sovereign immunity, so that they cannot be held responsible for how they distribute aid or for policies that facilitated disaster.

Climate related events such as hurricanes and droughts are weather events that are familiar to people. They are not new. The weather just seems to happen, making the common sense stories of causation as a background characteristic and without a human agent especially accessible. The weather-related disasters we have been facing have been completely familiar for centuries, even if the causal story told in the tension between the happenstance of where a storm lands and broader climate change is not.

CONCLUSION: DISASTER IN LEGAL FIELDS

Fires and floods and shootings are not new; they have moved and sometimes drawn more victims. In the Global North they no longer devastate the cities that were the sites of the terrifying urban fires that occasioned fire insurance, fire companies, compensation for them, and building codes (Novak, 1996). We build in dangerous areas, and we build projects that increase the chance of catastrophe after storms. Fire insurance emerged out of the devastating London fire in the seventeenth century, and regulating to manage fire to ensure an adequate response was at the heart of local building regulation and payments to firemen's pensions in the nineteenth century United States (Novak, 1996; Sterett, 2003). In the United States, programs to provide seeds to farmers in the nineteenth century after drought and plagues of locusts were the subject of litigation; the programs were challenged for using tax money unconstitutionally. Most of the time, the state courts held the programs constitutional. Courts in the Midwest that wouldn't respond to farmers would have been in an untenable position, and disaster relief had a long history in the United States (Sterett, 2003). These programs have a long history (Dauber, 2013). Getting people started again or compensating has long been politically appealing.

Adaptation and response to disaster require a different approach to risk from the old age, disability and mothers' pensions that have drawn most social welfare scholarship. Early social welfare advocates treated these risks as a knowable probability distribution. People will get old, or they will get injured and become unable to work at jobs for which they are qualified (Beck, 1992). The risks of injury and death from unspectacular events that do not result from society-wide catastrophe are still widespread; people still get old, and injured, and need unemployment payments or disability payments. Welfare states still design rules to distribute this assistance, and to plan on how to pay for it. Nevertheless, these injuries and deaths do not attract the same attention that disasters do, whether those disasters are hurricanes, tsunamis, or bombs (Birkland, 1997). Risk management tells us we can control risk even if we cannot, for it is the job of risk managers to manage it (Clarke, 1999). We do not manage uncertainty. We might try to reduce it. Instead, we manage everything around it: we wish to ensure that communities are prepared for uncertainties.

The rights-in-courts framework emergent in international governance and so familiar in the United States informs response as well. Indeed, there is a lively debate about whether to call people refugees when they have been displaced in part as the result of environmental problems (McAdam, 2010). Instruments from the United Nations promise rights for refugees and there is an international infrastructure to follow through on those rights. The debate over calling people environmental refugees centers on whether that is an appropriate use of the term refugee when causation is so difficult to ascribe, when the refugee system of relief is overburdened by those who have fled war and genocide, and when the internal guidelines on displaced people would seem to serve the purpose better than conventions on refugees (Kromm & Sturgis, 2008; Piguet, 2013).

Rights are often subject to the 'myth of rights,' (Scheingold, 1974) or the belief that rights are self-executing and will solve problems by being invoked; instead, rights work best where people and organizations mobilize to enforce them. International human rights or guidelines also require local translation and mobilization (Merry, 2006). Guidelines on internal displacement open the possibility of organizing a social field around questions of displacement. Organizing also requires that people find a way to gather, and define their interests in common; when people are dispersed and do not organize via tools that allow being dispersed, such as social media, the costs to forming a movement are high.

Expectations around disaster enter an already existing field of governance. The individualization, surveillance, and juridification that color legal responses outside disaster are frameworks that come to implementing disaster assistance. If we expect that people are only to suffer temporary setbacks, and all government-paid assistance except that for old age and disability (to speak to the United States welfare state) is temporary, then that will be true of disaster as well. The expectation that people should rely on their family members for assistance and build the human capital to allow them not to need social welfare payments will also color disaster assistance. Looking to what legal institutions can do requires understanding what they do in a broader organizational field, and from multiple points of view.

NOTES

1. For overviews of where gender has been included in the sociology of disaster and where it has not and why it is crucial, see (Enarson & Morrow, 1998) and (Enarson, 2012).
2. On law and the creation of new identities, see (Ewick & Silbey, 1998).
3. There continue to be exceptions. In the environmental field in the United States, see e.g. Massachusetts v. E.P.A. (2007).

ACKNOWLEDGMENTS

I am grateful for support from the National Science Foundation, including SES-1051408 and CMMI-0555117. I am also grateful for comments on earlier drafts from the editors of *Studies in Law, Politics and Society*, including the editors of the special issue. Lorita Daniels and Anne Zobell assisted with final research.

REFERENCES

Agamben, G. (2005). *Stato die eccezione*. [State of exception]. Chicago, IL: University of Chicago Press.

Aldrich, D. P. (2010). Fixing recovery: Social capital in post-crisis resilience. *Journal of Homeland Security*. Available at: http://works.bepress.com/daniel_aldrich/7

Barry, J. (1998). *Rising tide: The great Mississippi flood of 1927 and how it changed America*. New York, NY: Simon and Schuster.

Beck, U. (1992). *The risk society*. Thousand Oaks, CA: Sage.

Bilchner, L. C., & Molinder, A. (2008). Mapping juridification. *European Law Journal*, *14*(1), 36–54.

Birkland, T. A. (1997). *After disaster*. Washington, DC: Georgetown University Press.

Bloemraad, I., & Gleeson, S. (2012). Making the case for organizational presence: Civic inclusion, access to resources and formal community organizations. In M. P. Smith & M. McQuarrie (Eds.), *Remaking urban citizenship* (pp. 109–135). New Brunswick, NJ: Transaction Publishers.

Burton, L. (2008). The constitutional roots of all-hazards policy, management, and law. *Journal of Homeland Security and Emergency Management*, *5*(1). Available at: http://www.bepress.com/jhsem/vol5/iss1/35

Carman, D. (2005). Evacuees stories are moving but fence isn't. *Denver Post*, September 7, p. B1.

Cassels, J. (1993). *The uncertain promise of law: Lessons from Bhopal*. Buffalo, NY: University of Toronto Press.

Clarke, L. B. (1999). *Mission improbable: Using fantasy documents to tame disaster*. Chicago, IL: University of Chicago Press.

Conant, L. J. (2002). *Justice contained: Law and politics in the European union*. Ithaca, NY: Cornell University Press.

Cooper, P. J. (1988). *Hard judicial choices: Federal district court judges and state and local officials*. New York, NY: Oxford University Press.

Dauber, M. L. (2013). *The sympathetic state: Disaster relief and the origins of the American welfare state*. Chicago, IL: University of Chicago Press.

Dawson, M. C. (2012). Racial tragedies, political hope, and the tasks of American political science. *Perspectives on Politics*, *10*(3), 669–674.

Department of Defense Sexual Assault Prevention and Response Office. (2013). *Annual report on sexual assault FY 12* (Vol. 1). Washington, DC: Department of Defense.

Edelman, L. B., Uggen, C., & Erlanger, H. S. (1999). The endogeneity of legal regulation: Grievance procedures as rational myth. *American Journal of Sociology*, *105*(2), 406–454.

Enarson, E. P. (2012). *Women confronting natural disaster: From vulnerability to resilience*. Boulder, CO: Lynne Rienner Publishers.

Enarson, E. P., & Morrow, B. H. (1998). *The gendered terrain of disaster: Through women's eyes*. Westport, CT: Praeger.

Engel, D. M., & McCann, M. W. (2009). *Fault lines: Tort law as cultural practice*. Stanford, CA: Stanford Law Books.

Epp, C. R. (1998). *The rights revolution: Lawyers, activists, and supreme courts in comparative perspective*. Chicago, IL: University of Chicago Press.

Ewick, P., & Silbey, S. (2003). Narrating social structure: Stories of resistance to legal authority. *American Journal of Sociology*, *108*(6), 1328–1372.

Ewick, P., & Silbey, S. S. (1995). Subversive stories and hegemonic tales: Toward a sociology of narrative. *Law and Society Review*, *29*(2), 25–197.

Ewick, P., & Silbey, S. S. (1998). *The common place of law: Stories from everyday life*. Chicago, IL: University of Chicago Press.

Fassin, D., & Pandolfi, M. (2010). *Contemporary states of emergency: The politics of military and humanitarian interventions*. New York, NY: Zone Books.

Fassin, D., & Rechtman, R. (2009). *The empire of trauma: An inquiry into the condition of victimhood*. Princeton, NJ: Princeton University Press.

Federal Emergency Management Agency. (2006). *Reported mailing addresses of Katrina/Rita applicants from Louisiana, Mississippi, Alabama and Texas disasters as of 05-12-06*. Washington, DC.

Fortun, K. (2004). *Advocacy after Bhopal*. Chicago, IL: University of Chicago Press.

Fothergill, A. (2003). The stigma of charity: Gender, class and disaster assistance. *Sociological Quarterly*, *44*(4), 659.

Freudenberg, W. R., Gramling, R. B., Laska, S., & Erikson, K. (2009). *Catastrophe in the making: The engineering of Katrina and the disasters of tomorrow*. Washington, DC: Shearwater Press.

Galanter, M. (1974). Why the "haves" come out ahead: Speculations on the limits of legal change. *Law and Society Review*, *9*(1), 95–160.

Gilliom, J. (2001). *Overseers of the poor: Surveillance, resistance, and the limits of privacy*. Chicago, IL: University of Chicago Press.

Government Accountability Office [GAO]. (2009). *Disaster assistance: Greater coordination and an evaluation of programs' outcomes could improve disaster case management* No. GAO-09-561). Washington, DC: Government Printing Office.

Gusfield, J. R. (1981). *The culture of public problems: Drinking-driving and the symbolic order*. Chicago, IL: University of Chicago Press.

Haines, F. (2009). Regulatory failures and regulatory solutions: A characteristic analysis of the aftermath of disaster. *Law and Social Inquiry*, *34*(1), 31–60.

Haltom, W., & McCann, M. W. (2004). *Distorting the law: Politics, media, and the litigation crisis*. Chicago, IL: University of Chicago Press.

Hirschl, R. (2004). *Towards juristocracy: The origins and consequences of the new constitutionalism*. Cambridge, MA: Harvard University Press.

In re Katrina Canal Breaches 696 F. 3d 436 (2012) (5th Circuit).

Kalin, W. (2008). *Guiding principles on internal displacement: Annotations*. Washington, DC: The American Society of International Law.

Keck, T. M. (2007). Party politics or judicial independence? The regime politics literature hits the law schools. *Law & Social Inquiry*, *32*(2), 511–544.

Keck, T. M. (2009). Beyond backlash: Assessing the impact of judicial decisions on LGBT rights. *Law & Society Review*, *43*(1), 151–186.

Kromm, C., & Sturgis, S. (2008, January). Hurricane Katrina and the guiding principles on internal displacement: A global human rights perspective on a national disaster. Institute for Southern Studies.

Kupchik, A. (2010). *Homeroom security: School discipline in an age of fear*. New York, NY: New York University Press.

Levitsky, S. R. (2008). 'What rights': The construction of political claims to American health care entitlements. *Law & Society Review*, *42*(3), 551–590.

Mackay, C. (1841). *Extraordinary delusions and the madness of crowds*. New York, NY: Dover Publications.

Marshall, A., & Barclay, S. (2003). In their own words: How ordinary people construct the legal world. *Law & Social Inquiry*, *28*(3), 617–628.

Massachusetts v. E.P.A. 549 U.S. 497 (2007).

McAdam, J. (2010). *Climate change and displacement: Multidisciplinary perspectives*. Oxford: Hart Publishing.

McFalls, L. (2010). Benevolent dictatorship: The formal logic of humanitarian government. In D. Fassin & M. Pandolfi (Eds.), *Contemporary states of emergency: The politics of military and humanitarian interventions* (pp. 317–334). New York, NY: Zone Books.

Merry, S. E. (2006). *Human rights and gender violence: Translating international law into local justice*. Chicago, IL: University of Chicago Press.

Monahan, T., & Torres, R. D. (2010). *Schools under surveillance: Cultures of control in public education*. New Brunswick, NJ: Rutgers University Press.

National Research Council. (2010). *National security implications of climate change for U.S. Naval forces*. Washington, DC: National Academies Press.

National Research Council Committee on Assessing the Impacts of Climate Change on Social and Political Stress. (2013). *Climate and social stress: Implications for security analysis*. Washington, DC: National Academies Press.

Nelson, R. L., & Bridges, W. P. (1999). *Legalizing gender inequality: Courts, markets, and unequal pay for women in America*. Cambridge: Cambridge University Press.

Nielsen, E., & Kubrin, C. E. (2014). Rap lyrics on trial. *The New York Times*, January 13, p. A27.

Novak, W. J. (1996). *The people's welfare: Law and regulation in nineteenth- century America*. Chapel Hill, NC: University of North Carolina Press.

O'Malley, P. (2013). Uncertain governance and resilient subjects in the risk society. *Onati Socio-Legal Series*, *3*(2), 180–195.

Painter, J. (2006). Prosaic geographies of stateness. *Political Geography*, *25*(7), 752–774.

Perrow, C. (1984). *Normal accidents: Living with high-risk technologies*. New York, NY: Basic Books.

Piguet, E. (2013). From "primitive migration" to "climate refugees": The curious fate of the natural environment in migration studies. *Annals of the Association of American Geographers*, *103*(1), 148–162.

Reich, J. (2008). "The can't of CAN." Paper presented at the annual meeting of the American Sociology Association.

Roberts, P. (2009). A capacity for mitigation as the next frontier in homeland security. *Political Science Quarterly*, *124*(1), 127–142.

Roberts, P. (2013). *Disasters and the American state*. New York, NY: Cambridge University Press.

Roberts, P. S. (2006). FEMA and the prospects for reputation-based autonomy. *Studies in American Political Development*, *20*(01), 57.

Rozario, K. (2007). *The culture of calamity: Disaster and the making of modern America.* Chicago, IL: University of Chicago Press.

Sapat, A., & Esnard, A. (2013). Trans-boundary impacts of the 2010 Haiti earthquake disaster: Focus on legal dilemmas in South Florida. *Onati Socio-Legal Series*, *3*(2), 254–276.

Sarat, A. (1990). '... The law is all over': Power, resistance and the legal consciousness of the welfare poor. *Yale Journal of Law and the Humanities*, *2*, 343.

Scheingold, S. A. (1974). *The politics of rights: Lawyers, public policy, and political change.* New Haven, CT: Yale University Press.

Schuck, P. H. (1987). *Agent orange on trial: Mass toxic disasters in the courts* (Enl ed.). Cambridge, MA: Belknap Press of Harvard University Press.

Schwartz-Shea, P., & Yanow, D. (2012). *Interpretive research design: Concepts and processes. Routledge series on interpretive methods.* New York, NY: Routledge.

Shapiro, M. (1972). Toward a theory of *stare decisis*. *Journal of Legal Studies*, *1*(1), 125–134.

Shapiro, M. M. (1986). *Courts, a comparative and political analysis* (Paperback ed.). Chicago, IL: University of Chicago Press.

Shaw, I. G. R., Robbins, P. F., & Jones, J. P. (2010). A bug's life and the spatial ontologies of mosquito management. *Annals of the Association of American Geographers*, *100*(2), 373–388.

Silbey, S. S. (2005). After legal consciousness. *Annual Review of Law and Social Science*, *1*, 323–368.

Silver, N. (2012). *The signal and the noise: Why most predictions fail – but some don't.* New York, NY: Penguin Press.

Silverstein, H. (2007). *Girls on the stand: How courts fail pregnant minors.* New York, NY: New York University Press.

Skloot, R. (2011). *The immortal life of Henrietta Lacks.* Fort Collins, CO: Poudre River Public Library District.

Slaughter, A. (2004). *A new world order.* Princeton, NJ: Princeton University Press.

Sterett, S. (2009). New Orleans everywhere: Bureaucratic accountability and housing policy after Katrina. In J. Lezaun & A. Sarat (Eds.), *Catastrophe: Law, politics and the humanitarian impulse* (pp. 83–115).

Sterett, S. (2012a). State policy and disaster assistance: Listening to women. In E. David & E. Enarson (Eds.), *The women of Katrina: How gender, race, and class matter in an American disaster* (pp. 118–129).

Sterett, S., & Reich, J. (2007). Prayer and social welfare. In H. Potter, T. A. Fuller, M. Adya, & D. Austin (Eds.), *Racing the storm: Racial implications and lessons learned from Hurricane Katrina* (p. 135). Lexington, KY: Lexington Books.

Sterett, S. M. (1997). *Creating constitutionalism?: The politics of legal expertise and administrative law in England and Wales.* Ann Arbor, MI: University of Michigan Press.

Sterett, S. M. (2003). *Public pensions: Gender and civic service in the states, 1850–1937.* Ithaca, NY: Cornell University Press.

Sterett, S. M. (2012b). Need and citizenship after disaster. *Natural Hazards Review*, *13*(3), 233–245.

Stryker, R., Docka-Filipek, D., & Wald, P. (2012). Employment discrimination law and industrial psychology: Social science as social authority and the co-production of law and science. *Law and Social Inquiry*, *37*(4), 777–814.

Tetlock, P. E. (2006). *Expert political judgment.* Princeton, NJ: Princeton University Press.

Thaler, R. H., & Sunstein, C. R. (2009). *Nudge: Improving decisions about health, wealth, and happiness* (Update ed.). New York, NY: Penguin Books.

Tierney, K. (2006). Social inequality, hazards and disaster. In R. Daniels, D. F. Kettl, & H. Kunreuther (Eds.), *On risk and disaster: Lessons from Hurricane Katrina* (pp. 109–128). Philadelphia, PA: University of Pennsylvania Press.

Valverde, M. (2011). Seeing like a city: The dialectic of modern and premodern ways of seeing in urban governance. *Law and Society Review*, *45*(2), 277–312.

Yanow, D., & Schwartz-Shea, P. (2014). *Interpretation and method: Empirical research methods and the interpretive turn* (2nd ed.). Armonk, NY: M.E. Sharp, Inc.

CASSANDRA, PROMETHEUS, AND HUBRIS: THE EPIC TRAGEDY OF FUKUSHIMA

Masayuki Murayama and Lloyd Burton

ABSTRACT

Myth is a story of archetypical personas who behave in ways and with motives that we recognize in ourselves. We use myth as a way of reminding ourselves of the relationship between motives, actions, and consequences. Myths can serve either as inspirational or cautionary tales, and sometimes as both. But "myth" can also mean a fabricated story intended to create a false impression, and to achieve storytellers' ends when they have decided the truth will not suffice. We apply the myth of Cassandra to the millennium-long recorded history of giant tsunamis in Japan. After each of these catastrophes, survivors sought to warn future generations of their recurrences. But, each time, their progeny eventually lost the memory of these lessons, and lost their lives when the next monster wave overwhelmed them. Only when they kept the lessons as living knowledge in everyday life, could they manage to escape from monster tsunamis. In this chapter, we use the myth of Cassandra in conjunction with the myth of Prometheus, the bringer of fire to humankind, as a metaphor for Japan's growing reliance on nuclear power. Government

Special Issue: Cassandra's Curse: The Law and Foreseeable Future Disasters
Studies in Law, Politics, and Society, Volume 68, 125–153

ISSN: 1059-4337/doi:10.1108/S1059-433720150000068005

and utility companies built powerful but inherently dangerous cauldrons in the nation's disaster-prone landscapes, assuring the public they could control the fire's fury and defend it against nature's. As images of atomic bomb victims were still vivid and widely shared in Japan, they had to overcome the public fear of radioactivity by fabricating a "myth of safety." The nuclear disaster made the public distrust the government and utility companies, which lingers in the process of reconstruction from the disaster. Myths can either reveal hidden truths or mask hidden lies. The Japanese people must now learn to distinguish one from the other.

Keywords: Fukushima; tsunami; folk knowledge; public trust

INTRODUCTION: REVISITING THE MEANINGS OF *MYTH*

The introductory chapter in *Cassandra's Curse* discusses two meanings of the word "myth" in the English language that are central to the theme of this chapter as well. The first meaning is that of a tale of larger-than-life heroes, heroines, and villains doing deeds for reasons we recognize in ourselves. Their fate cautions us to be mindful of the intentions that precede our own actions as well; this is myth as morality play. And the second meaning is that of a fabricated story that has little or no basis in fact, concocted by the tale-teller to mislead or dupe the audience.

Both of these meanings of myth inform the epic tale we tell here, of two calamitous disasters: a foreseen and foretold natural one, and an entirely human-caused one that authorities had promised would never occur. First, we apply the myth of Cassandra to the millennium-long recorded history of giant tsunamis striking the east coast of Japan. After each of these catastrophes, survivors sought by various means to warn future generations of their recurrence. But each time, their progeny eventuality lost the memory of these lessons, and then lost their lives when the next monster wave overwhelmed them, as they repeatedly do.

Then we use the myth of Prometheus as a metaphor for Japan's growing reliance on nuclear power to fuel its post-World War technological and industrial rebirth. Not only did government and utility company experts call down the power of nuclear fire to fuel this economic miracle. They built their greatest and most powerful cauldrons in some of the nation's most disaster-prone landscapes, all the while assuring the public they could control their fire's fury and defend it against nature's. In their hubris, they fabricated a mythical world in which the laws of nature did not apply. And now the entire nation is suffering the punishment for violating those laws.

We now know how tragically deluded these government and industry leaders were, and how they managed to delude the Japanese public as well. Postdisaster, critics now refer to this relentless pronuclear propaganda campaign as the "myth of safety." The regulatory state the Japanese depended on to protect them from the very real dangers associated with nuclear energy technology failed them. Just as the redundant "failsafe" systems at the Fukushima Daiichi power plant failed to shut down its runaway reactors, so too did a compromised regulatory state fail to put the protection of the public above the profitability of the Tokyo Electric Power Company (TEPCO).

The Japanese people have humankind's most extensive experience with the unearthly power of nuclear fire. It killed tens of thousands of them at Hiroshima and Nagasaki in 1945, and fatally sickened many more. Building American-designed nuclear reactors along a disaster-prone coastline was not an easy sell. Getting the public to believe the "myth of safety" was a feat of social engineering that had to be accomplished before the nuclear engineering could begin.

Mythic narratives play an influential role in the discourses of public affairs. As we noted above and illustrate below, myths can either reveal and personify deeper truths, or they can effectively obscure them. In 2011 they did the latter. In this chapter, we seek to do the former.

THE CASSANDRA MILLENNIUM

Tsunamis Past and Present: The Thousand-Year-Old Warning

In the early afternoon of March 11, 2011, a huge Magnitude 9 earthquake occurred on the floor of the Pacific Ocean, about 130 km (80 miles) east of Japan's Ojika Peninsula, in the Miyagi Prefecture.[1] This and following earthquakes violently shook East Japan, heavily damaging Sendai, the capital city of Miyagi Prefecture.[2]

However, the earthquakes were only the first of the succession of huge disasters they would trigger. Fifteen minutes after the first earthquake, the first wave of tsunamis attacked Miyako City in Iwate Prefecture. Within an hour, along the 700-km (435 mile) coastline from Aomori to Chiba Prefecture, multiple tsunamis – each one larger and more destructive than the last – slammed into the coastal and near-shore communities on Japan's eastern seaboard.

Three minutes after the first earthquake, the Japan Meteorological Agency (JMA) issued a large tsunami warning to the coastal areas of the six eastern prefectures facing the Pacific Ocean. But at this early time, JMA did not estimate correctly the sizes of the earthquake and tsunami, which were too large for JMA machines to measure.[3]

JMA first predicted that the height of tsunami would be 6 meters (20 feet) in Miyagi and 3 meters (10 feet) in Iwate and Fukushima. But 25 minutes later JMA increased the estimated height to be 10 meters (33 feet) and 6 meters (20 feet) respectively. Finally, about an hour after the disaster struck, JMA issued a warning of a 10 meter (33 foot) tsunami for a much broader area, including the six prefectures from Aomori to Chiba.

Yet the actual height of the tsunamis was even larger. These massive tsunami destroyed the monitoring posts set in the sea off the east Japanese coast, so JMA could not get exact data on the enormous walls of water about to strike the coastline. When JMA issued the warning of 10-meter tsunamis, some places along the coastline had already been overwhelmed by tsunamis of this size or bigger.

The size of a tsunami when it meets a shoreline depends partly on the shape of the coast. A powerful tsunami coming ashore into a U-shaped or V-shaped bay or inlet will get very high. Such was the case with Iwate Prefecture, with a deeply indented coastline directly parallel to the seabed fault line whose rupture had caused the tsunamis to arise.

But even along a flat shallow beach, the tsunamis invaded inland fields 6 km (about 4 miles) inland from the beach in Miyagi Prefecture.[4] As a result, 15,883 persons died, while 2,671 persons went missing. Almost all the victims were killed by the tsunamis.[5]

The earthquake and tsunamis were entirely foreseeable events. The same fault line at the same place on the ocean floor had produced similar earthquakes and similar massive tsunamis along Japan's eastern coast many times in the past, with historical records of their occurrence dating back hundreds of years.

Small earthquakes are an almost everyday phenomenon in Japan. Tsunamis are also nothing new for people living in coastal areas. Particularly in the Sanriku Region of Iwate and Miyagi Prefectures,[6] where villages, towns, and cities are located on deeply indented coastlines, tsunamis have brought tremendous calamities in the past. In the Pacific Ocean near the prefectures, there are zones of frequent earthquakes, where the Pacific plate goes under the North American plate, creating the Japan Trench.[7]

The repeated devastation of the east coast of Honshu (Japan's largest island, and home to the national capital, Tokyo) resulting from shifts in the Japan Trench subduction zone is woven deep into the fabric of Japanese history and culture. In the severely damaged regional capital of Sendai there stands a little Shinto shrine, *Namiwake Jinja*, or "wave-dividing shrine." Rebuilt several times over the centuries, it commemorates the Jogan Earthquake and Tsunami of 869 CE, and stands at the very location – several miles inland – to which the Jogan tsunami extended. The shrine is a warning that the area toward the sea from that point is not safe.[8]

The city of Sendai was developed at first mainly on high ground on the hillside. But as the population increased, the residential area spread toward the sea and the warning was forgotten. In 2004, geologists began to study the strata of the ground of the Sendai Plain in order to find out how far Jogan Tsunami inundated the plain.[9] In their 2010 report, the scientists warned that a gigantic earthquake and tsunami such as the CE 869 Jogan would occur every 500–1,000 years. More ominously, they also predicted, that such an earthquake and tsunami could come anytime soon.[10] Just one year later, their warning came true.

Earthquakes occurring in Japan Trench do not really feel large in Sanriku Region because it is far from their epicenters, but they can still cause large tsunamis to strike the area. Moreover, as many small bays of the region are open to the direction where tsunamis come over the Pacific Ocean from Chile, large silent tsunamis caused by earthquakes in Chile have also caused serious damage in the region, and are expected to do so in the future.[11]

Tsunamis resulted in huge devastation in the region three times since the late 19th century: Meiji Sanriku Tsunami in 1896, Showa Sanriku Tsunami in 1933, and Chile Tsunami in 1960. No one now alive experienced the Meiji Sanriku Tsunami in 1896, but its survivors tried to warn succeeding generations of the danger. The stone monument of tsunami warning in Aneyoshi District, Miyako City, is known for its clear message:

Houses on a high place are for peace and pleasure of children and grandchildren

Remember miseries brought by big tsunami

Don't build houses below this place

Tsunami came up here in 1896 and 1933

The whole village perished and only two survived in 1896 and four in 1933

Be careful no matter how many years go by.

In Aneyoshi District, the whole village was destroyed by the tsunamis in 1896, so no warning message was left for younger generations; and the disaster was repeated in 1933. The monument was built after the disaster in 1933. Since then, no family has built a house below that level, and all the 11 households in the village survived the March 11, 2011 tsunami undamaged.[12]

Numerous similar stone monuments remained in 2000, 124 monuments being built after Meiji Sanriku Tsunami and 157 after Showa Sanriku Tsunami.[13] However, many of them went unheeded, and could not prevent residents from falling victim to the 2011 tsunamis. A warning message alone – even one literally written in stone – is not enough to save lives and homes unless it creates a pattern of behavior among residents to avoid the danger of tsunami.[14]

However, it is also true that there is often not much space up on a nearby hill to build a village along the Sanriku coastline. This is the case with Taro District of Miyako City.[15] In 1896, entire households of the Taro village perished, and more than 80% of the population died onsite or was washed out to see. Again in 1933, the village suffered the largest casualties in the Sanriku Region.

Unable to find a space for their village on a hill, villagers began to build a seawall against tsunami by themselves next year. In 1978, 44 years after the construction started, the seawall of 2.4 km long and 10 meters high was finally built. Because of its gigantic appearance, people called the seawall "the Great Wall." However, it was known that the Meiji Tsunami was 15 meters high in Taro village. Just a year before East Japan Disaster, a retired professor warned villagers not to rely too much on the seawall.[16] On March 11, 2011, the tsunamis came over the seawall, partially breaking it, and destroyed the whole village once again.[17]

Folk Knowledge and Contemporary Responses to Tsunami Disasters

As we have illustrated, Cassandra's voice in the form of shrines, sentinel stones, and cautionary literature has been echoing down through Japanese history for the last 1100 years. And it is not as if her warnings have gone unheeded at the folk level – among the people most affected by these disasters whose generations pass these memories on from generation to generation.

We cannot prevent natural disasters from occurring, and we have learned that levees and seawalls are not always able to prevent tsunamis from destroying the built environment. In these extreme situations, the only way for residents to save their lives is to run for their lives. In fact, some people and villages have woven this 'folk knowledge' into their daily lives, in a tradition now commonly called "Tsunami Tendenko."

"Tenden" is an expression of the dialect of Northeast Japan, which means "each." "Ko" is a postfix in the dialect, which does not have any specific substantive meaning. The message of "Tsunami Tendenko" is "When tsunami comes, escape immediately without thinking about others." Since the 2011 East Japan Disaster, "Tsunami Tendenko" has been often cited as an old oral tradition of Sanriku Region. But the phrase is actually a new invention.

A researcher on history of tsunami disasters, Mr. Fumio Yamashita, talked about his personal experience at a conference on tsunami held in Taro in 1990. When the Showa Sanriku Tsunami struck in 1933, he was seven years old, the youngest of seven children, living with his family in Ofunato City, Iwate Prefecture. When they felt big quakes, his father immediately ran out of the house without helping his family. As Mr. Yamashita was told to escape to a higher place when an earthquake came, he also ran as fast as possible all by himself. His father had experienced Meiji Sanriku Tsunami in 1896, which killed nine members of his family. In 1933, 26 out of 28 households perished in tsunami, but all the family of Mr. Yamashita survived. He explained about his experience of that time, saying "We escaped tendenko." "Tsunami Tendenko" came from this talk.[18]

However, as this origin of the phrase shows, the message has not been systematically and widely communicated, although individual families tried to keep the message among themselves based on their own experiences of the Chile Tsunami in 1960.[19] When generations of Japanese who personally experienced tsunami disasters pass away, so too does the living memory of the catastrophe they endured.

In the East Japan Disaster, there were two contrasting responses at grade schools to the tsunami: the "Miracle of Kamaishi" and "Tragedy of Okawa Elementary School." In Kamaishi City of Iwate Prefecture, a professor at a national university who worked as the city advisor for disaster prevention and crisis management began to work on tsunami disasters in 2008. Based on his instruction, teachers told children at elementary and junior high schools to be responsible for their own lives.

He emphasized three principles for escape from tsunami: (1) Don't believe in previous assumptions (including not even believing in hazard maps made by the city, because we never know how large the next tsunami would be); (2) Do escape to as high a place as possible; and (3) Escape first (Be the first to run). He told children to tell their parents, "After an earthquake, I will escape by myself, so please escape without being concerned with me."[20] Junior high school students were told that they were probably not going to be saved by others, but they could help save others.

When the first biggest quake came, children were not only at school but also playing near the beach and parks. They immediately began to move to a park on a hill and then to a nursery home designated as an evacuation shelter. However, junior high school students saw that the shelter was not safe from the tsunami and moved to an even higher hill. They helped elderly men and women from the nursing home to escape. They also took hands of preschool children on the way for escape.

After they left for a higher place, the evacuation shelter was inundated by tsunami. Although more than 1,000 persons died or went missing in the center of the city, all the children that had been to school on the day escaped from tsunami. All but 6 of 2,921 children were saved.[21]

By contrast, at Okawa Elementary School in Ishinomaki City of Miyagi Prefecture, 74 of 108 school children were killed or went missing. The 1960 Chile tsunami had not reached the district where the school located, so the school district was also not included in the area that the prefecture estimated tsunami would inundate.

Due to this lack of foresight, the school had an evacuation plan for fires and earthquakes, but not for tsunamis. When the earthquake came, teachers gathered the children at the school playground. Then, teachers discussed whether and where to escape.[22] They stayed there almost 50 minutes, until tsunami overwhelmed them. In addition to the lost children, ten teachers and employees at school also died.[23]

Though what really happened is not clear, it is obvious that the city and the teachers believed that they would not be victimized by a tsunami. They accepted the assumptions of the hazard maps, that never took into account the possibility of tsunamis larger than the ones that had affected eastern Japan over the previous 50 years.[24]

Data based on GPS information taken from cellphones and car navigation systems portray a surprising and disturbing picture of people's behavior. In Sanriku Region, people barely managed to evacuate tsunami inundation zones; many did not. In the Sendai Plain, the concentration of people in the inundation zone actually increased before the tsunamis attacked.[25]

Why did people not get out of the dangerous areas in Sanriku Region? As we saw above, the 1960 Chile tsunami resulted in serious damage in the region. However, since that event, the JMA issued a tsunami warning several times after large earthquakes in North Japan, but there were few casualties in those cases. It is a phenomenon described in the West as "crying wolf," based on a European folk tale of a shepherd who kept raising false alarms of the community's flocks being attacked by wolves. Eventually no one believed his warnings, including that of a real wolf attack that did destroy the flock.

Disaster managers worldwide worry about the problem of warning of the possibility or probability of a disaster that never occurs or is not as serious as feared. What happens then is that the public becomes complacent, and tends to ignore warnings of very real and massive threats. This seems to be what happened in the Sanriku Region.

On February 27, 2010, there was a huge M 8.8 earthquake in Chile. JMA issued a large tsunami warning in the morning on February 28, 2010. Municipalities warned their residents with emergency siren. The four prefectures of Northeast Japan that faces the Pacific Ocean issued evacuation orders to 320,000 people.[26]

However, the scale of tsunami was much smaller than expected. Despite of the prediction of a 3 meter tsunami, the first wave was only 20˜30 centimeters high, though that of the second wave was 1.45 meters at highest in the region.[27] At many harbors, the tsunami was more or less 1 meter high. Although railways were stopped and traffic was blocked on national roads in fear of inundation, only small parts of streets were a little submerged in the water near the harbors of Kesennuma and Ishinomaki.[28]

Less than expected was not only the scale of tsunami but also the responses of the people. In Miyako City, where Taro also located, 18,996 persons of 8,011 households were ordered to evacuate immediately after the JMA tsunami warning. However, only 1,261 persons actually fled to a higher place or evacuation centers. Those who fled were mostly elderly people who had actually experienced Chile 1960 Tsunami.[29]

Younger generations had never experienced a tsunami that came over seawalls. Therefore, they seemed to trust that tsunami would not inundate their villages and towns.[30] It is to be noted that cellphones were generally carried by younger people, but not by elderly people. The data based of GPS information must have indicated that younger people did not move.

However, even those who fled to evacuation centers did not stay there throughout the evacuation period. In Kuji City of Iwate Prefecture, before the first wave came, 1,133 persons evacuated to the evacuation center, but in four hours the number fell to 184 persons. Also in Kamaishi City, the number of evacuees decreased to a half after the first wave had come, as most evacuees went back home before the larger second wave came.[31]

A city official of Kamaishi speculated that as the tsunami did not come until a long time after the large tsunami warning, people could not maintain a sense of crisis. Some people in the city of Sendai Plain complained that the coastal area of Sendai Plain should be distinguished from Sanriku Region with the indented coastline, as they believed that Sendai Plain would not be as susceptible to inundation of a tsunami as Sanriku Region. Eventually, JMA apologized that their warnings were excessive for all the regions.[32]

As the complaint above indicated, cities of the plain did not seem to expect that huge tsunamis could occur in their region. Yuriage District of Natori City was the main harbor for fishery that provided fish to the Sendai area. When the earthquake struck, it is said that about 4,000 persons stayed at home in this district. About 800 of them died in inundation of the tsunami. This was the area where the number of staying people increased after the earthquake.

According to the GPS data, few people moved after the biggest earthquake. Later it was found that emergency sirens did not work because the earthquake damaged the antenna for transmission at the city hall. As electricity was down, people had to rely on radio information. Gradually, people began to move inside the district to obtain information. But many people stayed in the district because the city expected the biggest tsunami would be four meters high, though the actual tsunami was 8 meters high. Therefore, places that were inundated had been expected to be safe on the city hazard map and many people seemed to believe it.[33] This is the opposite of the "crying wolf" problem – that is, underestimating the degree of danger and not doing enough to evacuate vulnerable populations.

After the 2010 Chile Tsunami, which betrayed the expectation of danger, the city of Sendai conducted a survey of residents who lived in the areas of possible tsunami danger and neighboring areas.[34] When respondents heard the large tsunami warning issued by JMA, 46% of them did not expect that a large tsunami would come and 13% did not expect that a tsunami would come. Almost 60% of the respondents did not take the warning seriously. Yet 54% of the respondents actually evacuated, following the warning. But most of them evacuated very late, two to four hours after the warning was issued.[35] This was the pattern of behavior that people of Sendai took about a year before East Japan Disaster. It seems that this kind of behavior was repeated when the 3.11 earthquake struck the area.

When the Chile earthquakes occurred in 2010, most people in the Sanriku Region and Sendai Plain expected that the tsunami would be small and not dangerous, and behaved accordingly, despite the JMA's large tsunami warning. The subsequent experience confirmed their initial expectation and reinforced it. Insofar as the theoretical knowledge of the possibility of a huge tsunami remained abstract and was not sensed as something real, it could not trigger action. It seems that there was a desire on the part of many residents to not believe that such a catastrophic natural disaster could actually be bearing down upon them.

Therefore, keeping the memory of suffering and maintaining the changed expectation is crucial in making possible effective evacuations. We can also build houses on higher and safe places,[36] but insofar as human activities cannot be completely removed from coastal areas, "tsunami tendenko" must be the final solution to avoid damages.

In terms of the Japanese public's perception of risk, however, there is an additional problem, having to do with the difference between earthquakes and tsunamis . We can escape from a tsunami, but not from an earthquake, even if we have some idea of where it might occur, if not necessarily when.[37]

Knowledge of an impending tsunami and clear instructions on how to escape to safety when it strikes is crucial to the ability of coast-dwelling residents to survive such a disaster. But in the case of a catastrophic nuclear power plant failure, the centuries-old (but effective) folklore advice of "run to the highest ground" is not so helpful, unless there is timely and accurate information available to the public on where the greatest dangers lie in terms of the spread of radioactive material.

In the case of the Fukushima power plant meltdown, residents were not informed of the volume, intensity, or even the form (gas, liquid, or solid) of the radioactive materials spewing uncontrollably from the stricken site. The government had some data obtained from System for Prediction of Environmental Emergency Dose Information (SPEEDI) that would predict the volume of radioactive materials in the air by simulation based on information of a radioactive source, weather conditions, and geographical data.[38] However, both the national and prefectural government did not disclose the simulation results to the public until March 23, 2011 – 12 days after the catastrophe.[39] By this time, of course, many frightened and ill-informed residents had already suffered significant exposure.

Because of the lack of information provided to either municipalities or local residents, many of those desperate to escape from the radiation fled directly into the path of clouds of radioactive pollution. Others stayed in place either because they could not run or had decided not to do so, not knowing that a toxic cloud of radiation was hovering above and around them.

THE MYTH OF PROMETHEUS AND "NUCLEAR FIRE"

Olympus Revisited

The earthquakes and tsunamis also severely damaged the Fukushima Daiichi Nuclear Power Plant.[40] The quakes and tsunamis damaged the control system that was necessary to cool down the reactors and the tanks in which highly radioactive spent fuel was stored. As a result, a meltdown occurred at three reactors and massive evacuations followed in the coastal region of Fukushima Prefecture.

Both the tsunami and the nuclear disasters were triggered by the earthquakes, yet these two disasters present contrasting cases. The latter disaster was entirely human-caused. With the government's blessing, the Tokyo Electric Power Company (TEPCO) had built a huge nuclear power complex along this historically vulnerable coastline, all the while making assurances that it would be absolutely safe when the next earthquake and tsunami assaulted the coastline. And those with knowledge of east coastal Japan's geological history knew it would be only a matter of time before the next "harbor wave" (the literal translation of 'tsunami') assaulted the coast.[41]

The resulting – and as of this writing, still unfolding – industrial disaster at Fukushima now rates as the world's worst nuclear disaster since Chernobyl. It is a human failure of almost mythic proportions, and resort to myth helps put it into perspective. To us, the most relevant of the classics is the myth of Prometheus.

According to Greek mythology (Hamilton, 1969), Prometheus was one of the Titans: the children of Mother Earth and Father Heaven. Titans were the first fully conscious creatures to walk the Earth. And their children were the gods and goddesses of Olympus, Zeus being chief among them.

As too often happens in royal families, an intergenerational power struggle ensued, with Zeus and the Olympians overcoming and enslaving the Titans. Zeus especially had it in for Prometheus, who had fashioned human beings in their upright form and had given them the gift of fire, since they were otherwise so weak and defenseless that they stood little chance of surviving against the tempers and jealousies of the gods of Olympus. For this and other threats to his omnipotence, Zeus had Prometheus bound to a rock, and sent an eagle to feast daily on his vital organs, yet not kill him.

Prometheus is an important figure in Greek mythology for two reasons. To humans he is a hero, because he gave us powers to withstand those of the gods. We used fire to forge the metals out of which we fashioned the tools to control natural forces as well as each other. But to Zeus and his fellow Olympians, Prometheus was a traitor to the Greek pantheon of deities. Zeus feared – and rightly so – that just as he had stolen the powers of the Titans in order to conquer them with it, so too would humans, once they had seized the powers of the gods, cease to recognize and respect the gods, and would no longer worship any source of power they themselves had not harnessed. The gods would become irrelevant, disempowered, and forgotten. Humans would revel in their own power, and disregard as irrelevant the natural forces they could not control. Their characters would be afflicted by *hubris* – a deluded sense of their omnipotence and superiority that would render them incapable of respecting forces beyond their control.

And this is the very aspect of the myth of Prometheus that makes it so compelling for our purposes. The curators of nuclear fire – which is among the most powerful human-crafted forces in the world – somehow thought they had such complete control over its strength that they could defy the forces of nature in their handling of it, by constructing nuclear reactors on the fragile grounds of an earthquake-prone archipelago.[42]

Nuclear Fire and Modern Japanese History

Japanese people of post-World War generations grew up seeing vivid photos of the nuclear bombing victims in Hiroshima and Nagasaki, and hearing first-hand the stories of survivors of history's only nuclear attack against fellow human beings. Stories of leukemia caused by exposure to radioactivity were common knowledge. When the government began promoting nuclear energy as lighting the path to future prosperity, the Japanese people already knew that radioactivity was dangerous. So the nuclear power plants were built in the least populated areas, far from large cities.

Because a nuclear plant is not something the people would welcome without reservation, utility company executives and government promoters used two strategies to convince rural communities to accept their nuclear future: (1) various financial incentives for local people to ease the acceptance of a plant, and (2) creation of the "myth of safety." The siting and construction of the Fukushima Daiichi and Daini Nuclear Power Plants are typical examples of these twin strategies at work.

There are few industries other than the nuclear plants in the central part of the coastal area of Fukushima Prefecture where the two nuclear plants are located. The power plants brought employment, first in their construction and later in running the plants.[43] Previously, local farmers had seasonally migrated to big cities during winter, to earn adequate supplementary income. But after accepting the power plant, they did not have to go out anymore, improving the family life of residents in the area.

With nuclear power being advanced as a national policy,[44] the state started giving subsidies to a prefecture and a municipality hosting a nuclear power plant 10 years in advance of the plant going online.[45] Though the subsidies were halved when a plant began to operate, a municipality and a prefecture could impose property tax on a nuclear plant, once built and operating.[46] As a result, a prefecture, and in particular, a municipality, with a small budget, could obtain subsidies disproportionate to their budget's size.

In this way a municipality could get rich, though heavily dependent on the nuclear power plant to do so. A year after the Fukushima Daiichi disaster, four municipalities where the Fukushima Daiichi and Daini Nuclear Power Plants are located still rely heavily on state subsidies and property taxes on TEPCO: 43% of their budgets came from the state subsidies and the TEPCO property tax, though the percentage of the previous year was 52%.[47] TEPCO also donated 2 billion Yen to municipalities of nuclear power source as well as to researchers, though TEPCO stopped the donation a year after the Fukushima accident.[48] Until the accident, such dependence effectively muted any local concerns about the safety of the nuclear cauldron boiling in their midst.[49]

Conjuring the Myth of Safety

Since the Japanese people feared radioactivity, the government and the electric utility companies (the most powerful of which was TEPCO), had to persuade local people that a nuclear power plant was safe. In response to opponents of the national policy favoring nuclear energy, the government and electric companies developed a "safety myth" asserting that a nuclear power plant was immune to technical failures.

Such a safety myth was nourished and sustained by creation of a "nuclear village [Genshiryoku Mura]" which consisted of business people, public officials, and academics.[50] For instance, TEPCO donated research fund to academics and provided jobs to retired public officials in the national and local governments.

TEPCO was also a powerful corporation in business networks and a major company to pay a lot to the mass media for advertisements. There were (and still are) public interest corporations and Incorporated Administrative Agencies concerned with nuclear power plant and radioactivity that received national government subsidies and donations of TEPCO and other electric companies. These organizations also provide positions to retired public officials.[51] "The nuclear village" promoted nuclear power, and those to control a nuclear power plant for safety was captivated by those to be controlled.[52]

TEPCO's safety myth asserted that their nuclear power plants would never create a dangerous situation for local residents. Even if some malfunction would occur, TEPCO promised that it could be contained, and backed up by multiple redundant safety measures.

But in fact, the extent to which safety measures were actually established depended heavily on business calculations of cost and benefit. Although a geological scientist warned TEPCO of the possibility of another Jogan-like monster tsunami (like the one for which the inland shrine was built in Sendai in 869 CE) TEPCO disregarded the warning, since building the plant to protect it against a tsunami of that size would be too costly. TEPCO's risk probability calculations indicated that investing in that level of protection was unwarranted.

In essence, TEPCO bet with the lives of its Fukushima Daiichi neighbors that another event of the magnitude of the 1869 Jogan catastrophe would not happen during the lifetime of their nuclear complex. Not only did the power company lose the bet; so did residents used as poker chips in this very high stakes game.

The Myth of Denial and Its Consequences

The myth of safety thus became a myth of denial – a refusal to acknowledge the possibility of a worst-case catastrophe. Planners assumed that losing all electricity to the plant would never occur, and that high levels of radioactive gases and other materials would never have to be released. As a result, at the time when the emergency venting was indeed required, the Fukushima Daiichi Plant reactors did not have filters to reduce radioactive materials, In short, the nuclear plant was designed and operated based on the assumption that a critical control situation would never arise.[53]

Also in keeping with the myth of safety and the culture of denial that it spawned, no systematic plans were ever developed for the rapid safe evacuation of large numbers of local people in the case of an accident. After the earthquake struck, a little before 3 in the afternoon, the large tsunami warning was issued by JMA. At this point, people near the Fukushima Daiichi and Daini Nuclear Power Plants were only concerned with earthquakes and tsunamis, and not with any possible problem with the reactors, because they had not been informed of the possibility of radioactive environmental contamination.

According to an official of Naraha Town in charge of disaster prevention and response, TEPCO at the Fukushima Daiichi contacted the town government after the earthquake only once, with the information that all the electricity was lost at the plant. At 7:00 PM that evening, four hours after the earthquake, emergency status was declared at the Fukushima Daiichi plant, even though its radioactive waste storage facilities had started to go critical almost four hours earlier. But it took two more hours – until about 9:PM – for the national government to issue an evacuation order to residents within 3 km (about 2 miles) of the crippled Daiichi reactor complex.

About 6:00 AM the next morning, government officials widened the evacuation zone to residents within 10 km (6 miles) of the site. At this point, only 20% of the residents of five municipalities to which the evacuation order was issued knew that a serious accident had occurred at the Fukushima Daiichi Nuclear Power Plant.[54] Naraha town issued its evacuation order to all the residents at 8:00 AM on March 12. At that time, the only immediately useful relevant information local officials were obtaining was mainly from watching television, rather than from either government officials or TEPCO.[55]

Having little current, reliable information to act on, municipalities near Fukushima Daiichi tried to evacuate their residents to the north and northwest, while municipalities near Fukushima Daini (the other stricken plant) tried to evacuate their residents to the south, mainly to Iwaki City. However, when the first explosion occurred at Fukushima Daiichi at 3:30 PM on March 12, many people began to escape from Iwaki City and Minami Soma, a northern city, though these areas were not designated as evacuation zones. While nuclear reactors exploded one after another from March 12 to 15, about 150,000 people evacuated from the area, some of them prior to government having ordered an evacuation, and without knowing in what direction they should travel to escape the cloud of toxic radiation now emanating from the fatally stricken plant.[56]

Although many people fled Fukushima Prefecture to other parts of Japan or even to foreign countries, most of the evacuees remained in the prefecture, mainly in Iwaki City and the central region of the prefecture.[57] In areas where an evacuation order was not issued, many people stayed for their jobs even if they could not trust what the government told them after the accident.[58]

A city official of Iwaki said that he somehow trusted the messages of the national government every time when the Chief Cabinet Minister said that the situation was "not immediately dangerous" at a press conference. Because they believed the message of "not immediately dangerous," public officials worked outside wearing only dust masks, and recommended that residents stay in their homes. However, when this same Chief Cabinet Minister visited the area, he appeared in a full radiation protection gear, wearing a white hazmat suit.

The local official was struck with his attire, and suddenly realized that the Chief Cabinet Minister had kept telling them what he had not believed personally. When his own life was at stake, the minister was taking protective measures he had assured local governments and residents were not necessary. Hardly a more compelling image of government failure to inform and protect its citizens can be imagined. Little wonder, then, at the corrosive effect this disaster and its aftermath would have on the public's ability to trust anything either the government or TEPCO says or does.

As the level of radioactivity tended to be lower in the southern area than in the other areas of the coastal region, people are now relocated into Iwaki. Yet people living there are not free from anxiety, as it seems that nobody knows the longtime effects of exposure to low-level radioactivity upon health. But Iwaki is better off than Koriyama and Fukushima, which have higher levels of radioactivity in general and has so-called hot spots at many locations. Some lawyers in Fukushima Prefecture continue to believe an evacuation order was never issued to the central region because the government had never planned for and had no idea about how to evacuate and relocate so many people on such short notice. They also believe that the central region was too vital for the Japanese economy to be designated as evacuation zones.[59]

The highway and bullet train line running in the central region connects the Tokyo Metropolitan Area with Sendai, the largest city of Northeast Japan. Had Koriyama and Fukushima been declared evacuation zones, this main line of transportation running through the evacuation zone would have been severed. That would have cut the island in two, with Sendai and Northeast Japan almost isolated from the rest of the country.[60] In turn, that would have more disastrous effects upon the Japanese economy as a whole. Therefore, the government decided to advise residents in the central region to stay in place rather than leave the area immediately. The continuous exposure to uncertain and fluctuating levels of radioactive environmental contamination experienced by this unevacuated population has left them anxious and fearful of what the long-term effects of this exposure might be.

Some of the 150,000 people who evacuated without adequate instruction or information suffered exposure to radioactive materials as they fled.[61] Many other people in Fukushima Prefecture wanted to evacuate but could not do so.[62] Unlike tsunamis, people have to stay and endure anxieties about radioactivity, as only the fortunate can escape to a safe place.[63]

Once a nuclear accident occurs, there is no way to get away from radioactivity. Like Prometheus, the residents of Fukushima Prefecture were also chained to a rock – the rock in this analogy being the circumstances that would not allow them to flee the toxic contamination that was to harm their homelands and perhaps their health.

EPILOGUE

As this book goes to press, Japan continues to suffer the effects of two gaping wounds – one inflicted by natural forces, and the other by the hubris of utility companies and their friends in the government agency that was supposed to be regulating them. In their forbearance and resilience, the Japanese people will recover from this all-too-familiar natural disaster, just as they have been doing for well over a thousand years. Earthquakes and tsunamis are a way of life in Japan, as are wildfires in the mountains of the American West.

But the disaster created by calling down the nuclear fire government and industry leaders could neither control nor shield from poisoning innocent people is another matter indeed. This disaster did not just spread toxic pollution in the land and sea around the disaster site for many years to come. It also poisoned the Japanese people's faith in the government they had trusted to protect them. Both the ongoing inability of TEPCO to contain the disaster it created and the seeming inability of government to do so either has become a source of national disgrace.

The harbors and coastal villages of Northeast Pacific coastline will eventually be rebuilt and reinhabited, just as they have been after every other earthquake and tsunami over the last thousand years. But what may not be so easily repaired is the relationship between the Japanese people affected by the disaster and their government. Better warning systems, more timely and locally accurate information about postearthquake tsunami expectations and activity, and more responsible and realistic evacuation plans in response to natural disasters can help restore some degree of confidence. But the people's memory of how they were misled by their own government's "myth of safety" may take much longer to repair.[64]

Japan is an island nation with very little in the way of fossil fuel energy sources, nearly all of which need to be imported from afar. Nuclear power played an instrumental role in helping Japan get back on its feet after World War II. It was a dominant feature of Japan's energy portfolio right up until March of 2011, when both the industry and its government regulators proved themselves fundamentally incapable of safely managing the nuclear fire they had drawn down into the communities of rural Pacific coastal Honshu.

The ancient shrines and sentinel stones warned future generations not to live too close to areas of known natural hazards. Perhaps modern-day Japanese will need to find a way to warn future generations not to be deluded by the myths of their leaders.

Japan's post World War II Prometheans defied the natural forces of wind and wave when they built their nuclear cauldrons in the path of monster waves, and paying little heed to where the winds would carry the toxic smoke from their fires, and who might be poisoned as a result.

Perhaps now the Japanese can create for themselves an energy future that involves working in partnership with these natural forces rather than ignoring or dismissing them. Perhaps Zeus had a point. Respecting and accommodating natural forces far beyond our control is a far wiser and safer way to live than residing in the illusion that our powers exceed theirs. And just as importantly, we need to understand and respect limitations on our ability to control the technological forces we conjure up and unleash as well.

NOTES

1. One of the coauthors was waiting for an elevator on the 12th floor of a university building in Tokyo, when the first largest earthquake came. The building trembled and then swayed too hard to stand on the floor. Soon all the firewalls

contained in the wall were coming out and moving. When the earthquake stopped, we ran down the stairs to a nearby park. Then, the second one came. We saw nearby buildings sway back and forth. We knew some really big earthquakes happened far from Tokyo, but did not know exactly where.

2. In fact, the earthquakes afflicted damages in scattered wide areas where grounds were not very strong and secured, but the number of casualties caused by the earthquakes was much smaller than that caused by the tsunamis.

3. JMA first estimated the size of the earthquake as M 7.9 as that was the highest value that the JMA machine could measure, and issued the large tsunami warning based on this estimate. Ten minutes after the earthquake, an observatory in Nagano reported the scale of the earthquake as M 9, but as the observatory was not a part of the domestic observation network, the datum was not used by JMA. US Geological Survey estimated the scale of the quake as M 8.9, but later updated it to M 9.0. http://www.usgs.gov/newsroom/article.asp?ID=2727, accessed on August 19, 2013.

4. A huge area of the Sendai Plain became a flat land with skeletons of devastated houses and buildings. In some areas, concrete foundations indicated where houses were built. When we visited one of those areas in June 2011, a daughter was back to the place where her family house used to be, sitting on the foundation and staring on the ground. She just came back from a funeral of her friend. About 100 meters from there, stood a school building, which was designated an evacuation center for residents of the area. After the earthquakes, adults gathered on the first floor of the school building and children were on the second floor. After the tsunamis came, all the people on the first floor were gone. When we visited there, a clock in a classroom stopped at 3:35.

5. Another 2,688 persons died for causes related with the disasters, including evacuation from the Fukushima Daiichi Nuclear Plant accident. The numbers are for June 10, 2013 (Fukkocho [Reconstruction Agncy], 2013).

6. Deeply indented coastline lies from the north of Miyagi Prefecture to the north end of Iwate Prefecture.

7. While driving on a motorway along the Sanriku coastline in fall, 2011, the author was struck with warning messages above the motorway, such as "Showa Tsunami 1933 came to this level," or "Meiji Tsunami 1896 came to this level." The motorway runs up on the hill. These messages clearly show that villages near beach are vulnerable to tsunami.

8. Kahoku Shinpo is the major newspaper of Northeast Japan, which has the headquarters in Sendai, the capital city of Miyagi Prefecture and the largest city of Northeast Japan (Kahoku Shinpo, 2011a).

9. Shinsai Shishikura et al. (2010).

10. Kensho (2011).

11. In May 1960, an earthquake of M 9.5 in Chile caused tsunamis that attacked the Sanriku Region and left serious damages there: 142 persons dead or missing. The tsunamis were not expected by residents who had believed that tsunami would come after quakes. After this disaster, Pacific Rim countries set up an international warning system on tsunami information. Kahoku Shinpo, March 1, 2010, Article ID: K20100301A106X0010.

12. On a small island named Miyatojima, Miyagi Prefecture, a stone monument with a message "Place below this level is dangerous" carried a warning left by ancestors who suffered a huge earthquake more than 1,000 years ago. Nobody on the island suffered this time (Fukushima Minpo, 2011). Fukushima Minpo is one of the two major local newspapers in Fukushima Prefecture.

13. Monuments built after 1896 were generally memorials for the deceased, while those built after 1933 were generally to leave message for later generations. But a monument with a clear message, "Don't build a house below this place," is rather rare (Kagaku, 2013).

14. It was not rare that meanings of stone monuments had been forgotten among residents (Kahoku Shinpo, 2011d).

15. Because of repeated devastating damages by tsunami, the village was called Tsunami Taro (Kahoku Shinpo, 2010g).

16. Kahoku Shinpo (2010h).

17. There was the world largest seawall built against tsunami in the harbor of Kamaishi, Iwate Prefecture. It was built at a depth of 209 feet, a length of 1.2 miles, and a cost of $1.5 billion. But the tsunami surmounted the seawall and invaded the city (New York Times, 2011). Inside the city, cars were trapped in traffic jams and people inside cars were killed by inundation. The seawall was destroyed but it was said that it delayed the tsunami attack six minutes. However, people at a nearby village said that the seawall had made waves higher which destroyed their village.

18. Kahoku Shinpo (2010).

19. Many people who survived the Chile Tsunami seemed to tell to each other in their families that everybody should run on their own when tsunami came (Kahoku Shinpo, 2010j).

20. A mother who worked at a hair salon at the city center did not go to the school where her three daughters were, believing that they would escape by themselves. They did. If she would have been there, she would not be able to escape from tsunami. This is a practice of "Tsunami Tendenko" (Kahoku Shinpo, 2011h).

21. Kahoku Shinpo (2011g).

22. Parents of some children came to school to pick up their children. They saw teachers discussing what to do. Some of the parents told teachers to escape to a higher place, but apparently teachers did not take an immediate action. They seemed to believe that it was safer to stay at the school playground than trying to escape to a hill just behind the school (Kahoku Shinpo, 2011e).

23. There seemed to be only one teacher who could escape from tsunamis. But since he talked with the city education commission and also at a meeting with parents, he has not appeared in public. What he said to the commission could be contradictory to what others saw. Therefore, why the teachers did not move immediately is not precisely known (Ikegami, 2012).

24. Kikuchi (2011).

25. 'Inochi no Kiroku' wo Mirai he ~ Shinsai Big Data ~ Director Shuzai Note ['Record on Lives' for Future ~ Big Data on Disaster ~ Director's Note of Investigation]" (2013).

26. Kahoku Shinpo (2010f).

27. Kahoku Shinpo (2010a).

28. Kahoku Shinpo (2010a).

29. Also in Yamada Town, evacuees were mostly elderly people who experienced Chile 1960 Tsunami. At Yamada harbor, it was found later that tsunami was 1.61 meter high, the highest for Chile 2010 Tsunami (Kahoku Shinpo, 2010d).

30. Kahoku Shinpo (2010b).

31. Kahoku Shinpo (2010e).

32. Kahoku Shinpo (2010c).

33. The city expected the worst tsunami as 4 meters high, but according to a city official, the state and the prefecture expected the highest as 2.6 meters. Officials knew Jogan Tsunami, but did not revise the hazard map, as they were concerned with the possibility that it would unnecessarily inflame public anxieties (Ikegami, 2013).

34. The population was the citizens who lived in those areas and older than 15 years old. The sample size was 5,000 individuals and 1,808 responded. Details of the way the survey was conducted are not known.

35. Kahoku Shinpo (2010i).

36. Kahoku Shinpo conducted research on evacuees in the coastal area of Miyagi Prefecture from April 6 to 9, 2011. They distributed a questionnaire to 500 evacuees and obtained 396 responses. 48% of the respondents answered that they did not want to live at the same place, 23% were wondering, and 7% were not sure. 22% answered that they wanted to live at the same place. This result indicates that most people changed their expectations about possible tsunami damages. But at the same time, a significant minority still wanted to live where they used to live, though it is not clear whether these people lost their houses because of the tsunami (Kahoku Shinpo, 2011f).

37. In Japan, we now have an Earthquake Early Warning System that sends a warning from a few seconds to thirty seconds before an earthquake comes. But there are not many that we can do even for 30 seconds.

38. For an official explanation on SPEEDI given by the Ministry of Education and Sciences, see, http://www.nsr.go.jp/archive/nsc/mext_speedi/, accessed on March 20, 2013.

39. According to the government explanation, the simulation results were not disclosed because they could not obtain data of the source of radiation, thus making the simulation results inaccurate. But people, including mass media, considered that the real reason was that the government had been afraid that the disclosure would cause panic and disorder (Kahoku Shinpo, 2011c). It is conceivable that the government did not disclose the simulation results in fear of disorder, but it is more probable that the government wanted to exclude the central region from the evacuation areas.

40. Tokyo Electric Power Company (TEPCO) argued that the tsunamis destroyed the electric power system at the nuclear plant, because the scale of the tsunami was unprecedented. But the government investigation committee and the Diet investigation committee both did not rule out the possibility that the earthquakes could have damaged the system (Investigation Committee on the Accident at Fukushima Nuclear Power Station of Tokyo Electric Power Company, 2011; The National Diet of Japan Fukushima Nuclear Accident Independent Investigation Commission, 2012b).

41. The government standard for aseismic design of a nuclear plant was revised in 2006. However TEPCO did not construct additional protections against earthquakes, which would satisfy the requirements of the new standard. TEPCO and the government also knew that, if tsunamis would come over the nuclear plant, they could lose all the electricity and cause damages of a reactor, but did not take any effective preventive measures (The National Diet of Japan Fukushima Nuclear Accident Independent Investigation Commission, 2012e).

42. As four plates, Pacific, North American, Philippine, and Eurasian Plates, meet under the Japanese archipelago, the country is full of faults. Therefore, when a nuclear reactor is planned to be built, a crucial question is not whether there is a fault below or near the reactor site, but whether a fault is "dead" or "active." As a "dead" volcano does not exist anymore, whether a fault is "dead" or "alive" is a matter of duration in which the fault did not move.

43. After Fukushima Daiichi Nuclear Power Plant accident, other active power plants stopped working for regular checks and others. But such a temporal stop resulted in an unemployment problem. For instance, Fukui Prefecture issued emergency measures to respond to economic problems triggered by the stoppage of the power plant there (Fukui Shinbun, 2012).

44. The government of the Liberal Democratic Party (LDP) that dominated the Japanese political scene until 1990s pushed the policy since 1950s. The government of the Democratic Party of Japan (DPJ) reconsidered the policy but the LDP government reinstated the policy after the LDP won the lower house election in 2012.

45. The subsidies are Dengen Ricchi Chiiki Taisaku Kohukin [Subsidies for Measures for Power Source Area].

46. Keizai Sangyo Sho Shigen Energy Cho [Ministry of Economy, Trade and Industry, Agency of Natural Resources and Energy], Dengen Ricchi Seido no Gaiyo – Chiiki no Yume wo Okiku Sodateru [Overview of the Power Source Area Scheme – Facilitate to Expand a Local Dream], March 2009.

47. Kahoku Shinpo (2012).

48. Asahi Digital (2012).

49. The Mayor of Naraha town where Fukushima Daini Nuclear Plant located demanded TEPCO to restart the operation of the Fukushima Daini Plant only a week after the accident of the Fukushima Daiichi Plan. From an interview with a lawyer in Iwaki City, in July, 2011.

50. Six months after the accident, TEPCO disclosed that they employed 51 retired public officials at the end of August, 2011. Before the 3.11 accident in 2011, the Director of Agency for Natural Resource and Energy moved to TEPCO after his retirement, but facing public criticisms he resigned after the accident (Kahoku Shinpo, 2011b). "Descending from Heaven" typically means the practice that public officials find positions in private companies, public interest corporations or Incorporated Administrative Agencies after their retirement. It is assumed that the practice is a part of the give and take between two organizations. A similar practice can be seen for senior employees above a certain level in a large private company, descending to a position in a subordinate or affiliated company. These practices do not result from personal relations but arrangements between two organizations.

51. Kahoku Shinpo (2011i) wrote about "Nuclear Village" in Kasumigaseki where METI, MEXT and other Ministries locate. "Kasumigaseki" is a district of

Tokyo where national government ministries locate. METI is Ministry of Economy, Trade and Industry. MEXT is Ministry of Education and Sciences. Not only METI but also MEXT has a jurisdiction over nuclear matters, as MEXT integrated Science and Technology Agency that was established to promote nuclear energy (Kahoku Shinpo, 2011i).

52. "The Regulatory authorities became 'captives' of TEPCO and the FEPC (the Federation of Electric Power Companies of Japan)" (The National Diet of Japan Fukushima Nuclear Accident Independent Investigation Commission, 2012f).

53. The Diet Investigation Commission pointed out that the Fukushima Daiichi Power Plant did not have robustness against possible large earthquakes and that TEPCO did not set up countermeasures against possible tsunamis though TEPCO and NISA (Nuclear and Industrial Safety Agency) shared the perception of the vulnerability (The National Diet of Japan Fukushima Nuclear Accident Independent Investigation Commission, 2012c).

54. The National Diet of Japan Fukushima Nuclear Accident Independent Investigation Commission (2012d).

55. According to him, a hot line for emergency had been set up, but it did not work. As TEPCO did not call them, they called the office of the Fukushima Daini Nuclear Power Plant, trying to get more information. Interview in October, 2011.

56. People who were afraid of dangers of radioactivity evacuated without an evacuation order. Evacuation was not always organized well. In Minami Soma, 60% of the evacuees did evacuated on their own (The National Diet of Japan Fukushima Nuclear Accident Independent Investigation Commission, 2012a). Even if an evacuation order was issued, some people were not informed. A resident of Minami Soma stayed at a shelter overnight on March 11, 2011. He was only concerned with earthquakes and tsunamis. On March 12, he came back home, believing that big quakes and tsunamis would not come any more, and was drinking sake in the evening, when his friend ran to his house and told him to evacuate immediately. Being surprised with the news, he called city councilmen and others and found all of them had been gone. Interview in April 2013.

57. Fukushima Prefecture consists of three regions: the coastal region, the central region, and the west region. Iwaki is the largest city in the coastal region, while Koriyama and Fukushima are two largest cities in the central region. Many people initially fled to the west region where the level of radioactivity was rather low. But many of them later returned or wanted to return to Iwaki, as the climate of the west region is harsher.

58. Fathers who had jobs there wanted to stay, while mothers who had small children wanted to move as far away as possible. As a result, disputes between spouses occurred. When spouses lived separately, the separation also created tension between them. Lawyers the author interviewed in Fukushima said that an increasing number of spouses, often wives, came to seek advice on divorce. Interviews with lawyers in Fukushima in September 2011 and February 2012.

59. The central region is the most industrialized and populated area in Fukushima Prefecture, as the population of the region is about 1.2 million, 59% of the prefectural population on January 1, 2012 (Fukushima Ken Kikaku Chosei Bu Toukei Ka [Fukushima Prefecture, Planning and Adjustment Department, Statistics Section], 2013).

60. Then, there would be no route between Tokyo and Sendai, except a really long detour through Niigata and Yamagata along the Japan Sea. This route does not have highways or a high speed train line.

61. People of Namie Town fled to the direction that radioactive plume moved. This was confirmed later by simulation results of SPEEDI. If the data had been disclosed to the public, they would not have been exposed to the higher level of radioactivity.

62. According to results of a survey conducted by Fukushima City in May 2012, 34% of the respondents kept wanting to evacuate, while 31% used to want but not wanted to evacuate anymore. However, more than 80% were concerned with their health because of the radioactivity (Fukushimashi [Fukushima City]).

63. People who had financial resource or relatives at safer places could evacuate to safer places voluntarily. They are fortunate in this sense. But it is often not the whole family but only wives and children that evacuated to safer places. Such a situation often created difficulties for them, as we saw above.

64. There seems to be a cleavage between the people who evacuated or otherwise affected by the disasters and the rest of the Japanese. Most of the former have been deeply hurt and still cannot have normal life. They are afraid that most Japanese who were not affected by the disaster will forget the disasters rather soon as time passes.

ACKNOWLEDGMENTS

Professor Murayama's field research in Fukushima, Miyagi and Iwate Prefectures for this chapter was supported by a grant from the Foundation for Research in Civil Dispute Resolution. That support is hereby gratefully acknowledged.

REFERENCES

Asahi Digital. (2012). *Toden, Kihukin wo Zenpai he, Jichitai nadoni Nenkan 20 Okuen Shishutu* [*TEPCO Will Abolish Their Donations, Paid 2 Billion Yen to Municipalities and Others Every Year*], April 26. Retrieved from http://www.asahi.com/special/10005/TKY201204260299.html?ref=chiezou. Accessed on August 20, 2013.

Fukkocho [Reconstruction Agency]. (2013, July 2). *Fukko no Genjo to Torikumi* [*The Present Situation of Reconstruction and Our Initiatives*], p. 4.

Fukui Shinbun. (2012). *Genpatsu Teishi ni Tomonau Koyo Akka de Kinkyu Taisaku* [*Emergency Measures for the Worsening Employment Situation Resulted from the Nuclear Plant Stoppage*], June 18. Retrieved from http://www.fukuishimbun.co.jp/localnews/npp_restart/35290.html. Accessed on August 20, 2013.

Fukushima Ken Kikaku Chosei Bu Toukei Ka [Fukushima Prefecture, Planning and Adjustment Department, Statistics Section]. (2013). *Fukushima Ken no Suitei Jinko,*

Heisei 24 Nen Ban [*Estimated Population of Fukushima Prefecture, 2012 edition*], p. 8, Table 2. Retrieved from http://www.pref.fukushima.jp/toukei/data/02/jinkounen/24jin-kounen/honpen.pdf. Accessed on August 20, 2013.

Fukushima Minpo. (2011). 1000 Nen Ijo Maeni Tsunami, Sekihi Tate "Kokoyori Shita Kiken" Tomin no Inochi Sukutta Senjin no Iitsutae, Miyagi Higashi Matsushima Miyatojima [Tsunami came more than 1000 years ago, message "Place below here is dangerous" on a Stone monument built by ancestors saved lives of the people on the Island, Miyatojima, East Matsushima, Miyagi Prefecture], April 25, 8th ed., p. 15.

Fukushimashi [Fukushima City]. *Hoshano ni kansuru Shimin Ishiki Chosa' no Kekka (Gaiyo Ban)* [Results of 'Survey on Citizens' Consciousness Concerning Radioactivity' (Summary Version)], p. 4, 6. Retrieved from http://www.city.fukushima.fukushima.jp/uploaded/attachment/13557.pdf. Accessed on August 20, 2013.

Hamilton, E. (1969). *Mythology*. New York, NY: Penguin Books.

Ikegami, M. (2013, April 1). Yuriage no Machi wa Naze 'Soteigai' no Tsunami ni Osowaretanoka, Anzen Shinwa wo Umu 'Hazard Map' no Otoshiana [Why was Town of Yuriage attacked by 'unexpected' tsunami? A pit hall of 'the hazard map' that creates safety myth]. *Diamond.* Retrieved from http://diamond.jp/articles/-/34003. Accessed on August 18, 2013.

Ikegami, M. (2012, June 25). 'Hinanchu ni Otsunami' wa Uso Datta? Ishinomaki Shi Kyoi no Mujun de Akiraka ni naru 'Okawa Sho no Shinjitsu' ['Big Tsunami on the way to escape' was a lie? 'The truth of Okawa Elementary School Incident' comes to light through contradictions of the Ishinomaki City Education Comission]. *Diamond.* Retrieved from http://diamond.jp/articles/-/20521. Accessed on August 20, 2013.

'Inochi no Kiroku' wo Mirai he ~ Shinsai Big Data ~ Director Shuzai Note ['Record on Lives' for Future ~ Big Data on Disaster ~ Director's Note of Investigation]". (2013). *NHK Special Eyes* #22, March 1. Retrieved from https://www.nhk.or.jp/special/eyes/22/02.html. Accessed on August 22, 2013.

Investigation Committee on the Accident at Fukushima Nuclear Power Station of Tokyo Electric Power Company. (2011). *Interim Report* (*Main Text*), December 26. p. 25.

Kagaku. (2013). Sanriku Chiho no Tsunami, Sekihi Hibun ga Kataru Hisai no Kyokun Kokoro wo tsunagu Kizuna no Yakuwari ni [[Science] Tsunami in Sanriku Region, Lessons of Victimization that Stone Monument and Engraved Message Tell Play a Role to Bond People's Minds], *Sankei News*, March 18, Retrieved from http://sankei.jp.msn.com/affairs/news/130318/dst13031810070011-n1.htm. Accessed on August 19, 2013.

Kahoku Shinpo. (2010). Chile Jishin Tsunami 50 Nen Kienu Kioku (5)/Kyoiku/Gakko de Migaku Mi Mamoru Noryoku [50 Years after the Chile Earthquake and Tsunami, Memory is not gone (5)/Education/Capability to protect oneself trained at school]. May 23, Article ID: K20100523S206X0010.

Kahoku Shinpo. (2010a). Chile Daijishin de Otsunami Keiho/'Ki wo Yurumezuni Sonae wo/ Sendai Kishodai '1 meter koe, Kongo mo' [Big Chile Earthquake Prompted Large Tsunami Warning/'Keep Attention and Be Prepared'/Sendai Meteorological Agency 'Larger than 1 Meter Still May Come'], March 1. Article ID: K20100301A206X0070.

Kahoku Shinpo. (2010b). Chile Daijishin Tsunami Genchi Rupo/Hinan, Kotsu ... Mondaiten Arawa [Chile Big Quake Tsunami, Field Report/Evacuation, Traffic ... Problems Exposed], March 3. Article ID: K20100303EA0XX0090.

Kahoku Shinpo. (2010c). Chile Daijishin Tsunami/Hinanjo Riyo, Wazuka 6.5%/Dai 1 Pa Igo Tsugitsugito Kitaku Tohoku 4 Ken [Chile Big Quake Tsunami/Users of Evacuation Centers Only 6.5% of the warned / Went Back Home One after Another after the First Wave in Northeast Four Prefectures], March 2. Article ID: K20100302A206X0070.

Kahoku Shinpo. (2010d). Chile Daijishin Tsunami/Iwate Yamada Machi 1.61 Meter, Ozuchi Machi 1.45 Meter Dokuji Kansoku, Kuji no 1.2 Meter Uwamawaru [Chile Big Quake Tsunami/Iwate Yamda Town 1.61 Meter, Ozuchi Town 1.45 Meter by Their Own Measure, Surpassing 1.2 Meter in Kuji], March 4. Article ID: K20100304EA0XX0030.

Kahoku Shinpo. (2010e). Chile Jishin de Otsunami Keiho/Hinan Shiji wo Mushi, Jumin Tsugitsugito Kitaku/Iwate Engan Chiiki [Big Chile Quake Prompted Large Tsunami Warning/Ignoring Evacuation Order, Residents Went Back Home One After Another/ Iwate Coastal Area], March 1. Article ID: K20100301S103X0010.

Kahoku Shinpo. (2010f). Chile Jishin de Otsunami Keiho/Tohoku 32 Mannin ni Hinan Shiji [Big Chile Earthquake Prompted Large Tsunami Warning/Evacuation Order to 320,000 Persons in Northeast Japan], March 1. Article ID: K20100301A106X0010.

Kahoku Shinpo. (2010g). Chile Jishin Tsunami 50 Nen Kienu Kioku (2)/Densho/Kyohu to Kyokun, Sedai wo Koete [50 Years after the Chile Earthquake and Tsunami, Memory Is Not Gone (2)/Oral Transmission/Fear and Lessons Beyond Generations], May 20. Article ID: K20100520S106X0010.

Kahoku Shinpo. (2010h). Chile Jishin Tsunami 50 Nen Kienu Kioku (4)/Taisaku/Kiken Ninshiki shi Reisei na Kokoro wo [50 Years after the Chile Earthquake and Tsunami, Memory Is Not Gone (4)/Measures/Recognize Danger and Keep Cool Mind], May 22. Article ID: K20100522S206X0010.

Kahoku Shinpo. (2010i). Sonaeru/Chile Daijishin Otsunami Keiho Hatsurei … Tokoroga/ 'Konai' to Handan 6 Wari Sendaishi Shobokyoku Shimin Chosa/Hinan 2–4 Jikan Go/ Kitaku Tasu ga Kaijo Mae [Prepare/Chile Big Earthquake Large Tsunami Warning Issued … But/60% Figured 'It Wouldn't Come' Sendai City Fire Department Citizen Research/Evacuation 2–4 Hours Later/Majority Back Home Before the Cancel of the Warning], September 5. Article ID: K20100905M106X0010.

Kahoku Shinpo. (2010j). Sonaeru Jishin Bosai no Peji/Chile Jishin Tsunami Kyo 50 Nen/ Dakuryu ga Inochi wo Nonda [Preparing, Page for Prevention from Damages of Tsunami/Today 50 Years after the Chile Earthquake and Tsunami/Muddy Stream Swallowed Lives], May 24. Article ID: K20100524T10XX0010.

Kahoku Shinpo. (2011a). Kahoku Shunju [Kahoku in Spring and autumn] (Daily column on a special topic) April 3, Article ID: K20110403A106X0050.

Kahoku Shinpo. (2011b). Amakudari Yakunin Toden ni 51 Nin/Edano Keisansho ga Chosa Shiji [51 Former Officials Descended from Heaven to TEPCO/METI Minister Directed Investigation], September 27. Article ID: K20110927A40XX0080.

Kahoku Shinpo. (2011c). Fukushima Daiichi Genpatsu Jiko/Kunino Hoshano Kakusan Yosoku System Kochiku ni Fubi, Kakusan Yosoku no 'Kirifuda' Fuhatsu/Shisan Kekka Jissoku to Fugo/Konran Osore Kaiji Ninoashi [Fukushima Daiichi Nuclear Plant Accident/Defects with the Construction of the State Prediction System of Radioactivity Diffusion, 'the Trump Card' for Diffusion Prediction Did Not Work/ Simulation Results Matched Measured Results/Reluctant to Disclose in Fear of Disorder], April 19. Data ID: k20110419A306X0090.

Kahoku Shinpo. (2011d). Higashi Nihon Daishinsai/Iwate Kenritsu Hakubutsukan Shokuin, Tsunami Kinenhi Ou [East Japan Disaster/Employee of Iwate Prefectural Museum Seek Tsunami Monuments], December 5. Article ID: K20111205S206X0020.

Kahoku Shinpo. (2011e). Higashi Nihon Daishinsai/Jido 74 Nin Shibo Fumei/Ishinomaki Okawa Sho no 3.11 Anotoki. Nani wo Do Sureba ... [East Japan Disaster/74 School Children Dead or Missing/3.11 at Ishinomaki Okawa Elementary School, at That Time What and How to Do ...]", April 24. Article ID: K20110424S106X0010.

Kahoku Shinpo. (2011f). Higashi Nihon Daishinsai/Miyagi Engan Hinansha Anketo/Moto no Basho de Seikatsu 'Fuan' 7 Wari, Tsunami Bosai, Kahansu 'Ishiki sezu'/Kahoku Shinpo Sha [East Japan Disaster/Questionnaire on Evacuees in Miyagi Coastal Area/ 70% 'Uneasy' to Live Where Used to, Majority Not Conscious of Tsunami and Disaster Prevention/Kahoku Shinpo Company], April 11. Article ID: K20110411A106X0020.

Kahoku Shinpo. (2011g). Higashi Nihon Daishinsai/Shoten 3.11 Daishinsai/Bosai Kyoiku "Kiseki" Yobu (1) [East Japan Disaster/Focus 3.11 Disaster/Disaster Prevention Education Lead to "Miracle (1)", November 26. Article ID: K20111126A106X0010.

Kahoku Shinpo. (2011h). "Higashi Nihon Daishinsai/Shoten 3.11 Daishinsai/Bosai Kyoiku "Kiseki" Yobu (2) [East Japan Disaster/Focus 3.11 Disaster/Disaster Prevention Education Lead to "Miracle (2)", November 26. Article ID: K20111126S106X0010.

Kahoku Shinpo. (2011i). Zoom Up/Kasumigaseki ni 'Genshiryoku Mura', Keisan-Monbusho OB Zokuzoku, Koeki-Dokuritsu Gyosei Hojin he [Zoom Up/'Nuclear Village' in Kasumigaseki, Old Boys of METI- MEXT One after Another to Public Interest Corporations – Incorporated Administrative Agencies], May 19. Article ID: K20110519ZA0XX0010.

Kahoku Shinpo. (2012). Shoten/Jiko go mo Genpatsu Money Danomi/Ricchi no Fukushima, Okuma, Futaba, Tomioka, Naraha Machi [Focus/Dependent upon Nuclear Power Money even After the Accident/Power Source Fukushima Prefecture, and Okuma, Futaba, Tomioka and Naraha Town], May 13. Retrieved from http://www.kahoku.co.jp/spe/spe_sys1071/20120514_01.htm?style=print. Accessed on August 19, 2013.

Kikuchi, M. (2011, August). Naze Okawa Shogakko dake Dai Sanji ni Nattanoka (1)–(4) [Why Did Only Okawa Elementary School Meet the Big Disaster (1)–(4)]. *Chuo Koron*. Retrieved from http://www.chuokoron.jp/2011/07/post_87.html. Accessed on August 20, 2013.

New York Times. (2011). *Seawalls offered little protection against tsunami's crushing waves*. New York ed., , March 13, p. A8.

Shinsai Kensho. (2011winter). 1000 Nen Mae no Jogan Jishin no Jittai wo Akirakanishita 'Kyodai Tsunami' Kenkyu ha Ikasenakattanoka [Probing the disaster: Could we not utilize research findings on 'the Gigantic Tsunami' that had revealed realities of Jogan Earthquake 1000 years ago], Science Window. Retrieved from http://sciencewindow.jp/html/sw43/sr-earthquake. Accessed on August 20, 2013.

Shishikura, M., et al. (2010, August). *Heian no Hitobito ga Mita Kyodai Tsunami wo Saigensuru – Seireki 869 Nen Jogan Tsunami [Bringing Back Gigantic Tsunami that People Saw in Heian Period – Jogan Tsunami of 869 A.D.]*, AFERC News, No. 16, pp. 1–10.

The National Diet of Japan Fukushima Nuclear Accident Independent Investigation Commission. (2012a). *Appendix on survey of the evacuees from the Fukushima nuclear power plant accident*.

The National Diet of Japan Fukushima Nuclear Accident Independent Investigation Commission. (2012b). *Main report*, Chapter 1, Section 1.

The National Diet of Japan Fukushima Nuclear Accident Independent Investigation Commission. (2012c). *Main report*. Chapter 1, Sections 2 and 3.

The National Diet of Japan Fukushima Nuclear Accident Independent Investigation Commission. (2012d). *Main report*. Chapter 3, Section 6.
The National Diet of Japan Fukushima Nuclear Accident Independent Investigation Commission (2012e). *Main Report*. Chapter 1, pp. 2, 22–23.
The National Diet of Japan Fukushima Nuclear Accident Independent Investigation Commission. (2012f). *Main Report*, Chapter 5, Section 2.

BUSHFIRES AND AUSTRALIAN EMERGENCY MANAGEMENT LAW AND POLICY: ADAPTING TO CLIMATE CHANGE AND THE NEW FIRE AND EMERGENCY MANAGEMENT ENVIRONMENT

Michael Eburn

ABSTRACT

Modern emergency management policy is built around the concepts of shared responsibility and the development of resilient communities. Drawing on the Australian context, this chapter argues that giving effect to these policy directions will require negotiation between stakeholders and an inevitable trade in values, interests, and resources. The chapter identifies an apparent contradiction at the heart of modern disaster management: that improvements in establishing professional emergency and risk management services may have reduced the capacity of individuals and local communities to take responsibility for disaster preparation and response.

Keywords: Wildfire; Australia; shared responsibility; individual resilience

---

Special Issue: Cassandra's Curse: The Law and Foreseeable Future Disasters
Studies in Law, Politics, and Society, Volume 68, 155–188

ISSN: 1059-4337/doi:10.1108/S1059-433720150000068007

INTRODUCTION

Australia has always experienced the impact of natural hazards including destructive wildfires, storms, cyclones, and floods. Preparing for and responding to natural disasters was once a matter for local communities but is now a central function of government. Governments, however, realize that they are unable to manage emergencies on behalf of the community; what is required is a "national, coordinated and cooperative effort" involving individuals, communities, the business and nongovernment sectors, and all levels of government, local, state, and Federal.[1] The Australian *National Strategy for Disaster Resilience* is built around the concepts of shared responsibility for emergency management and the development of resilient communities that can prepare for, and withstand the impact of, natural hazards.[2] Giving effect to this high level policy statement will require negotiation between stakeholders about how responsibility is to be shared and how all aspects of prevention, preparation, response, and recovery will be managed in the new policy landscape. These changes will be negotiated against the backdrop of Australian society's norms and laws.

This chapter explores some issues that will influence implementation of the *National Strategy*. The chapter is presented in five sections. The sections "Introduction" and "Methodology" introduce the chapter and the methodology used. The section "Natural Hazards and Risks in Australia" explores the threat of natural hazards in Australia with discussion of the expected impact of climate change on the Australian risk profile. The section "Identifying The Measure of Success: What Level of Resilience Should We Aim For?" traces the history of Australia's emergency management policy and introduces the latest national policy statement, the *National Strategy for Disaster Resilience*.[3] The section "Building Resilience in the Face of Decreasing Individual Capacity and Increasing Expectations" identifies a number of issues and argues that these must be understood if the National Strategy is to be translated into effective action at the government and local levels. Finally "Conclusions" section provides some concluding comments.

Although written with an Australian focus the issues are universal. All governments and citizens have to consider how responsibility for risk and hazards will be allocated between governments, communities, and individuals, and what trade-offs they are willing to make in the name of safety.

METHODOLOGY

This chapter draws on relevant literature and primary legal sources. It also features insights offered by some of the chief officers of Australia's fire and emergency services who were asked to consider what are, or should be, the measures of success in emergency management. Semi-structured interviews of between 30 and 120 minutes were conducted with officers who attended an Australasian Fire and Emergency Services Authorities Council (AFAC) Command Forum and who agreed to take part.

Australia has very centralized emergency services with each of the six states and two self-governing territories operating police, ambulance, fire, and emergency services. Generally speaking, local governments do not operate their own emergency service but are serviced by the state or territory agencies. Most jurisdictions operate up to three fire services: an urban fire service, a rural or country fire service, and fire fighting services within public land agencies such as state forests and national parks. They also operate a state or territory emergency service to respond to floods, storms, and other emergencies. There were 36 officers at the Command Forum representing 27 separate fire and emergency service agencies from each Australian jurisdiction as well as New Zealand. Interviews were conducted with 18 officers (50%), representing 16 agencies (60%) and seven of the nine (including New Zealand) jurisdictions (77%).

Due to a technical failure, all but two of the interviews were recorded and fully transcribed. For the two interviews that were not recorded, notes made during the interview were relied on. The data were manually analyzed to identify the range of opinions on what the agency chiefs saw as issues in developing community resilience. The interviews were given with a commitment to anonymity, accordingly the identity of the relevant research participants, when quoted below, is undisclosed. The research was approved by the Australian National University's Human Research Ethics Committee (2011).

NATURAL HAZARDS AND RISKS IN AUSTRALIA

Australia is a large island continent lying between the Indian and Pacific oceans. With a land mass in excess of 7.6 million square kilometers,[4] Australia is only slightly smaller than the continental United States.

Australia is, however, sparsely populated with a population of just 23 million ABS (2013), or an average population density of 2.9 people per square kilometer. The majority of Australians live in the urban centers along the eastern seaboard ABS (2011).

The Australian population faces a number of natural hazards or risks.

- Tropical cyclones (hurricanes, typhoons) produce destructive winds, torrential rains, storm tides, and high seas. Tropical cyclones occur seasonally, with the majority occurring between December and April.
- Heavy rainfall can cause both riverine floods and flash floods. Floods are the most costly natural disasters in Australia and have caused over 2,300 deaths since 1790.
- Severe storms occur more frequently than any other natural hazard and have the potential to occur anywhere in Australia. They range from isolated thunderstorms to intense low pressure systems and can produce storm tides, lightning and thunder, hail, tornadoes, water spouts, damaging winds, and flash floods.
- Bush or wildfires pose a threat in nearly all parts of the country at different times of the year.
- Landslides are predominantly triggered by an increase in pore water pressure from intense short duration or prolonged rainfall.
- Earthquakes are rare as Australia is a tectonically stable region. Notwithstanding this stability, significant earthquakes have occurred. The 1989 Newcastle earthquake is Australia's single biggest earthquake event which left 13 people dead and 160 injured.
- Tsunamis have affected Australia but without any loss to life.[5]

To date Australia's worst natural disaster was the Spanish Flu epidemic of 1918/1919 that took in excess of 10,000 lives. Heatwaves are a leading cause of death; and the heatwaves of 1939 and 2009 were both followed by catastrophic wildfires. The 2009 Black Saturday wildfires were the worst wildfires on record, claiming 173 lives, but the event is listed as the 16th most costly event in terms of lives lost, and the 8th most expensive based on insured, nonadjusted dollars.[6]

Vulnerability and climate change. Natural hazard events are not disasters. An extreme flood, storm, or wildfire does not qualify as a disaster unless it strikes a vulnerable population or valued assets:

> ... a disaster occurs when a disaster agent exposes the vulnerability of a group or groups in such a way that their lives are directly threatened or sufficient harm has been done to economic and social structures, inevitably undermining their ability to survive.[7]

Climate change is expected to lead to an increase in the number and severity of hazard events,[8] and will also affect vulnerability; rising sea levels and coastal erosion may bring larger populations closer to the coastal edge making them more vulnerable to events such as storm surge or tsunami. Although there are uncertainties as to the extent of the impact, and there will be regional variations, current climate change science predicts a future experiencing greater frequency, and intensity, of wildfires, storms, cyclones, and other hazards and therefore, greater impacts on more people and places.[9]

Australia is, generally speaking, well prepared to deal with natural hazards. Australian emergency management doctrine is based on the comprehensive approach that embraces "the aspects of prevention, preparedness, response, and recovery (PPRR)."[10] Through community engagement, land use planning, mitigation strategies, and the development of early warning systems the government and communities prepare for expected events and take steps to minimize their impact. The states and territories have in place emergency plans, supported by well resourced, though largely volunteer, emergency services that are able to respond to fires and other hazards and are largely successful in controlling their impact without major loss of life or property damage.[11]

According to one view, adapting to the new hazard environment that climate change is expected to bring may be preparing for more of the same: more resources to deal with more fires, more floods, and more storms.[12] However, with any significant increase in the extent, impact, or number of natural hazard events, such an approach may be stretched, may not be affordable, or may not adequately protect at-risk populations. More of the same may not be sufficient to adapt to climate change.

The US Federal Emergency Management Agency (FEMA) considered what emergency management might look like in 2030. Its report concluded that:

> ... the emergency management community faces *increasing complexity and decreasing predictability in its operating environment*. Complexity will take the form of more incidents, new and unfamiliar threats, more information to analyze (possibly with less time to process it), new players and participants, sophisticated technologies, and exceedingly high public expectations. This combination will create a vastly different landscape for risk assessment and operational planning. Pressure to perform in this environment will be extraordinary.[13]

Adapting to a new climate environment and the increased extreme events that accompany it will require a different approach.

Australian Emergency Management Policy, Past and Present

Historically the fire and emergency services were made up of local volunteers effectively coming together to form a self-help group supplemented by brigades operated by local governments or insurance companies.[14] Over time the various brigades were brought under the control of an organizing authority or board but they remained largely independent.[15] In enacting legislation, the governments did not necessarily see their role as protecting people from fire. Victoria's first fire brigade legislation, the *Fire Brigades Act 1890* (Vic) was an Act to improve the administration of fire brigades. This Act empowered the local municipalities that had an interest in providing fire protection to do so if they wished;[16] it did not require them to do so. There was clearly no expectation that local government, let alone state government, would necessarily set up fire brigades to provide protection for the community, let alone to protect private assets or that emergency response was a central government activity.

Today emergency management is seen as a core or central government activity. In Victoria, statutory authorities such as the Metropolitan Fire and Emergency Services Board and the Country Fire Authority manage fire brigades and the delivery of fire services are subject to the direction and control of the Minister.[17] In New South Wales, the emergency services are centrally located as divisions of the Government service rather than independent statutory authorities.[18] The Federal Attorney-General is also the Minister for Emergency Management and the Commonwealth provides direct financial assistance to affected states and communities. Australian governments have moved from a laissez-faire or simply enabling approach to disaster response to providing direct personal assistance[19] in the event of an emergency.

Shared Responsibility and Resilient Communities

In the 1990s, in what may be seen as a return to the self-help days of the past, the "state agency-centered approach to hazard management began to be replaced by a model that sought to make community members increasingly self-reliant".[20] In the most recent, and high level policy statement, the *National Strategy for Disaster Resilience*, all Australian governments committed to strengthen

> ... the nation's resilience to disasters by:
>
> - developing and implementing effective, risk-based land management and planning arrangements and other mitigation activities;

- having effective arrangements in place to inform people about how to assess risks and reduce their exposure and vulnerability to hazards;
- having clear and effective education systems so people understand what options are available and what the best course of action is in responding to a hazard as it approaches;
- supporting individuals and communities to prepare for extreme events;
- ensuring the most effective, well-coordinated response from our emergency services and volunteers when disaster hits; and
- working in a swift, compassionate and pragmatic way to help communities recover from devastation and to learn, innovate and adapt in the aftermath of disastrous events.[21]

In this policy world, resilience will be supported by business, nongovernment organizations, and community organizations. It will be "based on individuals taking their share of responsibility for preventing, preparing for, responding to and recovering from disasters."[22] As the 2009 Victorian Bushfires Royal Commission explained "Shared responsibility … [will] create a situation in which the State, municipal councils, individuals, household members and the broader community all contribute to mitigating bushfire risk …."[23]

The vision is of resilient communities that share responsibility for hazard management. In this policy view, the community, or communities (however defined) will understand their risks, know how to, and in fact, prepare to face those risks. Community members will have identified steps that can be and are taken to minimize the impact of the event (e.g., by building hazard resistant homes or adopting other engineering solutions), there will be a plan on how to react when the hazard occurs and everyone will know who will do what to respond during and after the event. Communities will plan for the recurring event but also the extreme or catastrophic event. They may put in place mitigation for the 1 in 250 year flood event but will understand that mitigation measures will not protect them from more extreme events, such as the rare, but not impossible, 1 in 500 year flood event, and will plan accordingly. The emergency services will continue to respond but they will focus more on education and information, rather than response. As one of Australia's chief emergency service officers said:

> Our role is really to lead and educate so the community can understand, accept and manage their own risk … Focusing on response all the time, we're always going to be failing because a response is a failure. (Research participant interview #10).

Even so, natural hazards will occur and the emergency services will continue to respond. They will, particularly in rural and regional Australia, continue to be staffed by volunteers drawn from the community they serve, supported by a regional or State headquarters and resources. Maintaining volunteer emergency services will be part of the State's contribution to a resilient community.

A Word on Communities

The *National Strategy* aims to build resilient communities but does not define what is meant by community. Community may be defined by geographical location, for example the "Canberra Community" or by a community of interest such as the "Arabic community" or the community of "South's fans" or the "older community." People will belong to many communities and the strengths of the ties to their community will depend on many factors.[24]

Notwithstanding, or perhaps because of, these difficulties the *National Strategy* avoids defining community resilience. Rather than give a definition, the *National Strategy* describes disaster-resilient communities as having the following characteristics: "functioning well while under stress; successful adaptation; self-reliance; and social capacity."[25]

In the discussion that follows reference will be made to community and communities given that developing "resilient communities" is a fundamental objective of the National Strategy and, probably, we all have some understanding of the term community. Comprehensively defining "community" for bushfire and natural hazard management is, however, a matter of controversy[26] and beyond the scope of this chapter.

Creating Resilient Communities and Shared Responsibility

As an overarching policy goal the mutual ideas of the resilient community and shared responsibility are laudable, but translating that vision into a practical reality that will allow Australians to face the increased threats brought by climate change will require significantly more detail and a commitment to deal with impediments to the policy goal. The discussion that follows identifies some issues that need to be understood in order to translate the policy goal into a lived reality.

Assessing Risk is an Exercise in Politics, not Statistics

Risk can be assessed and described as a probability. For example, living in a 1 in 100 year flood zone means there is a 1% chance that, in any year, the land will be subject to flooding. Living in a 1 in 50 year flood zone increases the risk to a 2% annual chance of flooding; living in a 1 in 250 year flood zone reduces the risk to a 0.4% chance of flooding in any one year, but a person who buys a house in a 1 in 250 year flood plain, and who is flooded out the next year, has not necessarily misunderstood their risk nor has the risk assessment been wrong; a 0.4% chance event is unlikely but clearly possible.

Assessing and managing risk is not, however, simply a matter of having accurate risk figures or an understanding of their meaning. There is nothing inherent in a 2%, 1%, or 0.4% risk that says one risk is or should be acceptable, but another risk is too high. Policy both in the United States and Australia has been to restrict residential development to land above the 1 in 100 year flood level but not because that is an objectively acceptable risk. Wegner, Hussey, and Pittock (2013, p. 194) argue that:

> The 1 in 100 year flood was selected as an actuarial standard for the purposes of implementing the National Flood Insurance Program in 1971, and its effect has been to concentrate development just beyond the limits of the 1 in 100 year event. The selection of the 1 in 100 flood was arbitrary, and was not based on "sound scientific and scientific statistical foundations." Rather, it represents a compromise that balances flood losses against excessive floodplain regulation.

Everything carries risk, living in an urban area may not carry a risk of wildfire but there is still a risk that homes will be lost to fire. Living on the wildland urban interface (or WUI) may carry a very high risk of wildfire that living on cleared farmland does not, but that does not mean the farm land carries no risk or that the risk calculation was wrong when the farm house is razed by wildfire whilst homes on the WUI are spared.

A resilient community, one that can face, respond to, and then recover from a natural hazard event, not only has to understand its risks but also determine what risks are acceptable and what ones are not. Determining what is an acceptable risk, and what are acceptable mitigation measures necessarily involves compromise. It is apparent but not often made explicit that determining how compromise is to be made is political:

> Politics is *the* essential ingredient for producing workable policies, which are more publicly accountable and politically justifiable ... While some are uncomfortable with the notion that politics can enhance rational decision-making, preferring to see politics as expediency, it is integral to the process of securing defensible outcomes. *We are unable to combine values, interests and resources in ways which are not political*.[27]

As the argument below will show, defining what risks are acceptable and what price communities and individuals are willing to pay to improve personal and community safety, is absolutely about "values, interests and resources" and therefore requires political compromise. Merely establishing that an area, such as a flood plain or the WUI carries a high risk of danger does not, of itself, demonstrate what, if any, action should be taken to mitigate that risk.

Values

In their final report, the Commissioners inquiring into the 2009 "Black Saturday" wildfires said "the Commission examined particular localities, all of them close to bush and posing an unacceptably high threat to human safety."[28] They recommended that

> The State develop and implement a retreat and resettlement strategy for existing developments in areas of unacceptably high bushfire risk, including a scheme for non-compulsory acquisition by the State of land in these areas.[29]

The Royal Commission's recommendation, if followed, may be an effective policy to reduce exposure to risk but it assumes there is an objective measure of what is an "unacceptably high risk." The Commission did not explain to whom it is unacceptable or who should decide what is, or is not, an acceptable risk. The Commission did not recommend that individuals consider their risk and how they may adapt to it, rather the Commission told them, and the state, that the risk *is* unacceptable.

Notwithstanding the Commission's view, the Premier of Victoria said:

> We have hundreds of thousands of Victorians who choose to live in our bush and in areas close to our beautiful state and national parks. These places are, by their very definition, in high fire-danger-risk areas, but I will always defend people's right to live in these areas and enjoy the beauty of our natural bush.[30]

In the Premier's mind, a person's right to live in high risk areas is to prevail over the State's interest in removing them from risk; individual choice is to prevail. If, however, people are going to remain in these high risk areas, research emphasizes the importance of reducing or removing fuels immediately around houses to protect from wildfire.[31] Nonetheless, requiring everyone to build a 50 m concrete slab around their home may reduce the bushfire risk but that may impose such a financial cost, and represent a diminution in other values, that it may be a cost individuals or the community are not prepared to pay.

One chief officer, who inspected the areas affected by the 2009 Victorian fires, explained the problem:

> If you step back and you say, well, how could we have prevented that fire? Here's the strategy ... Clear every tree for 100 metres each side of the road winding up ... all that littoral forest and beautiful tall timber ... Get rid of all the timber cottages in the village. They're 100 years old ... made of timber and highly volatile. Put brick and concrete structures in place. Put perimeter hazard reduction around the village every two years ... I can tell you now if we had put that strategy in place the public would have said f___ off ... So if you step back and look at where [place name] sat in the landscape, and you look at the forest and 10 years of drought and accumulated fuel loads ... what part of inevitability didn't we get here? (Research participant interview #8)

Verchick (2010) says "Living near the arctic, or on a tropical shore, or in earthquake country, means taking a chance ..."; to that list can be added living on the wildland urban interface, a flood plain, in a crowded urban environment, an open plain, the "bush" or the forest. Everywhere carries its own risk so the objective is not to remove all risk but to "keep safe."

> "Keeping safe" means assessing and managing risk in ways that capture the full spectrum of values at stake in the context of preparing for catastrophic harm. Too often, important environmental or engineering decisions are made according to economic models that emphasize cost savings or commercial development but downplay public safety. (Verchick, 2010)

Decision-making is, no doubt, complex and people may be misled by heuristic shortcuts and biases[32] but if, for the sake of the argument, we assume that people are capable of putting their shortcuts and biases aside, and can properly understand and make a rational response to risk, then issues such as "cost savings or commercial developments" as well as living in high risk areas to "enjoy the beauty of our natural bush" or the American wildland urban interface can all be a legitimate part of the "full spectrum of values at stake." If governments are going to share the responsibility for risk management with individuals, or communities then there has to be room for those individuals and communities to prioritize those values in a way that is both rational and informed, even if others, including governments, would prefer to give greater priority to values of individual or public safety.

A simple example may demonstrate the point; driving a car 333 miles in the United Kingdom carries a one in a million chance of dying whilst riding a motorcycle 28 miles carries a four in a million chance of dying.[33] Assuming the risk remains constant, traveling approximately 333 miles carries a one in a million chance of death for the car driver and a 48 in a million chance of death for the motorcyclist.[34] Whilst the risk that either the car driver, or the motorcyclist will die is low, the motorcyclist is 48 times more likely to die than the car driver; clearly motorcycle riding is more dangerous than driving. Some people, including legislators, may think the risk of dying in a motorcycle accident is too high, but that does not mean that motorcycle riders cannot make an alternative assessment, taking into account the chance of dying balanced against the cost of running a motorcycle and the enjoyment they get from motorcycle riding. If a motorcycle rider dies in a motorcycle accident it does not mean their risk assessment was wrong or that their risk assessment failed to "capture the full spectrum of values at stake." Their decision to ride a motorcycle, assuming they understood the risk, reflected not only the values at stake, but also their personal prioritization of those values.

If individuals and communities are to take responsibility for their own risk, then governments, insurers, and other communities should accept that those individuals and communities are free to make choices that others would not make. Governments may need to take steps to ensure that people have the best information available to allow them to "capture the full spectrum of values at stake,"[35] but having considered their risk they should be allowed to make decisions about where and how they want to live (and that may include living in the bush or forest or on the flood plain) and be active partners in the negotiation of how responsibility for responding to and recovering from the impact of the risk when it does materialize will be shared between individuals, communities, and government. That negotiation may lead to a conclusion that responsibility for recovering after a predicted hazard is not a matter for government; in simple terms, if you want to live in some high risk areas, you have to own the risk that your property will be damaged or your life lost.

If, on the other hand, governments believe that individuals or communities are actually incapable of "assessing and managing risk in ways that capture the full spectrum of values at stake" then a different approach to the concepts of shared responsibility and resilient communities is required. If individuals and communities are incapable of making those assessments or rational decisions then someone else – the government, a Royal Commission or professional emergency managers and land use planners – may have to determine when a locality poses "an unacceptably high threat to human safety" and what should be done to mitigate that risk. In that case shared responsibility means government and emergency service agencies "have a responsibility to provide advice. They [the people at risk] have a responsibility to take up on that advice or to adhere to that advice" (Research participant interview #11).

At one extreme, hazard risk mitigation can be left entirely to individuals or communities (however defined) and provided that they have the tools and information to assess risk they can be left to their own choices no matter how foolish they appear to others. At the other extreme, governments will determine what an acceptable risk is and regulate or mandate the response to that risk by prohibiting some developments, imposing rigid building codes, mandating and policing obligations for ongoing hazard management practices, and the like. The appropriate share of responsibility lies between those two extremes.

As Burton argues in this volume, states sit along a spectrum of hazard regulation and where they choose to sit reflects "variations in the hierarchical ordering of ... values."[36] In Australia local governments are a creation of state government; that is, they are established and empowered by state or territory legislation[37] and required to give effect to state or territory land use planning policy.[38] All of the Australian states and territories would be what Burton calls "common standard" states.

Although the Australian states and territories do move to restrict development in high risk areas, the Australian common law tends to favor a libertarian approach. People are free to do what they like unless their actions are prohibited by law. The common law does not require governments or their agencies to rescue individuals, and there is no obligation to protect people from the impact of their own decisions. The High Court of Australia, Australia's ultimate court of appeal and the Australian equivalent of the US Supreme Court, had to consider whether or not members of a state police force owed any duty to detain a person they found sitting in a car apparently considering suicide and who did, later, take his own life. In the course of their joint reasons, dismissing the widow's claim, Justices Gummow, Hayne, and Heydon said:

> Personal autonomy is a value that informs much of the common law ... As Dixon J said in *Smith v Leurs*, "[t]he general rule is that one man is under no duty of controlling another man to prevent his doing damage to a third"... The common law has been described as "individualistic", the civil law as "more socially impregnated."
>
> It may be said that the notion of personal autonomy is imprecise, if only because it will often imply some notion of voluntary action or freedom of choice ... But expressed in the most general way, the value described as personal autonomy leaves it to the individual to decide whether to engage in conduct that may cause that individual harm. As Lord Hope of Craighead put it in *Reeves v Commissioner of Police of the Metropolis*, "[o]n the whole people are entitled to act as they please, even if this will inevitably lead to their own death or injury."[39]

Justices Crennan and Kiefel said:

> The common law generally does not impose a duty upon a person to take affirmative action to protect another from harm. Such an approach is regarded as fundamental to the common law ... So far as concerns situations brought about by the action of the person at risk, it is the general view of the common law that such persons should take responsibility for their own actions. In this, English law has been seen to have an affinity with Roman law, in its reluctance to interfere or to encourage interference with the freedom of the individual.[40]

Legislation, including land use planning laws, are written and understood in the context of the common law rights and freedoms. Although the states and territories can, and do, regulate to restrict personal freedoms to ensure others, whether rescuers, local communities, neighbors, or subsequent purchasers, are not exposed to risk or hidden dangers, they go a step further if they require people to take action for their own benefit. Legislation that does restrict personal freedoms will be strictly interpreted to maintain to the largest extent possible, recognized common law rights and freedoms.[41]

What follows is that risk assessment is not just about mathematical probability; it reflects our values and the values we place on those things at risk, whether that is life, liberty, or a home amongst the trees. Values are fundamental in determining what is or is not an acceptable risk.

Interests

Making decisions on developing resilience requires balancing interests: community interests against individual interests, short term interests against longer term interests.

In Australia's Byron Bay, located on the eastern-most point of the Australian mainland, the local government adopted a policy of "planned retreat" that:

> [I]n certain coastal areas the type of development is restricted within certain distances of the erosion escarpment. Development is to be relocatable so that as erosion moves landward, development can be removed, rather than development being prevented at all times. Planned retreat maximises the limited use of land until such time as coastal hazards are realised and only once land becomes too threatened by coastal processes is development meant to be removed and further use of the land for residential purposes prevented.[42]

Notwithstanding this policy, one landowner took active steps to rebuild a sea wall that was severely damaged by storms in 2009. Consistent with the council's policy, the council declined to repair the wall or give approval to the landowner to repair it. The landowner argued that when the council built the wall in 2001 they, by implication, agreed to maintain it, and if they would not, he was entitled to do so in order to protect his property. The council sought an injunction to restrain the landowner from repairing the wall. In the Land and Environment Court, Justice Pain said:

> The Council is seeking to enforce a public law, the EP&A [*Environmental Planning and Assessment*] Act. The Respondents argue the status quo is to allow them to erect the sandbag wall as built by the Council which previously existed on the Respondents' land. The Council argues that due to circumstances beyond the Council's control in relation to recent extreme and unpredictable weather events the situation has fundamentally altered and it does not follow that the sandbag wall as previously constructed should be erected. The wall was constructed in accordance with the 2001 consent and has now been effectively destroyed ... the situation is now different from when the consent was granted. Further, there is likely to be environmental harm resulting if that work occurs.
>
> ... to do any work in isolation on the Respondents' land will result in potentially adverse impacts elsewhere ... in the event that work was undertaken in front of the Respondents' land in the absence of work being done on the beach in front of neighbouring land, further damage will occur at other properties. All this evidence reinforces my view that work done in isolation on one property is likely to have adverse impacts on neighbouring properties ....[43]

In that case the court issued the injunction, putting the community interests and the interests of others ahead of the interest of this landowner, but in subsequent litigation the injunction was removed to allow the landowner to maintain the wall as it was before the 2009 storm.[44] The issue of the wall's longer term remediation remains before the court.

This extreme example, demonstrates that the issue of risk management is not simply a question of community choice (planned retreat) or application of a scientific formula of costs and benefits. Critical to the issue of risk management policy is the balance of interests, in this case between the individual and the community, represented by the local council. How those interests can be balanced can be determined judicially. Clarification by law reform to strengthen the power of governments or other relevant authorities is also a possibility. Regardless of the balance, or the means used to make final decisions, the point remains that managing risk necessarily requires a balance of interests and balancing competing interests necessarily involves a political decision and political decision-making.

Resources

Although risk exposure can be reduced, at some point the community has to identify when the costs exceed the benefits.

> Would society ever allow governments to spend the money necessary to establish a full-time, fully equipped, professional fire-suppression force with adequate training for dealing with large, rare, high intensity fires burning into the urban-interface under the worst possible weather and, possibly, fuel conditions? If it did, such supply would be excessive for the vast majority of the time .... (Gill, 2009, p. 156).

The 2009 Victorian Bushfires Royal Commission recommended that high risk power lines be buried.[45] Research by the Powerline Bushfire Safety Taskforce (2011) found that the Victorian community was unwilling to pay the cost of meeting that recommendation. Demands that the State do "whatever it takes"[46] to ensure that a similar disaster does not occur again[47] are unrealistic; they are unrealistic as natural hazards, whether floods, fires, or storms, are inevitable[48] and likely to increase and, as noted above, no government or community can afford to invest in the type of capacity required to meet "large, rare, high intensity" events but which would spend most of its time sitting idle.[49] Ashe, de Oliveira, and McAneney (2012) have further argued that there is already an overinvestment in fire prevention. If money were taken out of fire prevention there may be more fire and more lives lost due to fire, but more lives could be saved by diverting the funding to deal with other more common threats to public health.

Risk Assessment is Political

It follows that deciding how to prioritize safety against other values is not a simple matter of assessing the risk and measuring that risk against an objective measure of low, medium, high, or unacceptable. Deciding what is acceptable and what is not requires a consideration of "values, interests and resources," that is, it is a political decision.[50] To say the decision is "political" is not to dismiss it or to suggest that it is a matter only for politicians. How responsibility for risk assessment and risk mitigation is to be shared between individuals, communities, and central governments reflects, or should reflect, a political consensus on how and when obligations should be imposed upon individuals in the interest of community self-defense, the willingness of individuals to give up personal autonomy, and whether participation in community protection is mandatory or voluntary. To return to Burton's chapter, determining an appropriate response to statistical risk requires a debate on how to prioritize the values of historicity, identity, mutuality, plurality, autonomy, participation, and integration.

The process we have to balance those values and interests is politics, where people can argue and press their case and in a democracy try to persuade the electorate or the electorate's representatives, to act on their view.

The outcome is often messy with no single interest, including safety, the dominant winner. If, however, governments are to guide communities along the path to resilience they must engage the community to mutually determine what the acceptable levels of risk are and how competing "values, interests and resources" are to be balanced. Sharing responsibility for developing resilience, locally and at state and national level, requires a deliberate discussion on these issues and a willingness to live with the consequences.

IDENTIFYING THE MEASURE OF SUCCESS: WHAT LEVEL OF RESILIENCE SHOULD WE AIM FOR?

Perhaps more important than identifying how responsibility for risk management is to be shared, is identifying what resilience looks like or what level of resilience is to be achieved. A measure of success is required to identify whether the outcome of an event, even if it involves loss of life and property, represents an effective response to the particular hazard. In his review of the 2011 Perth Hills wildfires former Australian Federal Police Commissioner[51] said:

> There remains one question the answer to which eluded the Special Inquiry but it is an answer that requires further examination and that is: What is the measure of success of the outcome of a bushfire? Is the loss of no lives the only performance measure? If so, how many houses is an acceptable number to lose?

The objectives of Australian emergency management policies are not clearly defined. Neither the Commonwealth, nor the states and territories, have a clear statement on what emergency management policy is meant to achieve. Without a clear statement of objectives, it is hard to identify whether or not a particular outcome is a success or failure.

A policy statement should, inter alia, describe the desired policy direction and give details on how that will be implemented, measured, monitored, and evaluated.[52] Most statements on Australian emergency management policy fail to state the policy direction or goal and fail to indicate how that goal will be achieved or how it will be monitored and evaluated.

The *National Strategy for Disaster Resilience* identifies the objective of building resilience but gives no indication on how stakeholders will identify when the goal has been reached or how resilient communities should be;

should community infrastructure be designed to withstand the 1 in 100 year flood, or the 1 in 1,000 year event?

A disaster-resilient nation is "... one in which its communities, through mitigation and pre-disaster preparation, develop the adaptive capacity to maintain important community functions and recover quickly when major disasters occur."[53] Australia, at a national level, and even down to a state and regional level demonstrates a high degree of resilience. In 2003 uncontrolled wildfires burned into urban Canberra, the national capital, but there was no threat to the operation of the federal government. Four lives and approximately 500 homes were lost, but important community functions were maintained and the city recovered reasonably quickly.

The fact that Australia's populations and cities have not been devastated is testament to the nation's resilience; an ability to prepare for, and quickly recover from these events, but is our current level of resilience sufficient? Floods, fires, and storms, even in the nature of the 2003 Canberra and 2009 Victorian fires, the Victorian and Queensland floods of 2011 and 2012 and cyclones such as Cyclone Larry (2006) and Cyclone Yasi (2011) are, in the Australian context, relatively routine or, at least not out of the ordinary but "coping with moderate events may not be a true indicator of preparedness for a great one."[54] Although the Black Saturday fires that burned through Victoria in 2009 were devastating, claiming 173 lives and thousands of homes, worse fires can be imagined and are likely. In the context of climate change – and even within the current climate envelope – catastrophic fires will occur again, and if those fires impact upon many jurisdictions at the same time (as they did in February 1983 when the "Ash Wednesday" fires burned in Victoria and South Australia and which were, prior to 2009, the worst wildfires on record) and impact on heavily-populated areas such as Sydney's Blue Mountains, Canberra, or the Adelaide Hills, the consequences may be much worse. The cumulative impact on emergency management and response capacities of more concurrent and/or closely spaced events is an important implication of climate change.

The objective of emergency management policy cannot be to build a community that has been so engineered that no flood or fire can occur. There will always be earthquakes, fires, floods, and storms. Because we live on the planet, people will still be affected by those events, and tragically people will suffer losses and die. To expect anything else is unrealistic. Accordingly, disaster resilience policy has to identify what level of resilience is acceptable. That will involve asking serious questions about the level of loss that is acceptable.

The issue of who should be asking and answering such questions is of course at the heart of the politics of disaster management. Once those decisions have been made, living with the remaining residual risk must include being prepared to accept that adverse outcomes remain possible if not inevitable, and not all losses therefore represent a failure of policy.

BUILDING RESILIENCE IN THE FACE OF DECREASING INDIVIDUAL CAPACITY AND INCREASING EXPECTATIONS

Australia's emergency service chief officers are concerned that individual, and with it community, resilience is decreasing rather than increasing. As one chief officer reported, people now call upon the emergency services rather than looking to themselves to deal with the impact of natural hazards:

> If I think about every time we get a storm these days, if a tree falls over somebody's front fence or their garage, immediately they ring the SES [State Emergency Service]. So the SES … are seeing much more demand. I think that's because the government has done a fantastic job – and these agencies [have] done a fantastic job in marketing themselves and telling them that they're around. So, instead of people saying, listen I'll sort that out, their immediate response is to ring the SES and they'll come and cut it down for them …
>
> I think that's what's happening in fire too … a lot of our research is saying that people are still going to hang around until the last minute and generally they're going to want answers and somebody to tell them what to do. (Research participant interview #16)

This is perceived as a diminution in personal resilience and may be attributed to a number of factors including the creation of a risk averse society. Individuals have been encouraged to undertake a risk assessment of all aspects of their lives and to avoid unnecessary risk. The lead in this area is in workplace health and safety where, in one sense, shared responsibility is paramount. Modern workplace health and safety laws impose health and safety obligations on everyone involved in the workplace, from employees and visitors, to the person undertaking the business enterprise, and the supplier of goods and materials.[55] That model of shared responsibility may not, however, improve individual resilience. Under that model, responsibility is shared by recognizing a risk and calling on others to deal with it; today's office workers cannot change their office light bulb, rather they are trained to understand that standing on the desk or chair is not safe and to call in the workplace electrician. If that understanding is transferred to the home, a resilient home owner may recognize the risk posed by a tree that has fallen on their roof, and, being resilient, they know not to expose themselves to danger but to call on the very service that has been established to assist them. The presence of a volunteer emergency service, such as the State Emergency Service is further evidence of community resilience. It is members of the community who volunteer to undertake the necessary training, and it is the state that ensures that they have the necessary equipment, so that individuals can safely call upon them to remove fallen trees or fight fires.

In the context of wildfire, the idea that people can take action to develop their own resilience is controversial. Prior to the 2009 Victorian fires, Australian wildfire policy was summed up as "stay or go" but more comprehensively as "prepare, stay and defend or leave early." The policy was predicated on the assumption that the vulnerability of a prepared and informed resident is not self-evident. With adequate prior preparation property owners can reduce their vulnerability and effectively defend themselves and their home.

This policy, developed during the 1990s, represented "a broad paradigm shift ... away from an agency-centered approach and towards shared responsibility between emergency services and the community." The policy identified a "critical role of the public in preparing for and responding to bushfire threat" and encouraged "greater community self reliance" rather than relying on or expecting the state agencies to manage their safety during an emergency.[56]

Notwithstanding this policy view, when dismissing an application to strike out an action against the State of New South Wales alleging negligence in the State's response to wildfires in 2003, Chief Justice Higgins said:

> ... A bushfire hazard is clearly a danger to persons and their property and only an organised, trained and equipped service such as the Rural Fire Service could have any prospect of averting danger from a serious bushfire.
>
> The vulnerability of the prospective victims is self-evident, particularly if they are or may be assumed to lack the resources to protect themselves.[57]

In 2008 Chief Justice Higgins' view that *only* a fire brigade could avert danger and that homeowners and residents were self-evidently vulnerable was at least inconsistent with the then current bushfire response policy and the evidence, then available, that people can take positive action to defend themselves and their property.

The 2009 Victorian Bushfires Royal Commission was critical of the policy that framed the individual's options in such an oversimplified way as "stay or go" … Many factors affect the choice to stay and defend, or leave early, as well as what triggers people will wait for before deciding to act. The Royal Commission recommended that bushfire policy be adapted to more accurately reflect human behavior:

> The stay or go policy tended to assume that individuals had a fire plan and knew what to do when warned about a bushfire threat. But many people did not have a well-thought-out plan and were left to make their own decisions without the benefit of assistance from the authorities … The Commission heard that many people wait to see what eventuates before leaving in response to a range of prompts, such as a fire being in their area, the situation becoming dangerous or being told to leave. For these people the lack of alternatives – the provision of shelters and refuges or evacuation – can become critical because they have no fallback option … the reality is people will continue to wait and see, and a comprehensive policy must respond to this by allowing for more options and better warnings.[58]

As a result of the Commission's recommendations, a number of changes were made to bushfire policy. A new category of "catastrophic" fire danger was introduced to stress that if a fire occurs on those days, it cannot be controlled; statutory duties to warn were introduced;[59] councils and the Country Fire Authority were required to work together to identify neighborhood safer places to serve as places of last resort,[60] and legislative reform was made to allow the Country Fire Authority to give specific advice on whether a property is or is not defendable.[61] Such practices may well advance the goal of saving human life, but they also reflect a shift from the earlier policy view, that the decision to stay or go was always a decision for the individual and that they were responsible for their level of preparation and response. The changes imposed an increased responsibility on the state to not only assist residents to prepare, but to prepare for and provide for people who did not leave early, whose plans failed, or who refused or neglected to plan for their own fire safety.

Shifts in capacity and attitude such as those discussed, above, have created an environment where the expectations of individuals, communities (however that may be defined), and the emergency response organizations may not align. People "want to feel safe so they want us to protect them" (Research participant interview #13). The emergency services know that communities want to rely on the government to warn them, advise them of pending threats, and take action to mediate the impact, but "… it's one thing to have an understanding of community expectations. We need to do that. Whether we can meet those expectations is another thing" (Research participant interview #6).

Increased expectations allow little time for learning in high stakes disaster situations, with no tolerance for trial and error. In December 2009 (after the deadly Victorian wildfires), the Australian and Victorian governments launched an automated telephone warning system, the "Emergency Alert."[62] With this system, an incident controller can nominate an area that is at risk and all land line telephones in that area can be called to transmit a warning message. Mobile phones that have a billing address within the affected area can be called or sent a short text message. The system misses people who are in the area, but whose mobile phone billing address is elsewhere, and contacts those that are outside the area but who have a mobile phone billing address in the affected area. The system is being developed to allow calls to be made to mobile phones based on their physical location but that is not yet possible on all mobile networks.[63]

The first real test of the system came in September 2011 with a factory fire in the suburbs of Canberra, the national capital. The factory contained a number of dangerous chemicals that were giving off potentially toxic smoke. As fire fighters worked to contain the blaze, measure the pollutants in the smoke and generally gain control of the emergency, warnings were sent to the affected community. The first warning was sent at 1:38 a.m. and called for people to evacuate the suburb of Mitchell. The second alert, sent at 3:19 a.m., urged people to stay indoors, close windows, and turn off air conditioning.[64]

The first alert was programmed to go to 22,598 fixed phone lines. All numbers were dialed and 25% of those calls were answered. The remaining calls went unanswered (16%), received a busy tone (10%), or went to an invalid phone number (44%) or to a fax line (4%). Text messages were intended to go to 2,693 mobile phones, and 63% were delivered (ESA, 2011).

For the second alert, messages were to be sent to 86,801 landline numbers; 16% of the messages were sent, 4% failed, and 80% of the numbers were not dialed. Text messages were to be sent to 83,774 mobile phones and, again, 63% were delivered.[65]

Lessons were learned from this exercise, in particular lessons about the capacity of the system to dial so many numbers within a short time. Further, the system allowed the operator to enter a warning area that the system could not service, and it failed to report that the programmed warning exceeded its capacity. These were limitations that had not become apparent during preincident testing.

According to the Emergency Services Agency,

> Notwithstanding limitations arising from a discrepancy between the identified target area and the nominated campaign time, the Emergency Alert successfully provided warning messages to a significant number of people in the community that were acted upon.[66]

As a first live use of the system, it reached, in the first warning, 80% of the target phone audience. In both warnings, 63% of the target mobile phone recipients had a message delivered, though whether they chose to read it or act upon it cannot be known. But the press did not see the situation in that light. Headlines included "Fire warning system fails Canberrans,"[67] "Mitchell Fire Alerts Failed,"[68] and unsubtly, "ACT arsed up the use of emergency alerts during the Mitchell fire."[69]

A resilient community that shares responsibility for disaster resilience may recognize a message system that delivers some 74,000 recorded and text messages as a useful addition to other warning systems such as radio, door knocking by emergency service personnel, and being personally aware of one's own circumstances. This system was introduced after the 2009 Black Saturday wildfires so the outcomes represented a dramatic, if not perfect, improvement in communication ability since that tragedy.

On the other hand, if "shared responsibility" means that the emergency services "… have a responsibility to provide advice" and "to let [individuals] know what their dangers are" whilst the responsibility of the individual is to act on that advice (Research participant interview #11), then failure to send in excess of 100,000 programmed warnings (i.e., the approximate number of calls not dialed, or SMS messages not delivered) is a failure warranting condemnation of the emergency service agencies, even though, only 2 years earlier no automated warnings could have been sent. The belief that the emergency warning was a failure suggests that the popular view of shared responsibility is, as described above, that it is the government's responsibility to tell people what to do and when and the communities responsibility to do what they are told. That may be a way of sharing or allocating responsibility, but it is not a way to develop resilient communities.

Linked to the expectation that the government and emergency services will tell people what to do, and when, is the expectation that the emergency services will always be available to respond when a crisis occurs. A key message from the emergency services is that in extreme conditions, on those days when the risk to life and property is highest, there will be circumstances when agencies are unable to provide fire-fighting resources in sufficient time and strength to prevent all loss of life and damage to property.[70]

In those circumstances, on the days of severe, extreme, or catastrophic fire weather, people should not, and cannot, expect a fire truck to be dispatched to protect their property.[71] They need to have their own plan for what to do and how to react to the emerging situation; individuals and communities must share responsibility for the response and the outcomes. Notwithstanding these warnings, the lived experience of *most* people will be that there was, and are, sufficient fire-fighting resources and that the fire agencies *are* successful in combatting the fires. It is, perhaps, precisely because of that experience that events like the wildfires that burned into Canberra in 2003 and that devastated Victoria in 2009 are so shocking and lead to demands to understand what went wrong: why the fire services could not deal with the event when normally, they can.

In this context, individual and community resilience may be perversely affected by the success of the emergency response agencies:

> [I]n the majority of cases where the incident is small and at a scale that we can handle, we will get there and put the fire out in that house. Or get that fire in the bush next to a private property within a couple of hectares ... We create an expectation that we're really good at what we do, and the government has given us a lot of money to create that capability. But when we get to a particular scale of incident where we can't meet that expectation, we get whacked around the ear. (Research participant interview #16)

Another fire chief described "perverse behavioral effects in communities where there'd been bushfire education campaigns and households sort of becoming less and less prepared." He explained that he thought these effects occurred "because they felt that someone must be doing something because there's information in the post and there's meetings behind held. So I'll be less prepared" (Research participant interview #5).

If we consider just the hazard of wild or bushfire, the Australian fire services are in fact very effective. Using Victoria's Country Fire Authority as an example, the Authority's performance is measured against prescribed Service Delivery Standards. The Authority's response performance for the period 2007/2008 to 2010/2011 is shown in Table 1.[72]

The relevant response times were given in evidence before the 2009 Victorian Bushfires Royal Commission CFA (2004); they are shown in Table 2.

The conclusion is that between 2008 and 2011, in 94.5% of cases, a fire crew responded to a fire call on a rural property within 21 minutes, to a low urban property within 11 minutes, and to a medium urban property within 9 minutes. McFarlane, McGee, and Faulkner (2011) argue that this sort of success may dissuade people from preparing and increase the tendency to blame the fire services and the government generally, when fires are not controlled.

Table 1. Country Fire Authority Response Measured Against Service Delivery Standards.

	Number of Emergency Incidents	Response Within Standard Response Time	Response Within Standard Response Time + 60 Seconds
2010/2011	22,879	20,156 (88.1%)	22,879 (100%)
2009/2010	23,039	20,476 (88.9%)	21,485 (93.2%)
2008/2009[a]	25,183	22,525 (89.45%)	23,546 (93.5%)
2007/2008	24,795	21,994 (88.7%)	22,649 (91.3%)

[a]This includes the response to the Black Saturday fires of February 7, 2009.

Table 2. Country Fire Authority Response Time Service Delivery Standards.

Class of Hazard	Response Time Definition	Vehicle Response Time (Mins)
2 – Medium urban	Significant urban areas, primarily residential areas involving commercial centers, clusters of industrial and/or institutional hazards	8
3 – Low urban	Encompasses all structural hazards in urban areas not falling into Classes 1 and 2 and includes predominantly residential occupancies and small industries	10
4 – Rural	Primarily involves natural surroundings in terms of fuel, but also involves isolated dwellings and structures within those areas	20
5 – Remote rural	Structural and rural hazards similar to Class 4 and for which the location of the hazard is geographically distant from a fire station	No times specified

As emergency services improve their response capacity, their ability to communicate with the public, and their ability to predict the path and impact of hazards, Bushfire CRC (u.d.) individuals will expect them to apply those capacities for their benefit and may be able to rely upon the law to ensure that happens. When fire prediction involved experienced fire fighters making their best guess as to the direction the fire would take, and then directing fire fighters into the bush to "do their best," there could be no legal ramifications for failure to control the fire. Fire response was a private matter and individuals grouped together to form community fire brigades that were little more than mutual self-help societies.

Today responding to a fire with a group of citizens, dressed in cotton overalls using a knapsack spray and beater, would be unacceptable. Fires can now be observed by air or even satellite, predictions of the impact of the fire can be made at the property level[73] and emergency warning messages may be communicated by radio, telephone, SMS, Twitter, and Facebook. Modern fire crews turn out in specially designed vehicles with self-protection devices, radio communications, and GPS tracking, and are supported by extensive firefighting and observation aircraft as well as logistics and welfare support. Self-help local brigades could not bring the resources to bear that a modern fire brigade requires and the community expects, and in today's risk averse culture, would not be allowed to operate by the various state fire brigades and work health and safety inspectorates.

Determining when a government agency such as an Australian fire brigade or emergency service owes a duty to take positive action to prevent another person from harm is complex and depends on an assessment of a range of salient features.[74] Critical to that assessment are the degree of control the agency can exercise over the hazard and the vulnerability of those at risk.[75] As technology assists the emergency services to predict and respond to hazards, and to warn the community, their level of control, over both the hazard and over information about where the hazard will impact, increases. The consequence may be that failure to respond to a fire or other emergency in an effective manner, to inform an individual that they are under threat, or to evacuate communities that are not in fact at risk, will, in the future, be actionable for failure to reasonably use the available resources to protect the increasingly vulnerable. In short, the more the emergency services can do, the more they will be expected to do and, in turn, individuals may feel less need to look after themselves.

Dealing with those expectations will pose serious challenges for the emergency services and will impose particular burdens on the volunteer services. The amount of training those volunteers will be required to attend and the performance standards they must meet if they are to behave, and deliver the services that the law demands from a "reasonable" emergency service, may impose intolerable burdens on a volunteer organization. Society may no longer accept that protection of their lives and properties depends on the volunteer spirit. If that is true then adapting to future fire scenarios will have significant resource implications and may also reflect a further shift from community and individual resilience to a greater demand that the government be there to deal with future natural hazards.

The Australian Structural Context

There are some matters that will remain constant in the Australian structural context and that will affect the implementation of the National Strategy.[76]

The legal system will remain much as it is; the Constitution is unlikely to undergo significant change, so Australia will continue to operate across three tiers of governments with all the inefficiencies that this brings in terms of trying to ensure consistent approaches in the context of emergency management. However, the federal system also allows cross-jurisdictional policy and management experiments and learning from them to be shared.

Australia will remain a liberal democracy allowing the balance of competing values to be constantly negotiated, and policymaking and implementation will often be slow and messy.

A fundamental part of the legal system is the independent system of courts and tribunals. This will remain in place, with some modifications to encourage alternative dispute resolution and to reduce the negative impacts of adversarial litigation, but at its apex the Courts will remain and will continue to provide an avenue where people can challenge policy decisions and, in particular, decisions that have a negative impact on their private rights. This allows public interest groups to resist policy changes for private gain, but also allows individuals to resist policy change where there private interests are adversely affected.[77]

CONCLUSIONS

As the Victorian Bushfires Royal Commission noted, shared responsibility does not mean equal responsibility and as discussed above, society is changing in how it expects people to respond to emergencies.

Communities in Australia and around the world are expected to face greater exposure to natural hazards such as storms, floods, and fires; when matched with human vulnerability those changes will equal disasters. Our vulnerability to hazards is a product not only of the hazard, but also a product of the choices we make, both as individuals and as communities. To build resilience requires trade-offs and costs. Communities, governments, and individuals need to engage in a debate about what risks they are prepared to live with, and what benefits and life style choices they are prepared to forsake.

Australia is seeking to meet these challenges by a significant policy shift moving away from the state centered, Prevent, Prepare, Respond and Recover (PPRR) paradigm, to one where responsibility is shared between individual, communities, and governments. Translating that policy into practical reality will require changes in law, policy, and attitude. The critical first step is to start the serious debate about what risks individuals and communities (however defined) are willing to accept, what price they will pay to meet their risk objectives, and what trade-offs they will accept. Those issues cannot be determined by professional risk or emergency managers because determining what risk, or price, is acceptable requires consideration of the "full spectrum of values at stake,"[78] and those values are not just safety and economy. Only when communities have answered those questions can governments, federal, state, and locals begin to develop law and policy to give effect to those choices. When developing appropriate law and policy, governments will have to deal with increased demand for government services with, at least a perceived, decreased capacity for individuals to engage in self-help activities. Further, the policy response must take into account and reflect fundamental structural realities in Australian society.

Although the discussion here has focused on Australian law and policy, the issues of negotiating the tradeoffs in values, interests, and resources will apply universally but will be shaped by local norms, laws, and culture. Identifying and building resilience requires a reordering of values, interests, and resources. It confirms that the development of resilient communities is, at its heart, a political rather than scientific, technological, or legal question. The answer is not just in correctly assessing risk, buying more and better equipment, or legislating to require people to take more care of themselves or to understand the world the way the risk manager does. It will require negotiation and compromise and that is what politics is intended to achieve, but whatever is negotiated will still leave a residual risk. Everyone needs to understand that vulnerability to hazards is not just a product of the event, the landscape, or government failure; it is a product of our *collective* choices.

NOTES

1. CFA (2009).
2. CFA (2010).
3. COAG, 2011.
4. Australian Government, u.d.

5. Middelmann (2010).
6. AEMI, u.d.
7. Kent (1987, p. 4.)
8. Pachauri and Reisinger (2007); Garnaut (2011), Climate Commission (2011), IPCC (2012), FEMA (2012), Climate Commission (2013).
9. CSIRO and BoM (2012).
10. Emergency Management Australia (1988, p. 24).
11. Productivity Commission, 2012.
12. Dovers (2009).
13. FEMA (2012, p. 2), emphasis in original.
14. Ruoff (1966).
15. Ellis, 2001; Murray &White, 1995.
16. Victoria, Parliamentary Debates, Legislative Assembly, June 18, 1890, 381 (Mr. Deakin).
17. Metropolitan Fire Brigades Act 1958 (Vic) ss 6, 7 and 8; Country Fire Authority Act 1958 (Vic) ss 6 and 6A.
18. Public Sector Employment and Management Act 2002 (NSW) s 4C and Schedule 1.
19. Platt (1999).
20. Victoria (2009, vol II, part II, p. 352).
21. COAG (2011).
22. *Id.*
23. *Id.*
24. Eburn (2012).
25. COAG (2011, p. 5).
26. Phillips et al. (2011).
27. Davis (1993, p. 257), emphasis added.
28. Victoria (2009, vol II, part II, p. 249).
29. Victoria (2009, vol II, part II, p. 252, Recommendation 46).
30. Victoria, Parliamentary Debates, Legislative Assembly, August 10, 2010, 2984 (the Hon John Brumby, Premier).
31. Gibbons et al. (2012).
32. Gowda (1999).
33. Blastland and Spiegelhalter (2013).
34. 333 miles is approximately 12 times further than 28 miles (i.e., $333/28 = 11.9$); if traveling 28 miles carries a 4:1,000,000 risk of dying, traveling 12 times further (all else being equal) will carry a risk equivalent to 12×4 or 48:1,000,000.
35. Verchick (2010).
36. Burton (2013).
37. Local Government Act 1993 (NSW); Local Government Act 2008 (NT); Local Government Act 2009 (Qld); Local Government Act 1934 (SA); Local Government Act 1993 (Tas); Local Government Act 1989 (Vic); Local Government Act 1995 (WA).
38. See for example, Environmental Planning and Assessment Act 1979 (NSW).
39. Stuart v Kirkland-Veenstra (2009).
40. *Id.*
41. Pearce and Geddes (2011).
42. Byron Shire Council v Vaughan (2009).
43. *Id.*

44. Vaughan v Byron Shire Council (2011).
45. Victoria 2011, Recommendation 27.
46. Victoria, Parliamentary Debates, Legislative Assembly, July 29, 2010, 2834 (the Hon William (Bill) Tilley Member for Benambra).
47. Victoria, Parliamentary Debates, Legislative Assembly, August 10, 2010, 2984 (the Hon John Brumby, Premier).
48. COAG (2009).
49. Gill, 2009.
50. Davis, 1993.
51. Keelty (2011, p. 3).
52. Dovers (2005).
53. Committee on National Earthquake Resilience (2011, p. 3).
54. *Id.*
55. Safe Work Australia (2011).
56. Victoria (2009, p. 193.)
57. State of New South Wales v West & Anor (2008).
58. Victoria (2009, vol II, part I, p. 32).
59. Country Fire Authority Act 1958 (Vic) s 50B; Fire Services Commissioner Act 2010 (Vic) s 24; Forests Act 1958 (Vic) s 62AA; Metropolitan Fire Brigades Act 1958 (Vic) s 32AA.
60. Country Fire Authority Act 1958 (Vic) s 50E-50O.
61. *Id.*
62. Attorney General's Department (2012).
63. *Id.*
64. *Id.*
65. *Id.*
66. ESA (2011, p 7).
67. The Australian (2011).
68. Canberra Times (2011).
69. RiotACT (2011).
70. AFAC, 2010.
71. See RFS (2009), TFS (2013).
72. CFA (2009), CFA (2010), CFA (2011, 2012):
73. Bushfire CRC (u.d.).
74. Graham Barclay Oysters Pty Ltd v Ryan (2002), Caltex Refineries (Qld) Pty Ltd v Stavar (2009).
75. Pyrenees Shire Council v Day (1998), Stuart v Kirkland-Veenstra (2009).
76. Eburn (2012).
77. Byron Shire Council v Vaughan (2009).
78. Verchick (2010).

ACKNOWLEDGMENTS

This chapter was developed from a paper delivered at a workshop on Legal and Institutional Dimensions of Adaptation and Extreme Event

Management funded by the National Climate Change Adaptation Research Facility (NCCARF) and held at the Australian National University on November 23, 2011. This chapter draws on data from a survey of chief officers of Australia's fire and emergency services. Findings from that survey have also been reported in Eburn and Dovers (2014, 2015).

REFERENCES

Ashe, B., de Oliveira, F. D., & McAneney, J. (2012). Investments in fire management: Does saving lives cost lives? *Agenda*, *19*, part. 2. Retrieved from http://epress.anu.edu.au/apps/bookworm/view/Agenda+-+Volume+19%2C+Number+2%2C+2012/10161/cover.html. Accessed on May 3, 2013.

Attorney General's Department. (2012). *Emergency alert*. Retrieved from http://www.em.gov.au/Emergency-Warnings/Pages/Emergencyalert.aspx. Accessed on April 2, 2013.

Australasian Fire and Emergency Services Authorities Council [AFAC]. (2010). *Bushfires and community safety*. Retrieved from http://knowledgeweb.afac.com.au/positions/documents/AFAC_Position_Bushfires_Community_Safety_v4.1.pdf. Accessed on February 2, 2013.

Australian Bureau of Statistics [ABS]. (2011). 3218.0 – Regional population growth, Australia, 2011.

Australian Bureau of Statistics [ABS]. (2013). *Population clock*. Retrieved from http://www.abs.gov.au/ausstats/abs@.nsf/0/1647509ef7e25faaca2568a900154b63?opendocument. Accessed on May 3, 2012.

Australian Emergency Management Institute [AEMI]. (u.d.). *Knowledge hub: Disaster information*. Retrieved from http://www.emknowledge.gov.au/disaster-information/. Accessed on April 2, 2013.

Australian Government. (u.d.). *Our country*. Retrieved from http://australia.gov.au/about-australia/our-country. Accessed on May 3, 2012.

Blastland, M., & Spiegelhalter, D. (2013). *The norm chronicles: Stories about numbers and danger*. London: Profile Books.

Burton, L.. (2013). The 'Cassandra Zone' and Law's Moral Purpose.

Bushfire CRC. (u.d.). *Risk assessment decision toolbox*. Retrieved from http://www.bushfirecrc.com/projects/12/risk-assessment-and-decision-making. Accessed April 2, 2013.

Byron Shire Council v Vaughan. (2009). NSWLEC 88, [4].

Caltex Refineries (Qld) Pty Ltd v Stavar. (2009). 75 NSWLR 649.

Canberra Times. (2011). *Mitchell fire alerts failed (29 September 2011)*. Retrieved from http://www.canberratimes.com.au/act-news/mitchell-fire-alerts-failed-20110929-1wrt8.html. Accessed on May 3, 2013.

Climate Commission. (2011). *The critical decade: Climate science, risks and responses*. Canberra: Commonwealth of Australia.

Climate Commission. (2013). *The critical decade: Extreme weather*. Canberra: Commonwealth of Australia.

Committee on National Earthquake Resilience Research, Implementation, and Outreach, Committee on Seismology and Geodynamics and National Research Council. (2011). *National earthquake resilience*. Washington, DC: National Academies Press.

Commonwealth Scientific and Industrial Research Organisation [CSIRO] and Bureau of Meteorology [BoM]. (2012). *State of the climate 2012*. Canberra: Commonwealth of Australia.
Council of Australian Governments [COAG]. (2009). *COAG National Disaster Resilience Statement*.
Council of Australian Governments [COAG]. (2011). *National Strategy for Disaster Resilience*. Canberra: Commonwealth of Australia.
Country Fire Authority [CFA]. (2004). *CFA's Service Delivery Standards (SDS)*. Retrieved from http://www.royalcommission.vic.gov.au/Documents/Document-files/Exhibits/DOC-CFA-015-0003. Accessed on May 3, 2013.
Country Fire Authority [CFA]. (2009). *Annual report 2008*. Melbourne: Government of Victoria.
Country Fire Authority [CFA]. (2010). *Annual report 2009*. Melbourne: Government of Victoria.
Country Fire Authority [CFA]. (2011). *Annual report 2010*. Melbourne: Government of Victoria.
Country Fire Authority [CFA]. (2012). *Annual report 2011*. Melbourne: Government of Victoria.
Davis, G. (1993). *Public policy in Australia* (2nd ed.). Sydney: Allen and Unwin.
Dovers, S. (2005). *Environment and sustainability policy: Creation, Implementation and evaluation*. Sydney: The Federation Press.
Dovers, S. (2009). Normalising adaptation. *Global Environmental Change*, *19*, 4–6.
Eburn, M. (2012). Sharing responsibility and community resilience: The role of law in converting policy to action. In M. Clarke & G. Griffin (Eds.), *Next generation disaster and security management*. Melbourne: Australian Security Research Centre.
Eburn, M., & Dovers, S. (2014). How chief officers view the measures of success in fire policy and management. *Australian Journal of Emergency Management*, *29*(3), 16–21.
Eburn, M., & Dovers, S. (2015). Learning lessons from disasters: Alternatives to Royal Commissions and other quasi-judicial inquiries. *Australian Journal of Public Administration* (Online), 1–14. doi:10.1111/1467-8500.12115
Ellis, J.-A. (2001). *Tried by fire: The story of the South Australian Country Fire Service*. Adelaide: South Australian Country Fire Service.
Emergency Management Australia [EMA]. (1988). *Australian emergency management glossary, Australian emergency manuals series. manual 3*. Canberra: Commonwealth of Australia.
Emergency Services Agency [ESA]. (2011). *Use of emergency Alert during the Mitchell hazardous material fire*. Canberra: Australian Capital Territory.
Federal Emergency Management Agency [FEMA]. (2012). *Crisis response and disaster resilience 2030*. Washington, DC: Department of Homeland Security.
Garnaut, R. (2011). *The Garnaut review 2011*. Cambridge, MA: Cambridge University Press.
Gibbons, P., van Bommel, L., Malcolm Gill, A., Cary, G. J., Driscoll, D. A., Bradstock, R. A., … Lindenmayer, D. B. (2012). Land management practices associated with house loss in wildfires, 1–7. *PloS ONE*, *7*, Pt. 1.
Gill, A. M. (2009). Fire, science and society at the urban-rural interface proceedings of the royal society of Queensland (bushfire 2006 conference special edition) 115, 153–160.
Gowda, M. V. R. (1999). Heuristics, biases, and the regulation of risk. *Policy Sciences*, *32*, 59–78.
Graham Barclay Oysters Pty Ltd v Ryan. (2002). 211 CLR 540.

Human Research Ethics Committee. (2011). *Human ethics protocol 2011/480*. Canberra: Australian National University.

Intergovernmental Panel on Climate Change [IPCC] (2012). *Managing the risks of extreme events and disasters to advance climate change adaptation*. Cambridge, MA: Cambridge University Press.

Keelty, M. (2011). *A shared responsibility: The report of the Perth hills bushfire February 2011 review*. Perth: Government of Western Australia.

Kent, R. C. (1987). *Anatomy of disaster relief: the international network in action*. London: Pinter.

McFarlane, B., McGee, T., & Faulkner, H. (2011). Complexity of homeowner wildfire risk mitigation: an integration of hazard theories. *International Journal of Wildland Fire*, *20*, 921–931.

Middelmann, M. (2010). *Understanding natural hazard impacts on Australia (Australian bureau of statistics)*. Retrieved from http://www.abs.gov.au/ausstats/abs@.nsf/7d12b0f6763c78caca257061001cc588/00408ced366bb56aca2570de00029f46!OpenDocument. Accessed on July 26, 2012.

Murray, R., & White, K. (1995). *State of fire: A history of volunteer fire fighting and the country fire authority of Victoria*. Melbourne: Hargreen.

Pachauri, R. K., & Reisinger, A. (Eds.). (2007). *Climate change 2007: Synthesis report*. Geneva: Intergovernmental Panel on Climate Change.

Pearce, D., & Geddes, R. S. (2011). *Statutory interpretation in Australia* (7th ed.). Sydney: Lexis/Nexis.

Phillips, R., Chaplin, S., Fairbrother, P., Mees, B., Toh, K., & Tyler, M. (2011). *Defining community: Debates and implications for bushfire policy*. Melbourne: Bushfire CRC.

Platt, R. H. (1999). *Disasters and democracy*. Washington, DC: Island Press.

Powerline Bushfire Safety Taskforce. (2011). *Consultation paper (Melbourne)*. Retrieved from https://www.google.com.au/url?sa=t&rct=j&q=&esrc=s&source=web&cd=1&cad=rja&ved=0CDIQFjAA&url=http%3A%2F%2Fwww.esv.vic.gov.au%2FPortals%2F0%2FAbout%2520ESV%2FFiles%2FRoyalCommission%2FPowerline%2520Bushfire%2520Safety%2520Taskforce%2520%2520Consultation%2520paper%2520for%2520public%2520comment.pdf&ei=l-CBUafcB8mViQf9moDIDQ&usg=AFQjCNFSCssVql4u20NQY8OBhbkajRdxtA&sig2=fKbGonPmvccO1Bmt17xzFw&bvm=bv.45921128,d.aGc. Accessed on May 3 2013.

Productivity Commission. (2012). *Report on government services 2012*. Canberra: Commonwealth of Australia.

Pyrenees Shire Council v Day. (1998). 192 CLR 330.

RiotACT. (2011). *ACT arsed up the use of emergency alerts during the Mitchell fire (22 November 2011)*. Retrieved from http://the-riotact.com/act-arsed-up-the-use-of-emergency-alerts-during-the-mitchell-fire/59852. Accessed on May 3, 2013.

Ruoff, T. (1966). Links with London. *The Australian Law Journal*, *40*, 211–213.

Rural Fire Service (RFS). (2009). *Fire danger rating*. Retrieved from http://www.rfs.nsw.gov.au/file_system/attachments/Attachment_FireDangerRating.pdf. Accessed on May 3. 2013.

Safe Work Australia. (2011). *Model work health and safety bill*. Canberra: Commonwealth of Australia.

State of New South Wales v West & Anor. (2008). ACTCA 14 [26]-[27].

Stuart v Kirkland-Veenstra. (2009). 237 CLR 215, [88]-[89].

Tasmania Fire Service [TFS]. (2013). *New fire danger ratings.* Retrieved from http://www.fire.tas.gov.au/Show?pageId=colFireDangerRatings. Accessed on May 3, 2013.
The Australian. (2011). *Fire warning system fails Canberrans' (16 September 2011).* Retrieved from http://www.theaustralian.com.au/news/nation/canberra-fire-forces-suburb-evacuation/story-e6frg6nf-1226138487820. Accessed on May 3, 2013.
Vaughan v Byron Shire Council. (2011). NSWSC 824.
Verchick, R. R. M. (2010). *Facing catastrophe: Environmental action for a post-Katrina world.* Harvard, MA: Harvard University Press.
Victoria. (2009). *2009 Victorian Bushfires Royal Commission, Interim Report* (Melbourne).
Victoria. (2011). *2009 Victorian Bushfires Royal Commission, Final Report* (Melbourne).
Wenger, C., Hussey, K., & Pittock, J. (2013). *Living with floods: Key lessons from Australia and abroad.* Gold Coast: National Climate Change Adaptation Research Facility.

THE MULTI-LEVEL PREVENTION AND CONTROL OF CATASTROPHIC WILDFIRES IN MEDITERRANEAN EUROPE: THE EUROPEAN UNION, SPAIN, AND CATALONIA

Juli Ponce, Alexandre Peñalver, Oscar Capdeferro and Lloyd Burton

ABSTRACT

The law of catastrophic wildfire prevention and response in the Mediterranean member states of the European Union stands in stark contrast to that of common law nation states such as Australia and the United States. This is due primarily to the higher levels of reciprocal moral and legal obligations between governments and citizens established in various sources of European law. Focusing on the relationship between the EU, Spain, and the Autonomous Community of Catalonia within Spain, this chapter describes these three legal frameworks as they are nested within each other, followed by some case law examples of these

Special Issue: Cassandra's Curse: The Law and Foreseeable Future Disasters
Studies in Law, Politics, and Society, Volume 68, 189–225

ISSN: 1059-4337/doi:10.1108/S1059-433720150000068006

laws in action. We compare and contrast the philosophical assumptions underlying the utilitarian cost–benefit approach to regulatory justification used in the United States with the precautionary principle model emblematic of the European Union, the member state of Spain, and its Autonomous Community of Catalonia. Regardless of approach, protection of the public health, safety, and welfare will only be as robust and effective as the government agencies that have that responsibility, and the degree of cooperation with those agencies of the citizens they serve.

Keywords: Wildfire; European union; Spain; Catalonia; reciprocal

INTRODUCTION

Governmental Responses to the Growing Wildfire Menace in Mediterranean Europe

Three chapters in *Cassandra's Curse* deal with the rapidly growing threat of catastrophic wildfires in places where human communities and wild open spaces meet. Michael Eburn writes about the need to develop a more coherent and better coordinated national policy in Australia. Lloyd Burton analyzes state government policies in the mountainous western United States from the perspective of the duties of these governments toward their residents relative to some residents' resistance to rural land use regulation. And this chapter reports one example of how southern Europe is facing the same challenge.

The legal heritage of both Australia and the United States is that of the British common law tradition, in which the rights, freedoms, and duties of individual citizens are prominently featured, and the "wants and needs of the community" are but one of several considerations courts take into account in adjudicating those rights and duties. As a matter of custom and tradition, there is a general disinclination against government regulation, unless the government can carry the burden of showing that protection of the public health, safety, and welfare necessitates it. Agencies of the U.S. federal government are required by law to apply a utilitarian calculus to proposed new regulations, and they may be adopted only if their net benefits are shown to exceed their costs. Hence, the American penchant for placing a dollar value on human life.

By contrast, the philosophical starting point for discussions on the role of government in protecting the public is dramatically different, and proceeds mostly from a Kantian perspective. The debate instead tends to be cast in terms of *reciprocal obligation*: that is, what are the moral duties owed the citizenry by the state in terms of protecting their well-being, and what are the reciprocal responsibilities of the citizenry both to the state and to their fellow citizens in assuring that protection?

This chapter takes this distinction as its starting point, since it goes a long way toward explaining how and why the regulatory regimes of southern Mediterranean regions such as Spanish Catalonia differ so substantially from those of the common law countries, even while the technical methods of wildfire prevention and suppression are basically the same. For while the analytic framework for studying the impetus toward regulation in the United States is the explicitly utilitarian practice of cost–benefit analysis, in the member nation-states of the European Union (EU) it is the more Kantian precautionary principle.

Much has been made of the difference between the two, and how they require different modes of thinking about the relationship between citizens and their governments. It is not our intention here to replicate debates over the relative merits and shortcomings of both approaches; that has already been done quite ably elsewhere (e.g., Farber, Cheh, Verchick, & Sun, 2011, chapter 6). We are simply pointing out that this distinction exists, and that it is significant.

These two approaches also tend to be discussed in pure, theoretical terms, rather than with much reference to how they actually work in practice. In fact, discussions over duties to protect do make their way into regulatory proceedings in the United States and considerations of practicality and cost certainly do play a role as European governments apply the precautionary standards of (1) having project proponents making a showing of no harm instead of compelling the government to prove there will be, (2) compelling least harmful practices (or substitute practices) in meeting project goals, (3) presuming liability against project proponents if predicted harms in fact occur, and (4) allowing those affected by proposed projects a role in the decision processes governing project approval.

In terms of the themes of this book, what the precautionary principle does is to mandate that Cassandra's voice be heard and acknowledged, whether or not decision making authorities choose to act on her warnings. That in fact is the essence of taking prudent and reasonable *precautions* when seeking to protect the public from catastrophe.

This principle addresses the government responsibility to the citizenry side of the reciprocal obligation equation "The other side concerns citizens" (and here the term is used philosophically rather than legally) obligations to each other and to their communities, as expressed through compliance with regulations intended to protect public health, safety, and welfare. As we shall see throughout this chapter, the principal distinction between the EU approach (as manifested in Spain and in Catalonia by way of example) and that of countries such as the United States is that in the European context, there is a substantially higher level of reciprocal obligation – or duty of care – between governments and their citizenries. The sense of community at every level is stronger; and thus the role of government is too.

Disasters in the European Context

Natural and manmade disasters are a major European worry (Ponce, 2013). The economic impact of disasters in Europe has been estimated at €15 billion annually (European Commission, 2009, p. 4). Among disasters, the risk of wildfires in Southern Europe is high and has risen because of a number of different causes in the last decades (Vélez Muñoz, 2009, pp. 49–51). Increased risk is driven by social and economic factors, including rural depopulation and concentration of population in urban areas, abandonment of agricultural land, and an increase in spontaneously reforested forest lands, a growing forest–urban interface, the building of new infrastructure (railways, power lines, roads, etc.) that crosses forest areas, and more public recreational use of forests.

Another cause of that risk is forest management policy, such as the replacement of slow-growth forest species adapted to fire with other faster growing, but less fire-adapted, species. Decline in forest management has also resulted in high fuel accumulation, which means that natural events like lightning can cause large wildfires. Lastly, environmental factors are increasing wildfire risk.

And as in other forested areas of the world, such as the mountains of western North America and the Australian bush, climate change is steadily increasing wildfire danger, wildfire potential and frequency, and the severity of wildfires in the Mediterranean region (see IV Intergovernmental Panel on Climate Change Report 2007).

The Southern or Mediterranean States (Greece, Portugal, Spain, Italy, and France) are at the highest risk of suffering forest fires in western Europe. They tend to suffer many more forest fires than Northern Member States, and also accumulate a higher total of burnt area per year (EFFIS, 2011, p. 8). Moreover, risks levels vary across the seasons. Forest fires are much more frequent in summers (see Fig. 1), and fire extinction activities

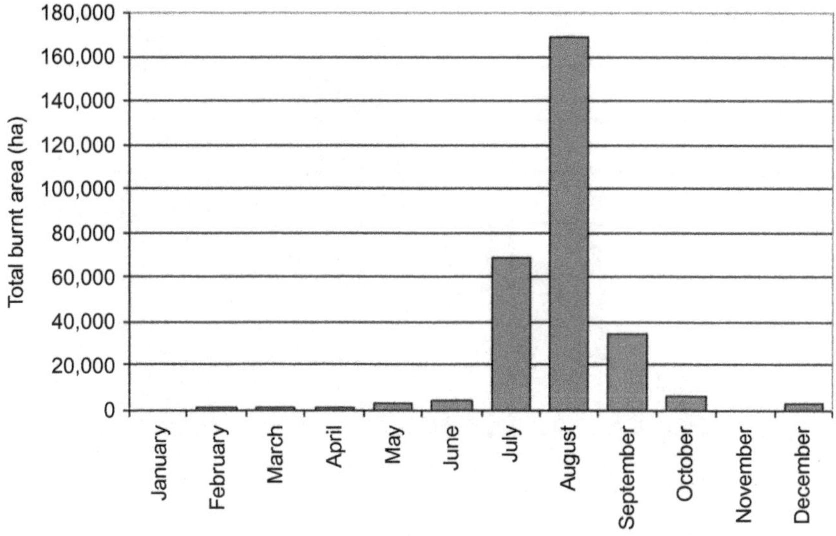

Fig. 1. Total Burnt Area per Month in Europe in 2010. *Source*: From EFFIS, Forest Fires in Europe 2010, p. 75.

are usually harder because adverse climatic conditions – including high temperatures, forest dryness, and strong wind – can intervene.

While the number of forest fires increased considerably from the 1980s to 2000 (see Fig. 2), the size of areas burned has decreased in the last 20 years (see Fig. 3). It has been observed that this phenomenon is "largely due to the improvements of the fire protection services of the countries" (EFFIS, 2011, p. 9). The five EU Mediterranean States spend € 2.5 billion ($3.3 billion USD) on prevention and fire extinction, but more financial resources are expended for fire extinction (60%) than prevention (40%) (Vélez Muñoz, 2009, p. 50).

By contrast, in 2007 the United States Forest Service spent over $1.1 billion USD on wildland fire suppression and about $300 million USD on fire prevention – about an 80% to 20% ratio (Gorte, 2011). What these figures indicate is that – at least relative to the wildland fire management budget in the United States – the fire-prone southern Mediterranean EU nation-states spend roughly twice as much on prevention as a percentage of their fire management budgets. And as is described below, in Mediterranean Spanish regions such as Catalonia, a good deal of this is expended on vigorously implementing and enforcing detailed standards for

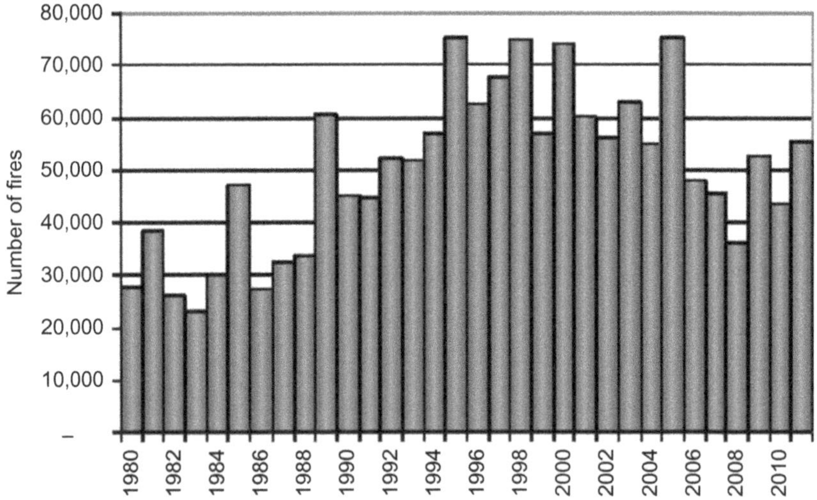

Fig. 2. Number of Fires in Southern European States 1980–2011. *Source*: From EFFIS (2011, p. 9).

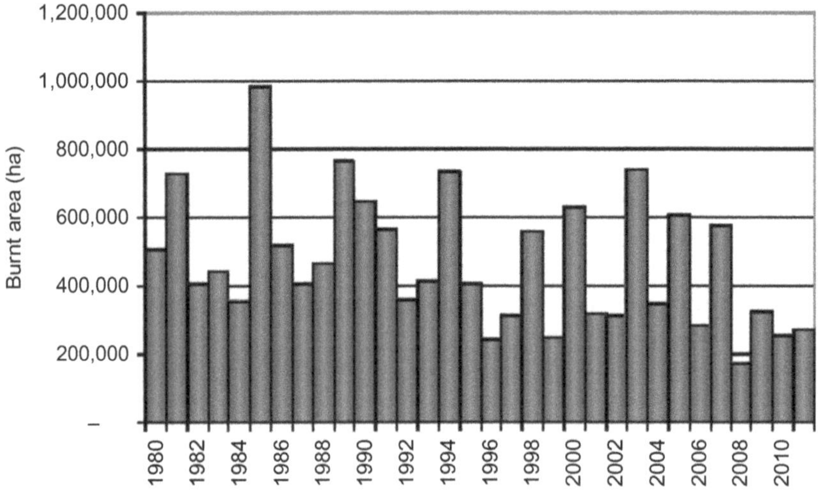

Fig. 3. Burnt Area in the Southern Member States 1980–2011. *Source*: From EFFIS (2011, p. 9).

wildfire prevention mitigation in areas at heightened risk for catastrophic fires. This is a rare practice in the U.S. mountain West, with the exception of states such as California and Oregon.

In Spain, the number and extent of wildfires increased dramatically from 1961 to 2010. But within the last decade of this time span, the number of fires as well as the area burned, has decreased. According to the Spanish Government report *Wildfire in Spain 2001–2010*, the reduction of forest area burned in Spain, like that throughout the EU more generally, is caused by the improvement of rapid extinction techniques of the fire service (see Figs. 4 and 5).

Catalonia has a forest area of more than 60% of the country (43% trees and 17% wooded bush and grass) and a fairly rugged relief. As we can appreciate in Figs. 6 and 7, the annual range of forest fires remained relatively constant throughout 1986–2012, whereas the burned area has tended to decrease since the late 1990s. The causes of wildfire in Catalonia between 1994 and 2005 are also included in Table 1.

In this chapter, we first consider the (limited) role of the EU in preventing and responding to wildfires. Second, we consider the role of the

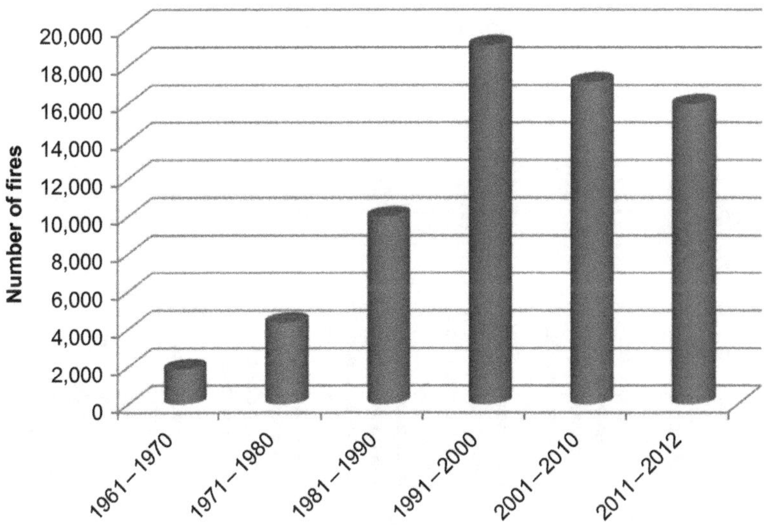

Fig. 4. Number of Fires in Spain (Annual Average). *Source*: Data from Ministerio de Agricultura, Alimentación y Medio Ambiente, 2012, Instituto Nacional de Estadística. Figures designed by authors.

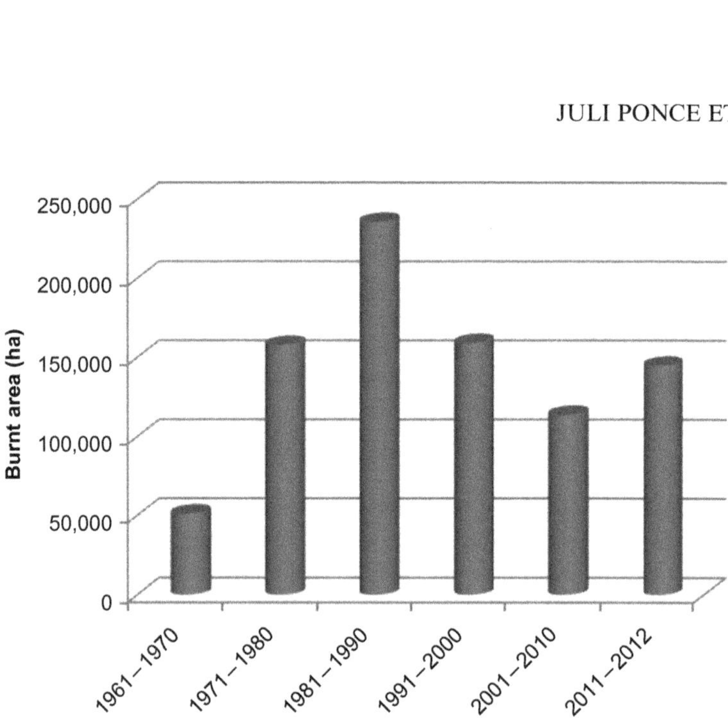

Fig. 5. Burnt Area in Spain (Annual Average). *Source*: Data from Ministerio de Agricultura, Alimentación y Medio Ambiente, 2012, Instituto Nacional de Estadística. Figures designed by authors.

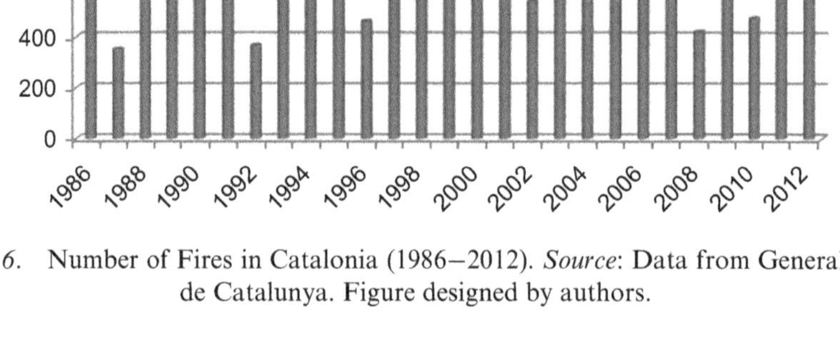

Fig. 6. Number of Fires in Catalonia (1986–2012). *Source*: Data from Generalitat de Catalunya. Figure designed by authors.

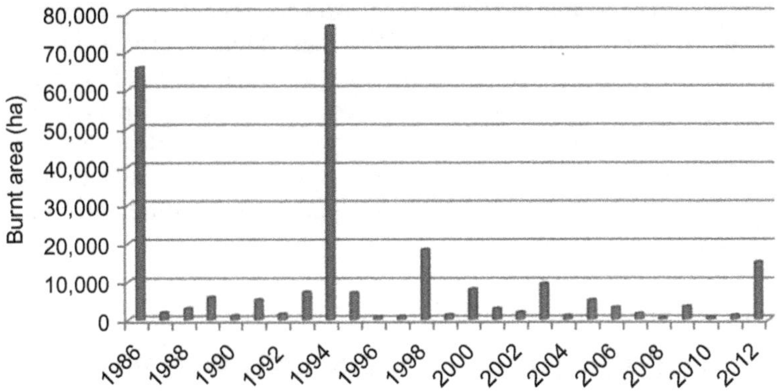

Fig. 7. Forest Area Burnt in Catalonia (1986–2012). *Source*: Data from Generalitat de Catalunya. Figure designed by authors.

Table 1. Wildfire Causes in Catalonia (Average 1994–2012).

Causes	Specific Causes	% Wildfires
Natural	Lightning	10.35
Negligence	Landfill	0.85
	Others negligence	9.96
	Agriculture fires	15.94
	Rubbish burning	1.12
	Bonfires	2.94
	Smoking	6.72
	Forest works	3.30
Accidents	Railway	0.83
	Power lines	5.55
	Engines and machines	3.55
	Others	0.88
Intentional		24.68
Unknown causes		12.33
Revitalized		1.01

Source: Data from Generalitat de Catalunya Departamentd'Agricultura, Ramaderia, Pesca, Alimentació i Medi Natural.

European Court of Human Rights in establishing the duty of care member nations (including EU member states as well as other countries) owe to their citizens at risk of harm to their possessions and persons in case of wildfires.

Then we analyze the distribution of powers regarding prevention and mitigation of wildfires in Spain as an EU State Member, focusing our analysis especially primarily on the example of the Catalan legal system. Next we reflect on the different actors involved and on several perspectives on wildfires, including land uses, housing, forests, environment, civil protection and prevention and safety fire risk. Finally, we consider private and public responsibilities in preventing and mitigating wildfires and mechanisms to compensate damages.

THE EUROPEAN UNION AND WILDFIRE MANAGEMENT

Background

At the current time, the EU has 27 European Member States, which means a global surface area of more than 4 million square kilometers and a population of 495 million inhabitants. That would be the third largest population in the world, after China and India (European Union, 2013).

The EU is regulated by two treaties: the *Treaty on European Union* (TEU) and the *Treaty on Functioning of the European Union* (TFEU), which came into force in their last modification in December 2009. According to the Treaties, the EU is empowered by the abovementioned Treaties to "*serve its interests, those of its citizens and those of the Member States, and ensure the consistency, effectiveness and continuity of its policies and actions*" (Art. 13 TEU).

The EU's main institutions are the European Council, the European Parliament, and the European Commission, and those institutions shall act according to the powers established in the Treaties. According to this legal framework, the EU does possess specified powers in several fields. These include the goals of sustainable development, solidarity, and the fight against social exclusion and for economic, territorial, and social cohesion (Chiti, 2003).

Attaining these goals has led to increasing EU intervention in member state affairs. The EU also has powers in the fields of the environment and other public policies with territorial impact (e.g., transportation) and in other areas connected with wildfires (e.g., civil protection) as we will see. In any case, it is necessary to also bear in mind the *principle of subsidiarity*. That is, matters ought to be handled by the lowest level of competent governmental authority, as long as the authority of the EU is not transgressed or ignored in areas where it has made policy.

The EU, the Member States and Wildfire Management: Distribution of Powers

The EU can only act within the limits of the powers conferred on it by its formative treaties. Therefore, whatever power does not belong to the EU according to the treaties, shall be a power of the Member States.[1] In this way, its founding documents bear some similarities to the enumerated powers of the US Constitution and those of other federalized nation-states, though the EU's powers are not enforceable against Member States by force of arms.

EU powers extend to wildfire management in terms of both prevention and suppression in two ways: environmental policy (as implied via agricultural policy) and civil protection. Each of these powers may authorize different approaches, mechanisms, and techniques to fight forest fires. The primary mechanism employed by the EU to promote forest fire prevention has been cofinancing forest fire prevention actions planned and implemented by the Member States. Thus, the European legislation against forest fires is formed by a succession of Council regulations that establish, with more or less specificity, the manner to obtain the European funding.[2]

In addition, some EU rules affect the protection of forests without specific reference to fire. These rules are directives, which means that they are binding rules, as to the result to be achieved, but they leave to the national authorities of each Member State "the choice of form and methods" (Art. 288 TFEU). In consequence, every State has to enact a national law, or more than one, transposing the content of the directive within a limited period of time.[3]

In the realm of environmental damages, there is a (narrow) EU common framework created by the Directive 2004/35/EC of the European Parliament and of the Council of 21 April 2004 on environmental liability with regard to the prevention and remedying of environmental damage. Member States were obliged to implement the Directive by 30th April 2007. Spain fulfilled its legal obligation with regard to environmental liability by means of the Act 26/2007, on 23rd October of the same year.

That Directive establishes a common European framework for environmental damages. But that framework is limited in different ways. That common framework applies only to environmental damages that are defined in article 2.[4] This Directive does not apply to cases of personal injury, to damage to private property, or to any economic loss and does not affect any right regarding these types of damages. For this reason, art. 3.4 establishes that this Directive shall not give private parties a right of compensation as a consequence of environmental damage or of an imminent threat of such damage.

The Directive only covers some operators that are occupational activities listed in Annex III to the Directive. Annex III includes mainly agricultural or industrial activities that require a license to be undertaken. These types of activities are deemed the responsibility of the operator even if he or she is not directly at fault. Out of Annex III there are other activities that can damage species or natural habitats protected by EU legislation (according to the definition of art. 1). In this second case, the operator will be held liable if, and only if, he or she is at fault or negligent unless for preventive measures.

In both cases, this Directive shall not cover environmental damage caused by "a natural phenomenon of exceptional, inevitable and irresistible character" (art. 4, paragraph 1, letter b). It also does not cover damages caused by nuclear risks (art. 4, paragraph 4). The Directive provides for two types of measures: (a) preventive measures: any measures taken in response to an event, act, or omission that has created an imminent threat of environmental damage, with a view to preventing or minimizing that damage; and (b) remedial measures: any action, or combination of actions, including mitigating or interim measures to restore, rehabilitate, or replace damaged natural resources and/or impaired services, or to provide an equivalent alternative to those resources or services as foreseen in Annex II.

Operators directly have the duty to take preventive and remedial measures against imminent threat of environmental damage or environmental damage. Competent authority shall require that these measures are taken by the operator or may take these measures itself. The operator shall bear the costs for these measures except in some cases listed in art. 8. In Spain, Competent authorities are Autonomous Communities.

In Spain, environmental damages can also be recovered by torts (art. 1902 Civil code) and by other administrative measures such as restitution to the previous state or restoration of damages (art. 77 Spanish Forest Act 43/2003).

Moreover, in 2001,[5] the EU created a system, the Community Mechanism for Civil Protection (MCP), to coordinate response to natural or manmade disasters, by pooling the civil protection capabilities of all the participating states (which can include external participants States). This mechanism aims to unify the European response and to produce much more efficient and effective joint action.

The MCP contains both measures for preparedness and response in the event of a major emergency. With regard to preparedness, the main EU contribution consists of establishing and managing the systems to coordinate the assistance among participant States (information, early warnings, capability to mobilize teams of experts, etc.), and especially, the Monitoring and Information Centre (MIC).

The MIC was the operational center of the MCP. It was the office in charge of coordinating support among States, by matching the needs of affected States and the offers of assistance made by participating States. The MIC is currently being replaced by the Emergency Response Centre (ERC). The new ERC is supposed to allow better assistance in advance and to facilitate a preplanned response.

Once a forest fire has occurred, the State itself has to control and extinguish the fire on its own. When the situation overwhelms national response capabilities (e.g., because of the number of active forest fires or their severity), the participating State suffering the forest fires can submit an assistance request to the ERC, with indication of the items needed. After that, the ERC communicates the request to the rest of the participants.

The items requested are usually aircraft self-protection items (masks and suits), and fire-fighting equipment (such as axes, ropes, and extinguishing foam). Then, any participating State, on the basis of the requested assistance, can present to the ERC an offer of help, specifying what resources could be sent to the affected area. These offers can be accepted or rejected by the requesting State. The MCP has been activated to respond to forest fires inside and outside the EU territory 51 times since 2007. The activation does not mean that equipment or personnel are going to be necessarily sent to the affected area: sometimes the activation is only an early warning or the assistance is no longer necessary before the effective delivery, generally due to situation improvement.

Under this arrangement, EU support is offered as a matter of last resort, and is only justified when the objectives cannot be satisfactorily achieved by the individual action of the Member States.[6]

This is the general system used by the EU to coordinate a joint intervention of Member States (plus the five external participant States) to face natural disasters. However, the solidarity (art. 222.1 TFEU) and final assistance (art. 122.2 TFEU) clauses of the Regulatory Treaties, can also play an important role when a major disaster, such as a severe forest fire, occurs within the EU.[7]

The EU does not have a legal responsibility for the protection of European citizens from wildfire dangers. It is not empowered either to enact prevention standards or to assist directly in wildfire mitigation or extinction efforts. Its role is limited in this field to helping the voluntary efforts made by Member States, both by cofinancing national fire prevention programs and facilitating international exchange of fire-fighting equipment.

The EU, through its intervention, tries to compensate for a lack of adequate Member State resources to respond to foreseeable future catastrophic wildfires (especially in the Mediterranean countries). On the other hand, it tries to help build national response capabilities since, usually, States are not adequately equipped to manage catastrophic wildfires.

The EU is aware of the dangers of wildfires to the security of European citizens.[8] But due to the current legal framework, the EU is limited to reminding Member States (and especially those subject to forest fires, like Spain) that they should take their moral and legal obligations under their own laws to prevent and mitigate wildfire damages to people and properties more seriously. The problem here of course is that each Member State has its own views on just what those obligations ought to consist of.

What is Next?: The Foreseeable Future

But, will this situation be the same in the future? Could the EU's concern about wildfires be converted into a more effective intervention in this field? As elsewhere in the world, climate change is wreaking havoc on the forests of the Mediterranean Member States. As the wildfire danger grows, so to must the ability of the Member States to respond in a coordinated fashion, and with sufficient resources to do the job.

There is no directive about how national laws should address forest fire prevention. However, recently, the European Parliament[9] has reiterated its call "for the Commission to adopt a directive on preventing and managing fires, which should include the regular collection of data, preparation of maps and identification of areas at risk, preparation of fire risk management plans, identification by the Member States of the resources allocated and facilities available, coordination of the various administrations, minimum requirements for training crews and establishment of environmental responsibility and the corresponding penalties" (par. 55).

Given the fact that wildfire risk continues to grow throughout the region, it is likely that some steps in this field will be taken in the foreseeable future, due to the devastating forest fires that swept over southern

Europe during the summer 2012. Spain, for instance, lost nearly 210,000 hectares (over half a million acres) to wildfire; and four motorists lost their lives trying to escape a wildfire over a narrow, cliffside coastal highway along Catalan Costa Brava just south of the French border.

DISASTERS AND THE EUROPEAN COURT OF HUMAN RIGHTS

The European Convention of Human Rights of 1950 is an international treaty signed by 47 states. Among them are all the EU state members, as well as other nations like Turkey and Russia. It applies to a population of 800 million people. The guardian of the Convention (which can be considered a European Bill of rights) is the European Court of Human Rights (hereinafter, ECHR) which is located in Strasbourg, France.

The Court of Justice of the European Union (hereinafter, ECJ), the guardian of the EU law located in Luxembourg, is not related to the European Court of Human Rights. But because all EU states are members of the Council of Europe and signed the Convention on Human Rights, there is a concern about consistency in case law between the two courts. The ECJ refers to the case law of the European Court of Human Rights and treats the Convention on Human Rights as a part of the EU's legal system, since it forms part of the legal principles of the EU member states. Indeed, since the Treaty of Lisbon of 2009, the ECJ is bound by the judicial precedents of the ECHR case law and thus must adhere to its human rights law.

According to the European Court of Human Rights, public authorities have a *positive obligation* to protect the rights of European citizens (typically, life and physical integrity, and possessions and properties). Such an obligation implies that public authorities have a duty to prevent and mitigate risks of disasters before they happen, including wildfires. The Öneryildiz case of 2004 and the Budayeva case of 2008 are examples of these positive duties in relation to disasters. (A brief analysis of both cases can be found in *Kälin* and *Dale*, 2008.)[10]

Öneryildiz v. Turkey, 2004

In 1993 a methane explosion took place in a municipal rubbish dump in Istanbul. There were several deaths and several dwellings were destroyed. The plaintiff lost nine relatives, and also lost his house, which was an illegal dwelling built in an illegal neighborhood. The applicant claimed a double breach of art. 2 ECHR and of art. 1 of the protocol of the ECHR: that is, violations of the right to life and the right to property. He won the case, receiving compensation for pecuniary and nonpecuniary damage.[11]

According to the ECHR, Article 2 does not solely concern deaths resulting from the use of force by agents of the State but also, in the first sentence of its first paragraph, lays down a positive obligation on States to take appropriate steps to safeguard the lives of those within their jurisdiction." That obligation has two components according to the ECHR: procedural and substantive.

Procedurally, when there is a disaster, there must be an official inquiry to determine responsibilities and liabilities. In this case, the court found that the procedures by which the Turkish government conducted its inquiry were insufficient for the task at hand. On the other hand, the *substantive aspect* of article 2 implies "The positive obligation to take all appropriate steps to safeguard life for the purposes of Article 2 (see paragraph 71 above) entails above all a primary duty on the State to put in place a legislative and administrative framework designed to provide effective deterrence against threats to the right to life."

As to the plight of the slum dwellers adjoining the refuse field, the Court found that

> the Government have not shown that any measures were taken in the instant case to provide the inhabitants of the Ümraniye slums with information enabling them to assess the risks they might run as a result of the choices they had made. In any event, the Court considers that in the absence of more practical measures to avoid the risks to the lives of the inhabitants of the Ümraniye slums, even the fact of having respected the right to information would not have been sufficient to absolve the State of its responsibilities.

In relation to the right to property, the Court followed the same reasoning and likewise found an obligation on government's part to discern the extent to which some property interest may have existed – an obligation not fulfilled.

Budayeva v. Russia, 2008

In 2000 a mudslide in a Russian province destroyed houses and caused personal damages. Several people brought a case before the ECHR accusing authorities of having allowed three major shortcomings in the functioning of the system for protection against natural hazards in Tyrnauz, which led to casualties and losses in July 2000.

First, they alleged a negligent failure to maintain mud-protection infrastructure, including the failure to restore the mud-retention dam damaged in 1999 and to clear the mud-retention collector, which was blocked by leftover debris. Second, they complained about the lack of a public warning about the approaching disaster, arguing that a timely warning would have helped to avoid casualties, injuries, and mass panic. Finally, they complained that these events, despite their scale and devastating consequences, did not give rise to an inquiry that would assess the effectiveness of the authorities' conduct before and during the mudslide, in particular whether everything possible had been done to mitigate the damage.

In sum, the European Court of Human Rights found that rights to life and property imply positive state obligations to prevent and mitigate disasters, including wildfires, which should be developed with due diligence and due care, in accordance with the *principle of good governance*. Citing the case of *Czaja v. Poland* (2012), outside the field of disasters but establishing a general doctrine, the Court pointed out the following:

> In examining the conformity of these events with the Convention, the Court reiterates the particular importance *of the principle of good governance. It requires that where an issue pertaining to the general interest is at stake, especially when it affects fundamental human rights, including property rights, the public authorities must act promptly and in an appropriate and above all consistent manner* (see Beyeler v. Italy [GC], no. 33202/96, § 120, ECHR 2000-I; Öneryıldız v. Turkey [GC], no. 48939/99, § 128, ECHR 2004-XII; Megadat.com S.r.l. v. Moldova, no. 21151/04, § 72, 8 April 2008; and Rysovskyy v. Ukraine, no. 29979/04, § 71, 20 October 2011). *It is desirable that public authorities act with the utmost care*, in particular when dealing with matters of vital importance to individuals, such as welfare benefits and other such rights ….

Although public authorities at the nation-state level have a wide margin of discretion to decide the means to comply with those duties, the ECHR will check that there is neither undue omission nor arbitrary and capricious behavior without justification and explanation. And the breach of such a duty can be the basis for liability, as we will see later.

DISTRIBUTION OF POWERS REGARDING PREVENTION AND MITIGATION OF WILDFIRES IN SPAIN

The Spanish National Government and Spanish Autonomous Communities

The Spanish Constitution of 1978 signified deep changes in Spain, with the introduction of democracy and the autonomy of historical regions that had been subjugated by a repressive regime since the end of the Spanish Civil War in 1939. The Constitution transformed Spain from a centralized state model to something more closely approximating a federal one. One of the newly re-recognized Autonomous Regions, or Autonomous Communities, is Catalonia. Like the Basque Autonomous Region, it understands itself as a nation within a nation. Its capital is the city of Barcelona. Catalonia has a long history, its own language, and a strong identity of nation status. It was a sovereign nation-state from the 10th century until to 1714, when it was defeated in the succession war. Our focus is on Catalan wildfire prevention policy and law because it is among the more extensively developed systems in both Spain and the rest of Europe.

Powers of the Spanish Government as Related to Wildfire Management

These are specified in the Constitution of 1978. The Spanish Government can enact laws related to wildfire risk management in accordance with the constitutional clause of art. 149.1.23. That article allows enactment of basic laws on environmental protection, forests, and forest exploitation. Using this power, the Spanish Forest Act of 43/2003 of 21 November was enacted.

But the Spanish Government also has some authority to manage wildfires that might produce serious or catastrophic threats to people, property, public service, and the environment. The Spanish Constitutional Court (since Decision 123/1984 until the recent one 49/2013 on Spain Forest Act of 2003) considered that emergency and civil protection is a part of the public safety clause of Spanish Government (art. 149.1.29 Constitution of 1978). According with these decisions, the Spanish government has the coordination and direction of civil protection in three emergency cases: (a) exceptional states (alarm, exception, and siege); (b) emergencies which require the coordination of personal and material resources from more than one Autonomous Community; and (c) when a global direction is required by an important emergency which affect Spanish interests. The Spanish Civil Protection Act 2/1985, of 21 January defines civil protection as a public service to study and prevent situations of serious risk, catastrophe, or public calamity and to protect and assist people and property in these situations.

Powers of the Catalan Government

The Catalan Government's powers are described in the Spanish Organic Act 6/2006 of the 19th July, of the Statute of Autonomy of Catalonia. As explained above, there is shared power to regulate environment protection, forests, and forest exploitation and thus to manage wildfire risk. According to art. 114 and art. 116.2.b of the Statute of Autonomy of Catalonia, legislative power, regulatory power, and the executive function are the responsibility of Catalonia, within the framework of the basic conditions established by the State as principles or lowest common legislative denominators in rules of legal rank. Thus Catalonia may establish its own policies in the exercise of these powers as long as there is no explicit conflict with the authorities of the Spanish government, as described above. The Catalan Parliament can implement and specify said basic provisions by means of adopting its own statutes. Using this power, it adopted the Forest Catalan Act of 6/1988 of 30 March. Fig. 8 depicts the range of mandatory

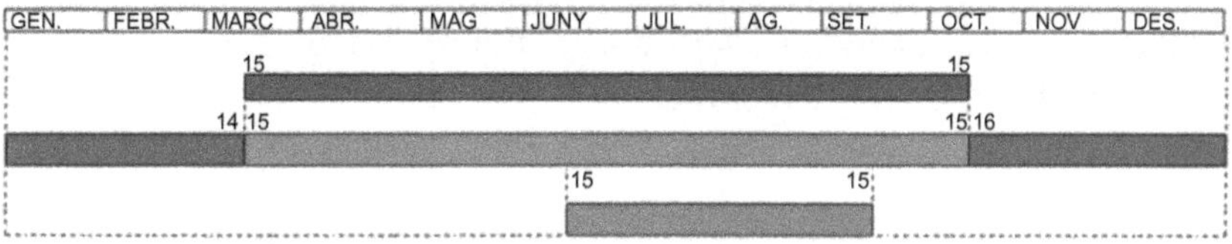

From Private Forestry Board http://www.forestal.cat/web/index.html and other information compiled by the authors.

- Landowners must mitigate fire conditions through vegetation management (for instance, radius of 3.5 m of cleaned area and removing tree branches below 3 m); prohibitions against depositing flammable litter on landscapes. These measures are in force year-round.
- Wildfire risk period.
- Fire and other dangerous activities related with fire (for instance, fireworks) are forbidden unless a permission from Environment and Biodiversity DG of Catalan Government
- All permits for fire in wildfire high risk areas which are specified in an annex are suspended (also works with vegetal rests as a result are forbidden) unless exceptional permission from Environment and Biodiversity Directorate General of the Catalan Government.

Fig. 8. Mandatory Wildfire Mitigation Measures, According to Seasonal Risk. *Source*: From Private Forestry Board http://www.forestal.cat/web/index.html and other information compiled by the Authors.

wildfire mitigation measures citizens must abide by, depending on the level of fire risk in different seasons of the year.

Residual Powers of Local Government

Local Government Law (Spanish Act 7/1985 and Catalan Act 2/2003) and Statute of Autonomy of Catalonia state that regulations in different areas must provide powers of fire prevention and suppression to municipalities; and that municipalities with more than 20,000 inhabitants must provide public fire prevention and firefighting services. Community residents also have the right to require the creation and the provision of this public service if it is not already being provided.

Under this rationale, environmental and forest laws allow the Local Government to adopt preventive additional measures in forest areas (art. 13.1 Executive Order *Decret* 64/1995, of 7 March about preventive measures of wildfires). Local Governments can also develop wildfire prevention plans, which must be approved by Agriculture and Environment Department of Catalan Government. These local plans are required for wildfire high risk areas (art. 40 Catalan Forest Act of 1988 and art. 17 Executive Order *Decret*34/1995).

ASPECTS OF THE MULTILAYERED APPROACH TO WILDFIRE PREVENTION AND MITIGATION

Land Use Regulation: Prohibitions and positives duties based on a property´s Social Function

Land use law (*Derecho urbanístico*, in Spain, or *Droit de l´urbanisme*, in France) deals with the public governance of private land use in the public interest. There is a clear relationship between land use and the likelihood of disaster.

Land use regulation that encourages residential and industrial development in fire-prone areas can actually make future disasters more likely. A good example of this urban development is along river banks and in flood plains (Spanish Government, 2010, p. 44). However, the proper regulation of land can also be a preventive tool, both by preventing disasters from happening and by minimizing their impact when disasters are unavoidable.

In accordance with the distribution of powers established by the Spanish Constitution, the 17 *Comunidades Autónomas* have enacted laws creating their own land use and housing laws. But there is still a body of national legislation that is applicable to all the Spanish land. Although central government had delegated many of its powers, it continued making laws concerning land use using several constitutional clauses (e.g., Art. 149.3, which allows it to enact supplementary legislation to complete the regional legal systems or basic rules about compulsory acquisition, art. 149.1.18, which are connected directly with property right). The important decision of the Spanish Constitutional Court *61/1997* established that land use law was a regional business and that the national level could only exceptionally regulate this matter based on the aforementioned constitutional clauses. The Spanish National Act of 1998 established some general rules about classes of land and limits to local plans, as well as some rules about the exercise of eminent domain. This act was modified in the current Spanish National Land Use Act 8/2007 with similar content, but greatly influenced by EU approaches.

Art. 12 of the Land Use Act stipulates that urban developments are prohibited in lands with natural or technological risks, in order to avoid natural disasters, including wildfires. This kind of land is declared rural (*suelo rural*). Therefore there is no right to build on those lands. Urban planners must recognize this restriction, and there is no compensation due to landowners when it is enforced.

A further step is imposing positive legal obligations on owners to prevent fires. In Spain, land owners cannot do whatever they want with their property. Although the Spanish Constitution recognizes and protects a right to property, it must be developed in accordance with its "social function" (art. 33 Spanish Constitution). It means that legislation (and urban plans within its framework) can limit the right to property, and guide development by establishing positive duties. These limits are not recognized as takings, and no compensation is required.[12] This Spanish legal obligation has been implemented by the Catalan Autonomous Community using its powers in the field of land use law. Thus, the Catalan legal system establishes some positive duties to the building's owner in order to prevent and mitigate wildfires.

As has been well established by wildfire science and field experience (Burton, 2013, pp. 242–243) "the presence or absence of fuel sources (trees, bushes, and flammable ground cover, as well as piles of firewood and other introduced fuel sources)" constitute one of the most important "determinants of whether a structure (and those who may be within it) will survive" a major wildfire. The role of fuel sources is the reason for the Catalan regulation *Decret* 64/1995 establishing preventive measures to avoid wildfires.

That regulation establishes security zones and protection zones (of different size depending on the construction) around certain infrastructure built in forest land. The security zones imply an area of land free of vegetation and other fuel sources. The protection zones mean a zone of land free of vegetation and with a density of trees under 150 feet/ha with a homogeneous distribution. The regulation applies to urban developments, isolated housing, industries, electric lines, roads, rubbish tips, camp sites, and recreational sites. Nobody can clean or perform maintenance work from March 15 to October 15. During that period, there is also a prohibition on several risky activities (including fires and fireworks) unless a permit is granted.

Following the path of that regulation, the Catalan legislature enacted Act 5/2003 to prevent wildfires in urban developments bordering wildlands and vegetated open space – what is referred to in American wildfire law as the "wild lands–urban interface," or WUI. (Burton, 2013, p. 237). Such developments at the wildland border must create a 25-m zone of protection surrounding them, keep plots clean of vegetation, have water enough to respond to wildfires, and create self-protection plans. Local governments are responsible for ensuring that the act is respected and can fine owners when they do not comply with these positive legal obligations.

Rezoning after Disaster: Limitations on Change of Use

Finally, Spanish land use law has a final measure to prevent wildfires: prohibiting the rezoning of plots after the disaster The Spanish Forest Act 43/2003 (modified several times since 2005 as a result of a terrible wildfire in Guadalajara) and the Spanish Land Use Act 8/2007 establish that after a wildfire a plot cannot be rezoned from rural to urban (i.e., with possibilities of urban developments) for at least 30 years. These measures were enacted at the national level when it was discovered that in some rural areas, land owners were setting fire to their lands to escape local land use regulations prohibiting change of use from agricultural to residential purposes (restrictions intended to preserve the open and scenic character of the rural provinces). Prior to these laws, once the land had been burned over, land owners were freed from change of use restrictions, which created an incentive for arson.

Housing and Wildfire Mitigation: Design and Materials Requirements

The other element (beyond fuel sources) that determines if a structure will survive a wildfire is "the design of structures and the materials" (Burton, 2013, p. 242). The Spanish Building Act 38/1999 establishes that "In order to guarantee people's safety, society's well-being and the protection of the environment, buildings must be projected, constructed, maintained and conserved in such a way" as to insure, "in case of fire," that "the occupants may evacuate the building safely, that the fire may be stopped from spreading inside the building and to neighboring buildings and that fire extinguishing and rescue services may operate" (article 3).

To guarantee that requirement, the Act provides the development of a Technical Building Code (*Real Decreto* 314/2006) and a specific regulation (Basic Regulation of Edification or *Norma Básica de Edificación*) in the field of "Fire Protection Conditions for Buildings." That regulation was enacted by means of the *Real Decreto 2177/96* which establishes very concrete technical requirements that buildings must follow to avoid fires. Interestingly, this structural mitigation statute is national law, as distinguished from wildfire mitigation measures in other fire-prone areas such as the American West and Australia, where such measures are a matter solely of local or provincial (state) law.

Forest Management

Big wildfires in Catalonia in 1986, 1994, and 1998 destroyed a total of more than 160 thousand hectares (nearly 400 thousand acres) of wildlands, forcing forest policy reforms that expanded forest services beyond firefighting alone. The change brought several new regulations: New Forest Law (1988), Forest Ownership Board (1990), Forest Plan of Catalonia (1994), and Forest Ownership Board Law (1999). The Forest law and plan changed from a defensive management and policy to a proactive management (Rojas-Briales, 2002).

Under the Catalan Forest Act of 1988, the Catalan Government can declare wildfire high risk areas. Then the local governments must develop wildfire prevention plans and the Agriculture and Environment Department of Catalan Government has the power to approve them (art. 40 Catalan Forest Act of 1988). The plan's fire prevention measures must be implemented by forest land owners, Forest Defense Groups (ADF) and Local Government, making them eligible to receive economic subsidies for wildfire prevention. ADF are associations of forest land owners, municipalities, environmental NGOs, and agriculture professional organizations. Their objectives are: development and implementation of prevention and control wildfires programs; enforcement on preventive measures enacted or issued by Government; carrying out information campaigns among owners of forest land on the actions of prevention and fight against forest fires; implementation of prevention programs, creation and maintenance of infrastructures, road network and water points; and support for forest extinction. ADFs are a good example of public participation on preventive measures which are very important (Vélez Muñoz, 2009, p. 52).Also according to Catalan Forest Act (art. 7), the General Plan of Forest Policy must specify wildfire risk areas. One of the most relevant was the Catalan General Plan of Forest Policy (1994–2003).

The Catalan Forest Act created a Private Forestry Board, the main function of which is to promote forest management plans in private forests. In 1999, a specific Act for this Board gave it broad autonomy including a specific private forest fund. The Board members include both forest owners and representatives of Catalan government. As a result, more than 1,000 forest management plans were approved in 10 years (1991–2000) in private forests. And a forest insurance system established for the first time in Spain. But only for forests with a management plan are eligible for insurance coverage (Rojas-Briales, 2002).

There are also some other preventive actions to assess wildfire risk. First, there is a daily danger map of forest fire risk for the whole region of Catalonia. This map is generated by collecting information from various sources that provide relevant data on the evolution of wildfire risk (http://www.gencat.cat/medinatural/incendis/mapaperill/). And second, the Alpha Plan is an operating procedure established by Rural Rangers to specify actions for fire prevention and extinction service in case of wildfire risk.

By 2012, Catalonia had deployed a total of 400 of these *Agents Rurals*, who patrol rural areas of the Region to monitor compliance with wildfire regulations and issue citations to violators. Though Catalan government employees, these rangers also report violators to the *Fiscalia del Tribunal Superior de Justicia de Catalunya*, the Spanish equivalent of the U.S. Attorney. This Spanish government prosecutor can then bring legal actions against violators. It was one of these prosecutors who successfully sued one Catalonia's largest electric utility companies for damages occasioned by culpability in starting one of the region's largest wildfires.

The Spanish Forest Strategy of 1999 encourages adoption of some wildfire preventive approaches (http://www.magrama.gob.es/es/biodiversidad/temas/politica-forestal/sfs_tcm7-30498.pdf). The Spanish Forest Plan was approved by the Spanish Government in July 2002 and it has a 30-year timespan 2002–2032 (http://www.magrama.gob.es/es/biodiversidad/temas/politica-forestal/politica-forestal-en-espana/pfe_plan_forestal_esp.aspx). It notes that public aids for forestry preventive wildfire have been 8% of total. One of its objectives is to improve preventive action with particular emphasis on preventive forestry and social awareness. It has 150 measures and some of them to prevent wildfire: introduction of legal regulations which would discourage use of fire for economic interest and the application of penalties; increase public awareness to avoid use of fire in forest land; reinforcement of mobile vigilance; promoting voluntary associations of landowners and citizen; funding of preventive forestry an infrastructure carried out by Autonomous Communities; guidelines for break areas in the urban/forest interface for the self-protection of housing complexes included in the urban planning. That plan required an urgent revision of Spanish forest legislation enacted in 1957, which was designed for a centralized state and paid little attention to wildfire prevention.

In 2003, the Spanish Forest Act of 43/2003 of 21 November was adopted. Following the Catalan model, wildfire high-risk areas must be declared by Autonomous Communities and a defense plan approved; Forest Policy plans must be approved by Autonomous Communities and must specify wildfire prevention measures. Others measures are the duty to restore burned forest and the prohibition on changing land use status from forest land to another status for 30 years. The Spanish Government must also collect statistical information on wildfire and Spanish Government and Autonomous Communities must coordinate preventive actions.

Environmental Protection

When there is an extreme meteorological risk of wildfire, the Environment and Biodiversity Directorate General of the Catalan Government can take measures such as prohibiting fire, logging, pedestrian and vehicular traffic, and free camping. This is very important because last year there were also wildfires in winter and in autumn. The government last implemented such measures during the extraordinary 2012 fire season.

The Spanish Forest Act of 43/2003 of 21 November reinforces the authority of Autonomous Communities to approve such wildfire preventive measures. The Spanish Government itself instituted such requirements nationally during the 2005 fire season.

As mentioned above, EU has approved several Directives on environmental matters that are binding as to the result to be achieved by each Member State to which they are addressed, but that leave the choice of form and methods to the national authorities. This classic EU legal technique of establishing a general principle and then deferring to member states to put it into practice explains why Spain, like other Member States, has been obliged to implement several Directives, by passing new legislation in relation to prevention and management of disasters, including wildfires.[13]

Protection of Public Safety
The Spanish Government adopted the Basic Civil Protection Directive for Forest Fire Emergency of 2nd of April 1993. It focuses on wildfire mitigation actions (detection, extinction, communication, public security, health care assistance, evacuation, and shelter). In the Civil Protection Plan for Forest Fire Emergency of 1996, the intention is of this plan is to encourage consistency and coordination across regional and local governments in Spain, insofar as protecting public safety during wildfire emergencies.

CIVIL AND CRIMINAL LIABILITIES IN WILDFIRE CAUSATION

Criminal Cases

Since 1995, the Spanish Criminal Code has dramatically altered its perspective on wildfires. Before 1995 intentional wildfires were considered a crime against ownership. Now, the Criminal Code includes that crime in Title XVII of Book II ("On felonies against collective safety") among felonies of catastrophic risk. Articles 352 to 355 and 358 establish the criminal framework in relation to wildfires (due to intention, e.g. Provincial Court of Cantabria decision of October 29, 2007, or serious negligence, e.g. Supreme Court decision of January 31, 2005; Corcoy, 2011, p. 591).[14]

Available data show that criminal cases related to wildfires have increased lately, and are a growing percentage of the cases handled by the Spanish Land and Environmental Special Public Prosecutor (Spanish Public Prosecutor, Rapport, 2012). From 2010 to 2011, criminal cases for intentional wildfires increased from 1780 to 2306.

Civil Liability: Personal Injury, Property Damage, and Other Economic Losses

Possible tort actions for disasters are established in accordance with each national legal system, which makes it difficult to generalize among the member states of the EU. Moreover the EU situation differs sharply from state and federal doctrines regarding tort in countries like the United States, in that the nation states of Europe are also subject to the jurisdiction of the European Court of Human rights, and edicts of the governmental institutions of the EU (Pierce, 2008, p. 167 and ff.).

Private liability and public liability can have different legal regimes, according to national administrative law systems (e.g., Spain). And even with this public–private distinction in mind, national legal characteristics can be quite different (e.g., England and Spain, where, as we will see, there is an "objective" public liability, that requires neither administrative fault nor negligence). In Spain, torts are under art. 1902 Civil Code. Fault and negligence are required. Tort complaints can also be attached to criminal or other civil proceedings.

Liabilities and Immunities of Governments

In the field of governmental responsibility for its own actions there is likewise no common European legal framework. Therefore, each Member State will apply its own legal regime, although all of them must take into account the ECHR case law described above.

This case law acts as a common standard in the field of disasters. If a public authority bound by the ECHR does not respect the positive duties linked to the rights to property and life, there is a legal consequence: citizens who are damaged can bring a lawsuit before national courts and, if not satisfied, before the ECHR to get a declaration of violation of their rights and a compensation.

The ECHR case law, however, distinguishes between natural and man-made disasters in relation to the right to property. In the case of natural disasters, there is no duty of full compensation of damages to property. As the court in the Budayeva case explained:

> [T]he Court considers that natural disasters, which are as such beyond human control, do not call for the same extent of State involvement. Accordingly, its positive obligations as regards the protection of property from weather hazards do not necessarily extend as far as in the sphere of dangerous activities of a man-made nature.
>
> For this reason the Court considers that for the purposes of the present case a distinction must be drawn between the positive obligations under Article 2 of the Convention and those under Article 1 of Protocol No. 1 to the Convention. While the fundamental importance of the right to life requires that the scope of the positive obligations under Article 2 includes a duty to do everything within the authorities' power in the sphere of

> disaster relief for the protection of that right, the obligation to protect the right to the peaceful enjoyment of possessions, which is not absolute, cannot extend further than what is reasonable in the circumstances. Accordingly, the authorities enjoy a wider margin of appreciation in deciding what measures to take in order to protect individuals' possessions from weather hazards than in deciding on the measures needed to protect lives. (Budayeva case, paragraphs 174–185)

The Court thus held that "the positive obligation on the State to protect private property from natural disasters cannot be construed as binding the state to compensate the full market value of destroyed property" (Budayeva case, paragraphs 174–185).

That kind of distinction, a little bit surprising and a total judicial creation, must be borne in mind by national European judges when deciding cases of natural disasters and controlling public management of their prevention and mitigation, even if applying national laws. In the Spanish case, art. 106.2 of the Spanish Constitution and arts. 139 and ff. act 30/1992 establish a legal framework applicable to all public administrations in Spain in all activity sectors.

According to this legal regime, a government agency will be liable if there is real damage that citizens do not have the legal obligation of bearing; if administrative activity (or lack of administrative activity, when action was legally compulsory) is involved in the damage; and if there is a relationship of causality between the public activity (or the lack of public activity) and the damage. In Spain, fault or negligence do not have to exist to establish government liability.

Payment is made through public budgets: as a general rule, public administrators are not held personally liable. The exception is when a public agency must pay for damages caused by the gross negligence or fault of a public employee. In such cases, the agency must seek to recover the sum it paid from the public employee. (art. 145.2 Act 30/1992).

This differs significantly from governmental liabilities and immunities in countries like the United States. Under U.S. federal and most state laws, a liability action against a public employee is considered a suit against the government, as long as the employee was acting within the scope of his or her employment. For actions outside that scope, however, the employee can be held personally responsible, and the government is relieved of any culpability. This can be a real problem for injured plaintiffs in the American system, since defendant public employees seldom have the assets to cover plaintiff damages, and the government has absolved itself of all legal and financial responsibility.

Government Liability Under Spanish Law

Regarding public responsibility for a lack of proper evaluation of risks, a question that can arise in case of disasters and damages, including wildfires, is whether preventive measures taken by government agencies were adequate. In other words, should government be liable for damages if it did not properly assess natural or man-made risks, and there are damages as a consequence of a disaster? The answer under Spanish law must take into account not only the Spanish legal system but the ECHR case law too.

The Biescas Campsite Case

The *Biescas* Campsite disaster in 1996 had a big impact on Spanish society. A sudden flood in the gorge of Arás (in Huesca, Northeastern Spain) destroyed the *Biescas* campsite, resulting in 87 deaths. After lengthy discussions about whether this disaster was an "act of God," a lawsuit was brought against the public authorities. A Spanish Court decision in 2005 directly confronted the question of possible public responsibility due to the lack of proper risk assessment when permitting the construction of the campsite in the ravine. As a result of its inquiry, the court ruled that state and regional government authorities were indeed to blame, and compensation for damages was required

In this historic case, the court ruled stated that government authorities did not evaluate the existing "natural and man-made risks of all kinds" to people and belongings. According to the Spanish *Audiencia Nacional* (a special high court in the Spanish legal system just below the Supreme Court, which hears precedent-setting cases dealing with public and international law) government authorities are always obliged to prevent risks even where there is a lack of specific legal provisions establishing such a duty. Due to the fact that the disaster was both predictable and avoidable, public authorities were obliged to compensate for damages in the amount of €12 million ($15.8 million USD). This case was brought in front of the ECHR but it rejected it considering it in its decision *Murillo Saldías and Others v. Spain* (application no. 76973/01).The Court noted that, "on 21 December 2005, the *Audiencia Nacional* had awarded Mr. Murillo Saldías compensation in an amount that could not be regarded as unreasonable and would probably be confirmed or even increased by the Supreme Court when it examined the applicant's appeal on points of law. The Court considered that, after the decision of the *Audiencia Nacional*, he could no longer claim to be a victim of a violation of rights set forth in the Convention within the meaning of Article 34. It accordingly declared the application inadmissible in respect of Mr. Murillo Saldías.

The Court also declared the application inadmissible in respect of the other applicants on the grounds of a failure to exhaust domestic remedies, finding that they should have brought administrative proceedings against the authorities before lodging their application with the Court," https://wcd.coe.int/ViewDoc.jsp?id=1077443&Site=COE#. This disaster and subsequent court ruling triggered several measures to develop policy for the prevention of disasters, such as amendments to the (above-mentioned) Spanish land use act and the creation of a Parliamentary Special Commission on Prevention and Assistance in Catastrophic Situations.

Case law Specific to Wildfires

There is an abundant case law addressing the question of public liability for wildfires in Spain (Sánchez Sáez, 2009, pp. 87–141). Public liability due to wildfires in Spain is decided by courts on a case-by-case basis. A government agency will be liable if there is a real damage which citizens do not have the legal obligation of bearing (*antijurídico*). To decide that point, Spanish Courts analyze legal obligations of public agencies and their due diligence to prevent wildfires (e.g., by cleaning public areas) and to respond to the fire (e.g., what kind of means are used).

Spanish law[15] establishes several duties the autonomous communities such as Catalonia must carry out, such as approving risk maps, classifying of fires according to their severity, creating of a system of detection and warning, declaring zones of high risk when necessary, establishing an effective operational system to face disasters, and preparing emergency response codes for reacting. If there is a breach in such obligations there will be public liability (e.g., Catalan Superior Court decision of July 1, 2006: lack of prevention in the surroundings of a rubbish tip during summer).

If there is a poor fulfillment of these obligations (i.e., a lack of due diligence or due care), courts also recognize public liability due to maladministration (e.g., Superior Court of Murcia, decision of September 19, 2001: the local government tried to fight a fire with an inadequate workforce). In Spain, fault or negligence do not have to exist to recognize administrative liability, but Courts nonetheless take into account whether public services were functioning as intended.

Even in cases where a third person starts the fire, Courts can declare public liability if public administration does not take due prevention measures (e.g., Spanish Supreme Court decision of April 20, 1991). Courts recognize the possibility of Acts of God (*fuerza mayor*), but deny them unless it is clear that an extraordinary cause is responsible for the wildfire and public administration must proof it (lightning strikes are not considered act of God if public administration was negligent in clearing forest and preventing the wildfire).

FINAL REFLECTIONS: RECIPROCAL OBLIGATIONS IN THEORY AND IN FACT

The purpose of this chapter has not been to demonstrate that the EU in general or that Spain and Catalonia in particular are in some way morally superior to other nations having to deal with the increasingly dangerous phenomenon of catastrophic wildfires, as in Lloyd Burton and Michael Eburn's chapter in this book. All of the Commonwealth countries and all of the EU member states share an ancient common legal lineage traceable to Justinian's Codes and Institutes, going back almost two millennia.

So notions of the reciprocal duties of governments and citizens are nothing new, even though our respective legal traditions, customs, and practices have evolved in innumerable diverse directions since that time. It is only to be expected that as the spacious former British colonies began to stand on their own and to appropriate resources formerly held by indigenous peoples, their legal systems would champion the individual and entrepreneurial rights of their citizenry, if sometimes at the expense of cohesive community or human rights in general.

Likewise, in the nation-states of modern Europe, which have been continuously populated at various levels of density for thousands of years and subjected to repeated and increasingly disastrous wars over the last two millennia, it is likewise to be expected that a higher premium is placed on the duties citizens owe to each other and to the state; and on the responsibilities of governments at every level to faithfully discharge the duties their citizens empowered them to perform on their behalf. What remains to be seen is whether these two substantially different systems have anything they can learn from each other in the realm of how to live more safely with the growing threat of catastrophic wildfires.

As discussed earlier, even as economically challenged as Spain is at this point in time, in Autonomous Communities such as Catalonia there is still a great deal more emphasis put on catastrophic wildfire prevention and investing public resources in achieving it than there is in countries such as the United States. As a result of these investments in prevention, there is correspondingly less that needs to be spent on fighting fires, even as the climatic threat of future fires continues to increase. There is a strong ethic of prevention at work here, which is reflected in these expenditures and these results.

The European, Spanish and Catalan legal frameworks have established the existence of public authorities´ legal duties, linked to human rights, in preventing and mitigating man-made and natural disasters, including wildfires. The content of the duties must be determined by each government in confronting specific circumstances, but the Courts, if necessary, will check the public behavior to decide if it fulfills legal requirements.

That legal duty implies positive measures and connects with moral obligations in the society. It is linked to classic European legal concepts such as *solidarity*, *public interest*, *social function of private property*, *human rights* and *good governance*.

The EU, strictly speaking, does not have a power in either prevention or extinction of forest fires. Its role is limited to co-financing national initiatives submitted by the Member States and to coordinating their voluntary international assistance, taking into account the subsidiarity principle.

To sum up, prevention and mitigation of wildfires is essentially a matter of competence at the member state level in the EU. Nevertheless, that situation could possibly change in the future, if regional conditions substantially worsen. Future directives in this field could spell out in more detail how to better mitigate against future fires, and how to better protect public health and safety when fires inevitably arise.

The distribution of powers in Spain changed dramatically with the Constitution of 1978, reintroducing democracy and the autonomy of historical nationalities, regions, and local governments. There are some clauses relating to prevention and mitigation of wildfire but, as a general rule, Spanish Government has the power to approve basic law and Autonomous Communities can approve developing law and enforce the whole legal framework. Catalonia is a special Autonomous Community and a leader in implementing and enforcing new laws on wildfire prevention. Local Governments have a relevant role to enforce the legal framework at the local level too.

In this regard, the incremental but continuous decentralization of government authority in Spain will have ongoing implications for the management of wildfire risk in its fire-prone Autonomous Communities. What remains to be seen is whether it is possible to maintain cooperative and effective coordination across all governmental sectors when we are facing a common threat, such as climate change in general or its catastrophic consequences in the form of deadly wildfires at the edge of our communities.

As several other chapters in *Cassandra's Curse* have pointed out, the problem now is less one of pretending that a threat does not exist, but in paying enough attention to and investing enough resources in the governmental institutions we depend on to both lessen the likelihood of future catastrophes and to shield us from their worst effects. We must remain as vigilant in maintaining the fitness of our disaster management agencies as we are in our efforts to prevent these disasters from happening.

NOTES

1. Art. 4.1 TEU: "In accordance with Article 5, competences not conferred upon the Union in the Treaties remain with the Member States."

2. At its origin in 1986, the EU established the first legal instrument to finance national projects for the period 1987–1992 through the Council Regulation (EEC) No 3529/86, of 17 November 1986, on protection of the Community's forests against fire. Community financial contribution was reserved for those national projects including preventive measures (forestry operations designed to reduce the risk of fire, the purchase of brush-clearance equipment, the provision of forest roads, fire belts, and water supplies ...) and supplementary measures (such as the training of highly specialized personnel). The next regulations, were for the periods 1992–2002, 2003–2006, and 2007–2013. All of them followed a similar structure and were based in the economic help to Member States' efforts in forest fire prevention, provided through grant agreements and public procurement contracts.

3. Some examples are the Council Directive 92/43/EEC of May 21, 1992 on the conservation of natural habitats and of wild fauna and flora and the Directive 2004/35/EC of the European Parliament and of the Council of April 21, 2004 on environmental liability with regard to the prevention and remedying of environmental damage.

4. The damages which are considered by this Directive are:

1. Damage to protected species and natural habitats, which is any damage that has significant adverse effects on reaching or maintaining the favorable conservation status of such habitats or species. The significance of such effects is to be assessed with reference to the baseline condition, taking account of the criteria set out in Annex I"; And protected species and natural habitats means:
   a. The species mentioned in Article 4(2) of Directive 79/409/EEC or listed in Annex I thereto or listed in Annexes II and IV to Directive 92/43/EEC.
   b. The habitats of species mentioned in Article 4(2) of Directive 79/409/EEC or listed in Annex I thereto or listed in Annex II to Directive 92/43/EEC, and the natural habitats listed in Annex I to Directive 92/43/EEC and the

breeding sites or resting places of the species listed in Annex IV to Directive 92/43/EEC; and

c. where a Member State so determines, any habitat or species, not listed in those Annexes which the Member State designates for equivalent purposes as those laid down in these two Directives;

2. Water damage, which is any damage that adversely affects the ecological, chemical and/or quantitative status and/or ecological potential, as defined in Directive 2000/60/EC, of the waters concerned, with the exception of adverse effects where Article 4(7) of that Directive applies;
3. Land damage, which is any land contamination that creates a significant risk of human health being adversely affected as a result of the direct or indirect introduction, in, on or under land, of substances, preparations, organisms, or microorganisms.

5. By the means of Council Decision 2001/792/EC, Euratom of October 23, 2001 establishing a Community mechanism to facilitate reinforced cooperation in civil protection assistance interventions; lately, object of substantial changes incorporated by the Council Decision of November 8, 2007 establishing a Community Civil Protection Mechanism (recast). This mechanism was at first established with a lack of specific power attribution by using a residual clause. Nowadays, after the last reform of the Regulatory Treaties in 2009, the EU is empowered in the field of civil protection (Art. 196 TFEU). According to that article, the EU power is limited to support tasks and coordination tasks.

6. Art. 5.3 TEU: "Under the principle of subsidiarity, in areas which do not fall within its exclusive competence, the Union shall act only if and in so far as the objectives of the proposed action cannot be sufficiently achieved by the Member States, either at central level or at regional and local level, but can rather, by reason of the scale or effects of the proposed action, be better achieved at Union level."

7. According to Art. 222.1 TFEU "*The Union and its Member States shall act jointly in a spirit of solidarity if a Member State is the object of a terrorist attack or victim of a natural or man-made disaster.*" This joint actuation inspired in the solidarity spirit is specified, for the case of forest fires when turned into disasters, in the same article: "*The Union shall mobilize all the instruments at its disposal, including the military resources made available by the Member States, to: [...] (b) assist a Member State in its territory, at the request of its political authorities, in the event of a natural or man-made disaster.*" Here, as in the MCP, in the respect of national sovereignty, this international aid must be requested by the Member State affected by the catastrophic forest fire. As far as financial assistance (Art. 122.2 TFEU), when a Member State is concerned by a natural disaster that causes to it difficulties or serious threats, it can receive financial assistance from the EU by a decision taken by the Council, after a proposal from the Commission and informing the European Parliament.

8. An example of this concern could be found on the Council Regulation (EEC) No 2158/92 of July 23, 1992 on protection of the Community's forests against fire: "*Whereas the protection of forests against fire is an urgent and important issue for the Community and whereas the Community must make a greater contribution to the efforts of Member States to improve such protection*".

9. European Parliament resolution of September 27, 2011 on "Towards a stronger European disaster response: the role of civil protection and humanitarian assistance" (2011/2023 INI) (2013/C 56 E/04).

10. European Court of Human Rights, Öneryildiz v. Turkey, Application 48939/99, judgment of November 30, 2004. European Court of Human Rights, Öneryildiz v. Turkey, Application 48939/99, judgment of November 30, 2004.

11. Art. 2, right to life: "1. *Everyone's right to life shall be protected by law.* No one shall be deprived of his life intentionally save in the execution of a sentence of a court following his conviction of a crime for which this penalty is provided by law.
Art. 1, protocol 1, right to property: "*Every natural or legal person is entitled to the peaceful enjoyment of his possessions.* No one shall be deprived of his possessions except in the public interest and subject to the conditions provided for by law and by the general principles of international law.
The preceding provisions shall not, however, in any way impair the right of a State to enforce such laws as it deems necessary to control the use of property in accordance with the general interest or to secure the payment of taxes or other contributions or penalties."

12. An example of this is Art. 9 of the Spanish land use act which establishes that land and building owners in Spain have a duty of conservation of their properties. That legal duty includes the obligation of keeping rural land (*suelo rural*) in good condition to avoid risks of possible disasters (fires, floods …).

13. Directives on Environmental Impact Assessment are good examples of the EU influence on Member States. Among these, we want to underline the Strategic Environmental Assessment Directive (European Parliament, European Council 2011). That Directive has been implemented in Spain by means of Spanish Act 9/2006, April 28 and Catalan Act 6/2009, April 28, on environmental assessment of some plans and programs (Ponce, J., 2013, pp. 12–13). This act demands an administrative procedure for the evaluation of environmental impact caused by urban or forest planning (civil protection plans are excluded). In connection with that, land use Act of 2007 establishes compulsory risk maps to be included in the environmental sustainability report that the developer must prepare. This report must be included in a document called Environmental Memory which explains environmental impact (art. 15).

14. Spanish Criminal Code:
"Article 352
Whoever sets woods or forests on fire shall be punished with imprisonment from one to five years and a fine of twelve to eighteen months.

If this has endangered the life or physical integrity of persons, the act shall be punished as set forth in Article 351, imposing the punishment of a fine from twelve to twenty-four months in all cases.

Article 353
1. The penalties stated in the preceding Article shall be imposed in the upper half when the fire is especially serious, according to whether any of the following circumstances concur:

1. When they cover a considerably large area;
2. When they cause major or serious soil erosion effects;

3. When they significantly alter the conditions of animal or plant life or affect any protected natural space;
4. In all cases, when there is serious deterioration or destruction of the resources affected.

2. Those penalties shall also be imposed in the upper half when the principal acts to obtain economic profit from the effects arising from the fire.

Article 354

1. Whoever sets woods or forests on fire without the fire there spreading, shall be punished with a sentence of imprisonment of six months to one year and a fine from six to twelve months.
2. The conduct foreseen in the preceding Section shall be exempt of punishment if the fire is not propagated by the proactive, voluntary action of the principal.

Article 355

In all the cases foreseen in this Subchapter, the Judges or Courts of Law may order that zoning classification of the land in areas affected by a forest fire may not be changed for a term of up to thirty years. They may also order limitation or suppression of uses to which the areas affected by the fire have been put, as well as administrative seizure of the burned wood from the fire.

Article 358

Whoever, due to serious negligence, were to cause any of the felonies of arson punished under the preceding Articles, shall be punished with the lower degree punishment, of those respectively foreseen for each case."

15. *Orden* of April 2, 1993.

REFERENCES

Burton, L. (2013). The comparative jurisprudence of wildfire mitigation: Moral community, political culture, and policy learning. *Oñati Socio-legal Series [Online]*, *3*(2), 234–253. Retrieved from http://ssrn.com/abstract=2012287

Chiti, M. P. (2003). Il ruolo del la comunità europea nel governo del territorio. In S. Civitarese, E. Ferrari, & P. Urbani Eds., *Il governo del territorio*. Milán: Giuffrè editores.

Corcoy, M. (2011). *Derecho penal*. Parte Especial, Valencia, Tirant Lo Blanch EFFIS, *Forest Fires in Europe 2010*, 2011. Retrieved from http://forest.jrc.ec.europa.eu/media/cms_page_media/9/forest-fires-in-europe-2010.pdf

Czaja v. Poland. (2012). *European court of human's right decision*. Retrieved from http://hudoc.echr.coe.int/eng#{"fulltext":["Czaja%20v.%20Poland,%202012"],"documentcollectionid2":["GRANDCHAMBER","CHAMBER"],"itemid":["001-113543"]}

EFFIS. (2011). *Forest fires in Europe*. Middle East and North Africa 2011. Retrieved from http://forest.jrc.ec.europa.eu/media/cms_page_media/9/forest-fires-in-europe-2011.pdf

European Commission. (2009).*Communication from the commission to the European parliament, the council, the European economic and social committee and the committee of the regions, A community approach on the prevention of natural and man-made disasters,*

[COM(2009) 82 final – Not published in the Official Journal] [online]. Retrieved from http://europa.eu/legislation_summaries/environment/civil_protection/pr0005_en.htm. Accessed on February 21, 2013.

European Parliament, European Council. (2011). *Strategic Environmental Assessment Directive (Directive 2001/42/EC of the European Parliament and of the Council of 27 June 2001 on the assessment of the effects of certain plans and programmes on the environment.* Retrieved from http://eur-lex.europa.eu/legal-content/EN/TXT/?uri=CELEX:32001L0042

European Union. (2013). *How the EU works*. Retrieved from http://europa.eu/about-eu/facts-figures/living/index_en.htm. Accessed on September 1, 2013.

Farber, D., Chen, J., Verchick, R., & Sun, L. (2011). *Disaster law and policy* (2nd ed.). New York, NY: Aspen Publishers.

Forest Ownership Board. (1990). Executive Order Decret 358/1989 on Ownership Board Regulation.

Forest Ownership Board Law. (1999). Forest Ownership Board Act 6/1999.

Forest Plan of Catalonia. (1994). Forest Plan of Catalonia of 13th of September of 1994.

Gorte, R. W. (2011). *Federal funding for wildfire control and management*. Washington, DC: Congressional Research Service. RL 33990.

Kälinand, D. (2008). Claudine Haenni Dale and Walter Kälin, "Disaster Risk Mitigation – Why Human Rights Matter". *Forced Migrant Review*, *31*, 38ff. Retrieved from http://www.fmreview.org/FMRpdfs/FMR31/FMR31.pdf

New Forest Law. (1988). Catalan Forest Act 6/1988.

Pierce, R. J., Jr. (2008). *Administrative law*. New York, NY: Foundation Press.

Ponce, J. (2013). Land use planning and disaster: A European Perspective from Spain. *Oñati Socio-Legal Series*, *3*(2). Retrieved from http://papers.ssrn.com/sol3/papers.cfm?abstract_id=2221235

Rojas-Briales, E. (2002). *A Spanish experience: The forest plan of Catalonia and its consequences for private forest management*. In O. Gislerud & I. Neven (Eds.), *National Forest Programmes in a European Context*, EFI Proceedings, 44, 2002, pp. 93–98. Retrieved from http://www2.euflegt.efi.int.qa.ambientia.fi/files/attachments/publications/proc44_net.pdf#page=93

Sánchez Sáez, A. J. (2009). Las responsabilidad patrimonial de las Administraciones públicas por incendios forestales. *Revista de Administración Pública*, *179*, 87–141.

Spanish Government. (2010). *River restoration: Basis of the nacional strategy for river restoration [online]*. Madrid: Spanish Government. Retrieved from http://www.magrama.gob.es/es/agua/publicaciones/River_B_Restoration_tcm7-27571.pdf. Accessed on February 21, 2013.

Spanish Public Prosecutor, Rapport. (2012). Retrieved from http://www.fiscal.es/cs/Satellite?c=FG_Actualidad_FA&cid=1247140789567&language=es&pageid=1242052000571&pagename=PFiscal/FG_Actualidad_FA/FGE_pintarActualidad&site=PFiscal

Vélez Muñoz, R. (2009). Cambio global e incendios forestales: Perspectivas de la Europea Meridional. *Recursos Rurais, IBADER, Instituto de Biodiversidade Agraria e Desenvolmento Rural*, *5*, 49–54. Retrieved from http://www.ibader.org/archivos/docs/recursos_rurais_05_07.pdf

EPILOGUE

As this book project was getting under way in the autumn of 2012, Hurricane Sandy struck the Atlantic Seaboard in the northeastern United States, killing more than 100 people and causing over $68 billion in property damage. With a diameter in excess of 1,000 miles, as of this writing it is the largest Atlantic hurricane ever to come ashore on the eastern seaboard.

As this book goes to press in 2015, we are observing the 10th anniversary of Hurricane Katrina, which, though smaller in size by half than Sandy, nonetheless killed well over 10 times as many people and destroyed more than $100 billion in property. The juxtaposition of these two events invites some comparisons – most notably, whether there were any lessons learned from Katrina that may have mitigated some of the worst potential impacts of Sandy.

Certainly, the Federal Emergency Management Agency's performance before, during, and after Sandy compares favorably with its fecklessness during Katrina, and more people were evacuated from the storm's immediate path. But at a deeper institutional level, some similarities are disquieting. As in Katrina, the poorest residents in the most vulnerable housing with the shakiest infrastructure were the hardest hit by Sandy. They were among the last to be evacuated and have fundamental survival needs attended to, and the last to have services restored and be allowed to return to their homes, if indeed their homes still existed. According to the Red Cross's after action report, the median age of the 117 Sandy-related fatalities was 65. As in Katrina eight years earlier, in the midst of Sandy, critical health care facilities in lower Manhattan lost all ability to serve their ill and injured because their emergency backup electrical generating systems were still located in their (now flooded) basements. As in Katrina, hospital staff had to carry bedridden patients down flights of unlit stairways to safety (Irfan, 2012).

This book is an issue in a series titled *Studies in Law, Politics, and Society*. Its chapters present case studies of repeated instances in which – with the possible exception of proactive wildfire mitigation in Mediterranean Europe – the law has failed to protect vulnerable populations because of politics, with the result that society has suffered egregiously and in many cases unnecessarily.

Dating as far back as the *Institutes of Justinian* in the late Roman Empire, the legitimacy of legal systems in the West has rested in part on the principle that a relationship of mutual obligation and interdependence exists between the body politic and its organs of governance. The people moving into housing in a flood plain, into a tinder-dry forest in the Mountain West, or to the base of a slide-prone mountainside have some faith that government would not have allowed such housing to be built if it was unreasonably dangerous to do so. They also believe that should the worst happen, their governments have thoughtfully planned how best to remove them from harm's way.

Little do they tend to understand the role of politics in making that faith misplaced. They believe the surrender of a measure of their liberty and property (living in accordance with the rule of law and financially supporting institutions that provide it) will secure for them the wise use of the police powers on which their health and safety depends. But especially in the realm of emergency management, time and again that trust has been forsaken.

As several chapters in this volume illustrate, all too often the political Powers That Be have successfully promoted discourses that weave an illusory cocoon of inviolability within which foretold disasters are themselves viewed as illusory, unlikely, or overblown. Even as the monster storms and mega-wildfires rend this veil of illusion with increasing frequency and ferocity, the dominant political will seems more inclined to reweave the torn veil than to relocate and rebuild infrastructure in a way that respects the natural forces that are the true governors of our world.

"Don't be such a Cassandra!" some contributors to this volume have been told, because the kind of research they do can be disquieting and disturbing. They encourage preventive planning for the likelihood of foreseeable future disasters that few want to contemplate. And it is not just those interest groups who profit from the status quo and disaster denial who resist messages of impending disaster. Much of the general public is resistant as well.

Two states of mind on the part of many listeners will always make Cassandra's task a challenging one: denial and despair. The message of those foreseeing and foretelling disaster is inherently anxiety-provoking. So one psychological defense is to simply deny the very existence of the threat, or its likelihood, or its severity. Unfortunately, the proof of threat that denialists demand before acting is usually the foretold disaster itself. It's almost a truism in disaster research circles that fundamental reform in disaster management systems and policies occurs only in the aftermath of great tragedy.

Alternatively, as the threat becomes increasingly self-evident, but the ability to mitigate against it seems beyond current political will or institutional capacity, there is the equally dysfunctional danger of an attentive public falling into enervating despair. No wonder then that a Cassandra's message is seldom a welcome one, if denial or despair appear to be the only response options. But they are not.

Citizens affected by government decisions that put them in harm's way are beginning to bring suit – and with increasing success – against those governments for a breach of duty to protect them against reasonably foreseeable disasters (Burkett, 2013). More and more, well-informed citizens are making well-documented arguments in public settings such as planning commission hearings, city council meetings, and similar venues, voicing the reasonable foreseeability of disasters those governing bodies might actually make more likely through improvident land use decision making or inadequate land use regulation. "Citizen scientists" are doing solid research on both foreseeability and – just as importantly – the untold aftermath of catastrophic disasters that government studies do not adequately assess (McCormick, 2012).

Perhaps a well-informed, organized, concerned, and motivated electorate has to take the lead in compelling their governments to do a more responsible job in the realm of proactive disaster mitigation planning. And seeking to vindicate rights to a functional government against dysfunctional politics that compromise government's moral obligations to its citizenry may be one means of doing so.

Cassandra's progeny have been speaking truth to power since Troy. And whether testifying in courtrooms, speaking out in planning commission hearings, or taking soil samples along polluted coastlines, we have never needed them more than we do now.

Lloyd Burton

REFERENCES

Burkett, M. (2013). Duty and breach in an era of uncertainty: Local government liability for failure to adapt to climate change. *Vermont Law Review*, *36*, 731.

Irfan, U. (2012). Superstorm sandy may have long-term public health impacts. *Scientific American* [Online]. Retrieved from https://www.scientificamerican.com/article/super-storm-sandy-may-have-long-term-public-health-impacts/. Accessed on November 6, 2012.

McCormick, S. (2012). After the cap: Risk assessment, citizen science, and disaster recovery. *Ecology and Society*, *17*(4). Retrieved from http://www.ecologyandsociety.org/vol17/iss4/art31/